Lecture Notes in Artificial Intelligence   13239

Subseries of Lecture Notes in Computer Science

More information about this subseries at https://link.springer.com/bookseries/1244

Andreas Theodorou · Juan Carlos Nieves ·
Marina De Vos (Eds.)

Coordination, Organizations, Institutions, Norms, and Ethics for Governance of Multi-Agent Systems XIV

International Workshop, COINE 2021
London, UK, May 3, 2021
Revised Selected Papers

 Springer

Editors
Andreas Theodorou (iD)
Umeå University
Umeå, Sweden

Juan Carlos Nieves (iD)
Umeå University
Umeå, Sweden

Marina De Vos (iD)
University of Bath
Claverton Down, UK

ISSN 0302-9743   ISSN 1611-3349 (electronic)
Lecture Notes in Artificial Intelligence
ISBN 978-3-031-16616-7   ISBN 978-3-031-16617-4 (eBook)
https://doi.org/10.1007/978-3-031-16617-4

LNCS Sublibrary: SL7 – Artificial Intelligence

This Springer imprint is published by the registered company Springer Nature Switzerland AG
The registered company address is: Gewerbestrasse 11, 6330 Cham, Switzerland

Preface

This volume collates selected revised papers presented at the 2021 edition of the Coordination, Organization, Institutions, Norms, and Ethics for Governance of Multi-Agent Systems (COINE). The workshop was held on May 3, 2021, and was co-located with the 20th International Conference on Autonomous Agents and Multi-agent Systems (AAMAS)—originally set in London, UK, but held virtually due to the COVID-19 pandemic situation.

This is the second iteration of the workshop since its relabeling in 2020 as COINE from its earlier form: COIN (Coordination, Organizations, Institutions and Norms in Agent Systems). This modification makes explicit the consideration of ethical aspects as a core part of the governance of social systems—the overarching theme of the COINE workshop series. Despite its new name, COINE continues the tradition of its predecessor by bringing together researchers in autonomous agents and multi-agent systems working on the scientific and technological aspects of social coordination, organizational theory, normative MAS, artificial or electronic institutions, and norm-aware and ethical agents.

COINE 2021 received 12 submissions all which underwent two rounds of single-blind peer review. Each submission received feedback by at least three reviewers; this initial assessment was part of the admission to the presentation. Given the recommendations made by the reviewers, nine papers were admitted: six submissions were accepted for full presentations and three for short presentations. All articles were subsequently refined and extended, based on feedback received as part of the reviews and the presentations, and underwent a second round of reviews before inclusion in this post-proceedings volume as full papers.

In addition to the peer-reviewed submissions, two invited speakers presented their work. The first speaker, Marija Slavkovik, introduced the field of machine ethics and its relationship with normative reasoning. Slavkovik presented open challenges and discussed how the COINE community can engage with the field. The second speaker, Julian Padget, argued how conscientious design can be used as a principled approach for the ethical design and deployment of value-driven agents. Padget discussed how such agents can reflect the way social institutions are connected through the governance of physical interaction and facilitate human-to-human interaction.

This proceedings volume organizes the workshop papers into three topics: 1) Invited Talks; 2) Conceptual Frameworks Architectures for Collaboration and Coordination; and 3) Modeling and Understanding Social Behavior Using COINE Technologies. The first topic contains an abstract from one of the two invited speakers. Next, we focus on articles presenting fundamental research on embedding and optimising social behavior in normative agents. The final topic contains papers where COINE technologies have been used to provide a better understanding human social intelligence.

Invited Talks

– Machine ethics - is it just normative multi-agent systems? by Marija Slavkokik. In this extended abstract, Slavkokik provides an overview of the field of machine ethics by discussing its relationship to normative reasoning.

Conceptual Frameworks Architectures for Collaboration and Coordination

This topic of the proceedings is dedicated to approaches that propose conceptual frameworks and other architectures for developing socially-aware agents. This theme contains work related to the emergence and optimization of COINE concepts, e.g. norms, which facilitate coordination and collaboration.

– A Framework for Automatic Monitoring of Norms that Regulate Time Constrained Actions by Nicoletta Fornara, Soheil Roshankish, and Marco Colombetti. This paper provides a framework for modeling norms, using operational semantics, to enable reasoning with these norms to automatically compute norms violation and fulfilment.
– Collaborative Human-Agent Planning for Resilience by Ronal Singh, Tim Miller, and Darryn Reid. This work investigates how human insights can be provided at run-time without changing the artificial agent's domain model in order to improve collaboration in human-machine teaming scenarios.
– Environmental consequences of the status-functions in artificial institutions by Rafhael Cunha, Jomi Hubner, and Maiquel de Brito. This work proposes the expression of the consequences in the environment of status functions in artificial institution to aid agents' reasoning over their social goals.
– Noe: Norms Emergence and Robustness Based on Emotions in Multiagent Systems by Sz-Ting Tzeng, Nirav Ajmeri, and Munindar P. Singh. The authors explore how considering emotional responses to the outcomes of norm satisfaction and violation affects the emergence and robustness of social norms. Their result demonstrate an improvement in norms compliance and promotion of societal welfare.
– Run-time Norms Synthesis in Multi-Objective by Multi-Agent Systems by Maha Riad and Fatemeh Golpayegani. This papers proposes a run-time utility-based norm synthesis approach as a mechanism for agents to understand the impact of a suggested norm on their objectives and decide whether or not to adopt it. The addition of this reasoning mechanism allows agents to optimize against multiple objectives: coordinating their behavior while achieving any norms-conflicting objectives.

Modeling and Understanding Social Behavior Using COINE Technologies

The papers in this thematic section draw upon real-world datasets or otherwise ground their assumptions in the literature to investigate social phenomena and provide new insights and solutions to social problems.

- A Bayesian model of information cascades by Sriashalya Srivathsan and Stephen Cranefield. This paper presents a Bayesian model of information cascades. The authors demonstrate how cascades will not necessarily occur and that adding prior agents' information will delay any effects of cascades.
- Interactions between social norms and incentive mechanisms in organizations by Ravshanbek Khodzhimatov, Stephan Leitner, and Friederike Wall. This paper focuses on how individual socially-aware behavior interferes with performance-based incentive mechanisms in multi-agent organizations. The authors discuss how promoting socially-accepted behavior might reduce an organization's performance, but that reduction can be mitigating by using individual-based incentives.
- Learning for Detecting Norm Violation in Online Communities by Thiago Freitas dos Santos, Nardine Osman, and Marco Schorlemmer. This paper demonstrates how the detection and generation of explanations for norms violations can be used to mitigate the ill-effects that arise when different members of an online community interpret norms in different ways. A real-world use case, based on the Wikipedia edits data, is presented.
- Solving social dilemmas by reasoning about expectations by Abira Sengupta, Stephen Cranefield, and Jeremy Pitt. This article investigates how explicit reasoning about expectations, i.e. future-directed beliefs that agents have, can be used to encode both traditional game theory solution concepts and social mechanisms in social dilemma situations. The authors model a collective risk dilemma, based on the plain-plateau scenario, and show how using expectations in the reasoning mechanisms enables cooperation to take place.

We would like to thank everyone who helped to make COINE 2021 a success and we hope that you enjoy these proceedings.

Marina De Vos
Juan Carlos Nieves
Andreas Theodorou

Organization

Program Chairs

Marina De Vos — University of Bath, UK
Juan Carlos Nieves — Umeå University, Sweden
Andreas Theodorou — Umeå University, Sweden

Program Committee

Huib Aldewereld — HU University of Applied Sciences Utrecht, The Netherlands
Andrea Aler Tubella — Umeå University, Sweden
Stefania Costantini — Università dell'Aquila, Italy
Virginia Dignum — Umeå University, Sweden
Nicoletta Fornara — Università della Svizzera italiana, Switzerland
Christopher Frantz — Norwegian University of Science and Technology, Norway
Pablo Noriega — IIIA-CSIC, Spain
Luís Moniz Pereira — Universidade Nova de Lisboa, Portugal
Jaime Simão Sichman — University of São Paulo, Brazil
Wamberto Vasconcelos — University of Aberdeen, UK
Javier Vazquez Salceda — Universitat Politecnica de Catalunya-BarcelonaTech, Spain
Harko Verhagen — Stockholm University, Sweden
George Vouros — University of Piraeus, Greece

Additional Reviewers

Petter Ericson — Umeå University, Sweden
Esteban Guerrero — University of Vaasa, Finland
Timotheus Kampik — Umeå University, Sweden
René Mellema — Umeå University, Sweden
Julian Alfredo Mendez — Umea University, Sweden

Additional Session Chairs

Timotheus Kampik — Umeå University, Sweden
Andreasa Morris Martin — University of Bath, UK

Contents

Invited Speaker

Machine Ethics - Is It Just Normative Multi-agent Systems?

Marija Slavkovik(⊠) (iD)

University of Bergen, Bergen, Norway
marija.slavkovik@uib.no
http://www.springer.com/gp/computer-science/lncs

Abstract. Researchers from normative multi-agent systems increasingly find familiar questions being asked but now in a field called machine ethics. I the invited talk I introduced machine ethics and focused on some overlapping topics of interest for the both field. This extended abstract offers a highlight on where these two fields overlap, where they differ, but foremost why pursuing advancements in both has a direct impact on society today.

1 Introduction

To live in the beginning of the twenty first century is to live with devices than increasingly have more computational power than the computer[1] used in the first moon landing. These devices also have numerous sensors and are Internet capable.. As our devices gain an increasing specter of unsupervised action ability, inevitably they become our moral arbiters.

Autonomous operation includes the ability of decision making. Successfully operating within society necessitates that the decisions taken are not only optimal with respect to the preferences, goals, and constraints of the individual making them, but also with respect to the interests of others in that society. When we enable devices to make decisions for us, we need to enable them to also consider the interests of others other than our own, i.e., to make moral decisions and thus be our moral arbiters. Machine ethics, or artificial morality, is a sub-field in AI that "is concerned with the behaviour of machines towards human users and other machines" [1].

A device that has the ability to accomplish goals, by having the ability to make decisions adjusted to an environment that it shares with people and other devices, is an artificial agent [13, Chapter2]. The field of multi-agent systems has studied various aspects of how artificial agents should operate in shared environment with other agents for a couple of decades now [17]. Within multi-agent systems research, the problem of how to specify norms for artificial agents,

---

[1] https://en.wikipedia.org/wiki/Apollo_Guidance_Computer.

Supported by organization x.

how can artificial agents reason with them and learn them is well recognised [3] and pre-dates machine ethics. Is then the case that we machine ethics just gives a new name for normative multi-agent systems research?

2   Who's a Good Device?

A good behaviour of machines towards people may not be satisfied even when they were to make the same decisions that a human that has a good behaviour would make in the same situation [10,11]. The problem of what is good, what is bad ,and how to discern them, is the subject of moral philosophy [7]. Machine ethics imposes new rigour and opens new study directions for moral philosophy such as: should machines be enabled with ethical reasoning [2,6] and can machines be moral agents at all [4].

Moral philosophy is considered to include three main areas of study: meta-ethics, normative ethics and applied ethics [7]. Normative ethics is concerned with developing moral theories, that is means to identify what are the right and wrong decisions, actions, states of the world etc. When we consider the specific problem of how to enable artificial agents to make moral decisions, we are primarily interested in normative moral philosophy and the moral theories developed within it.

Artificial moral agents can be accomplished both implicitly and explicitly [12,16]. To build implicit moral agents we use given moral theories an enable the agents to follow them. To build explicit moral agents we enable the agents to identify right from wrong without specifying a specific theory, but rather by enabling them to adopt the norms of the environment/society they occupy. The norms of society may or may not be constructed around a specific moral theory [15].

Not all norms in society are moral norms [8]. Why should then all normative agents be moral agents? Is an artificial agent that can reason with societal norms also an artificial moral agent? Is an artificial agent, since it necessarily follows programming rules to accomplish moral behaviour, necessarily a deontic moral agent? The answer of these question requires long-standing debates in moral philosophy to be settled.

3   Normative Conflicts and Moral Dilemmas

The idea that a device needs to be able to make moral decisions got fueled by the revolution of autonomous vehicles (AV) - AV's are both exciting and scary; traffic is a context in which successful operation heavily depends on concern for others. To illustrate the moral dilemma an AV may face, and also engage the audience, we overuse the trolley problems[2][3]. While we toy with imaginary driving scenarios, automated moral decision making is deployed somewhere else.

---

[2] https://www.brookings.edu/research/the-folly-of-trolleys-ethical-challenges-and-autonomous-vehicles/.

[3] https://www.moralmachine.net/.

Traffic is a context that is heavily legally regulated and in that sense stands completely opposite to the context of social media content curation. Misleading information, disinformation and outright fast-spreading lies have an unethical impact on our societies[4]. Choosing to censor or suppress the visibility of online content that may be misleading or misinforming, is a moral decision that we are very much interested to have software take over[5] How can we navigate these computational challenges of automating moral decisions regarding content when one man's lie is another man's gospel? Consider that we are not in consensus on whether content moderation is in itself a morally right thing to do[6]. The automation of moral decisions requires addressing the very practical problem of not what is the solution to long standing moral dilemmas, but on how to deal with moral conflicts.

Normative multi-agent systems as field has studied problems of norm compliance and resolving normative conflicts [14]. In contrast, the question of whether or not moral conflicts do really even exist has been long argued in moral philosophy [5]. A possible circumvention of solving hard moral philosophy problems has been argued through the observation that people do not tend to follow moral theories, but rules of thumb when choosing what to do in a morally sensitive situation [9]. If that is the case, then the machine ethics would very much require the expertise of normative multi-agent systems to operationalise artificial moral agents.

4   Conclusions

Is then the case that we machine ethics just gives a new name for normative multi-agent systems research? The answer has to be no. The scopes of machine ethics and normative multi-agent systems overlap, but neither subsumes the other. Machine ethics does bring the field of normative multi-agent systems closer to moral philosophy. The normative multi-agent systems field can offer valuable insights, tools and approaches to automating moral decision-making.

References

1. Anderson, M., Anderson, S.L.: The status of machine ethics: a report from the AAAI symposium. Minds Mach. **17**(1), 1–10 (2007). https://doi.org/10.1007/s11023-007-9053-7
2. Anderson, S.L.: Asimov's "three laws of robotics" and machine metaethics. AI Soc. **22**(4), 477–493 (2008). https://doi.org/10.1007/s00146-007-0094-5

---

[4] https://www.economist.com/open-future/2020/01/17/digital-disinformation-is-destroying-society-but-we-can-fight-back.

[5] https://economictimes.indiatimes.com/magazines/panache/twitter-content-warning-feature-lets-users-avoid-posts-they-dont-want-to-see/articleshow/89885837.cms.

[6] https://www.theguardian.com/technology/2022/apr/30/elon-musk-why-44bn-vision-for-twitter-could-fall-apart.

3. Boella, G., van der Torre, L., Verhagen, H.: Introduction to normative multiagent systems. Comput. Mathemat. Org. Theory **12**(2), 71–79 (2006). https://doi.org/10.1007/s10588-006-9537-7
4. Brożek, B., Janik, B.: Can artificial intelligences be moral agents? New Ideas in Psychol. **54**, 101–106 (2019). https://doi.org/10.1016/j.newideapsych.2018.12.002, https://www.sciencedirect.com/science/article/pii/S0732118X17300739
5. Donagan, A.: Consistency in rationalist moral systems. J. Philos. **81**(6), 291–309 (1984). http://www.jstor.org/stable/2026371
6. Etzioni, A., Etzioni, O.: Incorporating ethics into artificial intelligence. J. Ethics **21**, 403–418 (2017)
7. Fieser, J.: Ethics. In: Boylan, M. (ed.) Internet Encyclopedia of Philosophy. ISSN 2161–0002 (2021)
8. Gibbs, J.P.: Norms: the problem of definition and classification. Am. J. Sociol. **70**(5), 586–594 (1965). http://www.jstor.org/stable/2774978
9. Horty, J.F.: Moral dilemmas and nonmonotonic logic. J. Philos. Logic **23**(1), 35–65 (1994). http://www.jstor.org/stable/30227222
10. Malle, B.F., Scheutz, M.: When will people regard robots as morally competent social partners? In: 2015 24th IEEE International Symposium on Robot and Human Interactive Communication (RO-MAN), pp. 486–491 (2015). https://doi.org/10.1109/ROMAN.2015.7333667
11. Malle, B.F., Scheutz, M., Arnold, T., Voiklis, J., Cusimano, C.: Sacrifice one for the good of many? People apply different moral norms to human and robot agents. In: Proceedings of the Tenth Annual ACM/IEEE International Conference on Human-Robot Interaction, HRI 2015, pp. 117–124. Association for Computing Machinery, New York (2015). https://doi.org/10.1145/2696454.2696458
12. Moor, J.H.: The nature, importance, and difficulty of machine ethics. IEEE Intell. Syst. **21**(4), 18–21 (2006). https://doi.org/10.1109/MIS.2006.80
13. Russell, S., Norvig, P.: Artificial Intelligence: A Modern Approach. Pearson Education, 4 edn. Upper Saddle River (2020)
14. Santos, J.S., Zahn, J.O., Silvestre, E.A., Silva, V.T., Vasconcelos, W.W.: Detection and resolution of normative conflicts in multi-agent systems: a literature survey. In: AAMAS, pp. 1306–1309. International Foundation for Autonomous Agents and Multiagent Systems (2018)
15. Slavkovik, M.: Automating moral reasoning (invited paper). In: Bourgaux, C., Ozaki, A., Peñaloza, R. (eds.) International Research School in Artificial Intelligence in Bergen, AIB 2022, June 7–11, 2022, University of Bergen, Norway. OASIcs, vol. 99, pp. 6:1–6:13. Schloss Dagstuhl - Leibniz-Zentrum für Informatik (2022). https://doi.org/10.4230/OASIcs.AIB.2022.6
16. Wallach, W., Allen, C.: Moral Machines: Teaching Robots Right from Wrong. Oxford University Press Inc, New York (2008)
17. Wooldridge, M.: An Introduction to MultiAgent Systems. 2nd edn. Wiley, Chichester(2009)

Conceptual Frameworks Architectures for Collaboration and Coordination

A Framework for Automatic Monitoring of Norms that Regulate Time Constrained Actions

Nicoletta Fornara[1]([⊠]), Soheil Roshankish[1], and Marco Colombetti[2]

[1] Università della Svizzera italiana, via G. Buffi 13, 6900 Lugano, Switzerland
{nicoletta.fornara,soheil.roshankish}@usi.ch
[2] Politecnico di Milano, piazza Leonardo Da Vinci 32, Milano, Italy
marco.colombetti@polimi.it

Abstract. This paper addresses the problem of proposing a model of norms and a framework for automatically computing their violation or fulfilment. The proposed model can be used to express abstract norms able to regulate classes of actions that should or should not be performed in a temporal interval. We show how the model can be used to formalize obligations and prohibitions and for inhibiting them by introducing permissions and exemptions. The basic building blocks for norm specification consists of rules with suitably nested components. The activation condition and the regulated actions together with their time constrains are specified using the W3C Web Ontology Language (OWL 2). Thanks to this choice, it is possible to use OWL reasoning for computing the effects that the logical implication between actions has on the fulfilment or violation of the norms. The operational semantics of the model is specified by providing an unambiguous procedure for translating every norm and every exception into production rules.

1 Introduction

In this paper, we present the T-NORM model (where T stands for Temporal), a model for the formalization of *relational norms* that regulate classes of actions that agents perform in the society and that put them in relation to other agents, like for example paying, lending, entering a limited traffic area, and so on. Our proposal is strictly related to the specification of the operational semantics of such a model to make it possible to provide monitoring and simulation services on norms specifications. Specifically, the proposed model can be used to automatically compute the fulfilment or violation of active obligations and prohibitions formalized to regulate a set of actions that should or should not be performed in a *temporal interval*. The fact that the actions regulated by the norms are time constrained is an important distinguishing feature of the proposed model. We

Funded by the SNSF (Swiss National Science Foundation) grant no. 200021_175759/1.
Proc. of the COINE 2021 co-located with AAMAS 2021, 3rd May 2021, London, UK.
All Rights Reserved.

© Springer Nature Switzerland AG 2022
A. Theodorou et al. (Eds.): COINE 2021, LNAI 13239, pp. 9–27, 2022.
https://doi.org/10.1007/978-3-031-16617-4_2

would like to stress that the type of norms that can be represented with the proposed model are assumed to be *static*, in the sense that they do not change dynamically over time. What is represented in the model is that a norm may be activated over time and subsequently its activation may generate fulfilments and/or violations. Another important aspect of the model is that once a set of obligations and prohibitions are formalized they may be further refined by the definition of permissions and exemptions.

In NorMAS literature [16] it is possible to find numerous formal models for the specification of norms, contracts, commitments and policies. Many of them can be used for regulating the performance of actions or for requiring the maintenance of certain conditions, but very often those actions and conditions may only be expressed using propositional formulae. This choice makes it difficult to express the relation between the regulated actions (or conditions) and time. This is an important limit in the expressiveness of those models, because there are numerous real examples of norms and policies whose relation with time intervals is important for their semantics; for example in e-commerce, deadlines (before which a payment must be done) are fundamental for computing the fulfilment or violation of contracts.

When temporal aspects are important for the specification of norms and for reasoning on the evolution of their normative state, one may decide to use temporal logics (e.g. Linear Temporal Logic LTL) to express and reason about time-related constraints. Unfortunately, this solution has important limitations when it is necessary to use automatic reasoning to compute the time evolution of the normative state, as discussed in [12].

In our approach we propose to formalize some components of the norms, i.e. their activation condition and the regulated actions together with their time constrains using semantic web languages, specifically the W3C Web Ontology Language (OWL 2, henceforward simply OWL)[1]. This is for two reasons. First, it should be easier for those who want to formalize norms with our model to use a standard language that is fairly well known and taught in computer science graduate courses. Second, this language has a formal semantics on which automatic reasoning can be performed. Moreover, OWL is more expressive than propositional formulae[2], which are used in many other norm models. The idea of formalizing policies using semantic web languages is spreading also thanks to the success of the ODRL (Open Digital Rights Language) policy expression language[3], which has been a W3C Recommendation since February 2018.

Our idea is to propose a model of norms that norm designers can use for formalizing the intuitive meaning of having an obligation or a prohibition. That is, when something happens and certain conditions hold, an agent is obligated or prohibited to do something in a given interval of time. What is innovative

---

[1] https://www.w3.org/TR/owl2-overview/.

[2] Description Logics (DLs), which are a family of class (concept) based knowledge representation formalisms, are more expressive than propositional logic, and they are the basis for ontology languages such as OWL [10].

[3] https://www.w3.org/TR/odrl-model/.

with respect to other approaches is that instead of explicitly labelling a norm as an obligation or a prohibition, we let the norm designer explicitly express what sequence of events will bring to a violation or a fulfilment; this way, there is practically no limit to the types of normative relations that can be expressed. To do so the norm designer needs to be able to describe triggering events or actions and their consequences. The resulting model will let the norm designer to specify norms as *rules* nested into each other.

The main contributions of this paper are: (i) the definition of a model of norms that can be used to specify numerous types of *deontic relations*, i.e. different types of obligations and prohibitions, and their exceptions; (ii) the definition of its operational semantics (by combining OWL reasoning and forward chaining) that can be used to automatically monitor or simulate the fulfillment or violation of a set of norms; (iii) the proposal of a set of different types of concrete norms, that can be used to evaluate the expressive power of a norms model.

This paper is organized as follows: in Sect. 2 the main goals that guided the design of the norms model are presented. In Sect. 3 the T-NORM model is introduced and in Sect. 4 its operational semantics is provided. In Sect. 5 the architecture of the framework for computing the fulfillment or violation of norms and its implementation are presented. Finally, in Sect. 6 the proposed model is compared with other existing approaches.

2 Design Goals

In this section we list the main goals that guided us in the design of the proposed model and in the definition of its operational semantics.

Our first goal is to propose a model of norms able to regulate *classes of actions*; for example, we want to be able to formalize a norm that regulates all the accesses to a restricted traffic zone of a metropolis and not only the access of a specific agent. This objective is not achieved by those models, like ODRL and all its extensions or profiles [3,6] where the policies designer has to specify the specific debtor of every policy instance.

Our second goal is to define a model of norms able to regulate classes of actions whose performance is *temporally constrained*. For instance, the following norm regulates all the access to an area and the subsequent action of paying is temporally constrained by a deadline, which in turn depends on the access instant of time: *"when an agent enters in the limited-traffic area of Milan, between 7 a.m. and 7 p.m., they have to pay 6 euros within 24 h"*. The first and the second goal will bring us to define a model for expressing norms that may be applied multiple times to different agents and may be activated by numerous events happening in different instants of time.

Starting from the experience that we gained by using the model of obligations, prohibitions and permissions presented in our previous paper [6], we have developed a third goal for our model. The goal is to propose a model made of basic constructs that can be combined by a norm designer to express different types of deontic relations without the need to introduce a pre-defined list of deontic types, like obligation, prohibition, and permission. This has the advantage that whenever a new kind of norms is required, like for example the notion of exemption or the notion of right, there is no need to introduce a new type into the model with its operational semantics. With the model proposed in this paper, it is possible to use few basic constructs and combine them in different ways to express the obligation to perform an action before a given deadline or the prohibition to perform an action within an interval of time. Our idea is to allow norm designers to explicitly state what behaviour will bring to a violation and what behaviour will bring to a fulfilment, regardless of whether they are formalizing an obligation or a prohibition. Moreover, in this new model, permissions are not treated any more as first-class objects, but they are formalized as exceptions to prohibitions, while exemptions are formalized as exceptions to obligations.

Our fourth goal is to provide an operational semantics of our model of norms that will make it possible to *monitor* or *simulate* the evolution of their state. Our goal is mainly to be able to automatically compute if a policy is *active* (or in-force) and then if it becomes *fulfilled* or *violated* on the basis of the events and actions performed by agents. Monitoring is crucial from the point of view of policy's *debtor* for checking if their behaviour is compliant and it is relevant for policy's *creditors* to react to violations. Simulation may be used for evaluating in advance the effects of the performance of certain actions. Another useful service that can be provided on a set of policies is checking their consistency, checking for example if a given action is contemporarily obligatory and prohibited. This can be done at design time by using model-checking techniques, but it is not among the objectives of our model. However, by proposing a model that allows us to track how the state of the norms evolves over time, it will be possible to detect inconsistencies that occur at a precise instant of time during the execution of their monitoring process.

3   The T-NORM Model of Norms

The idea that has guided us in the definition of the T-NORM model is to give norm designers a tool to describe what sequence of events or actions would bring an agent to the violation or fulfilment of a norm. This approach has the advantage of providing norm designers with a model that in principle can be used to define any type of deontic relationship, like obligations, prohibitions, permissions, exemptions, rights and so on. This is a crucial difference with respect to the models having a pre-defined set of deontic types, like it is the case for ODRL, OWL-POLAR [13], and also our previous proposal of a model for monitoring obligations, prohibitions, and permissions [6].

The intuitive meaning of having an obligation (resp. a prohibition) that we want to capture is the following one: when an activation event happens and some contextual conditions are satisfied, it is necessary to compute some parameters (for example the deadline) and to start to monitor the performance of a specific regulated action or class of actions. In turn, if an action, which matches the description of the regulated one, is performed before another event (for example a time event that represents a deadline), then the obligation is fulfilled (resp. the prohibition is violated); otherwise, if the regulated action cannot be performed anymore (for example because the deadline has elapsed) the obligation is violated (resp. the prohibition is fulfilled).

To capture this intuitive meaning we decided to represent norms as rules that determine the conditions under which a fulfilment or violation is generated. Below, we discuss how different types of norms can be represented in this way. Then in the next section we describe how T-Norm norms can be translated into production rules, thus assigning an unambiguous operational semantics to our norm formalism.

The idea of representing norms in the form of rules is not new in NorMAS literature [7]. However, in order to explicitly specify the sequence of events that bring to a violation or a fulfilment, we propose a model of norms where the basic building blocks for norm specification consists of rules with properly nested components. Thanks to this choice, as we will discuss in Sect. 4, the operational semantics of our model of norms can be easily expressed using productions. Our idea is to express the meaning of having an obligation or a prohibition by nested rules of the following form:

```
NORM Norm_n
[ON ?event1 WHERE conditions on ?event1
THEN
    COMPUTE]
    CREATE DeonticRelation(?dr);
    ASSERT isGenerated(?dr,Norm_n); [activated(?dr,?event1);]
    ON ?event2 [BEFORE ?event3 WHERE conditions on ?event3]
        WHERE actor(?event2,?agent) AND conditions on ?event2
    THEN ASSERT fulfills(?agent,?dr); fullfilled(?dr,?event2)|
                violates(?agent,?dr); violated(?dr,?event2)
    [ELSE ASSERT violates(?agent,?dr); violated(?dr,?event3)|
                fulfills(?agent,?dr); fulfilled(?dr,?event3)]
```

In the proposed model the first (optional) ON...THEN component is used for expressing *conditional norms*, i.e. norms that start to be in force when a certain event happens and where the *temporal relation* between the activating event and the regulated action is crucial in the semantics of the norm. For example in Norm01 (*"when an agent enters in the limited-traffic area of Milan between 7 a.m. and 7 p.m., they have to pay 6 euros within 24 h"*) the event of entering in the limited-traffic area must occur for the obligation to pay to activate; moreover the entering instant is fundamental for computing the deadline of the payment. The second ON...THEN component is used for expressing the actions regulated by the norm and the consequences of their performance or non-performance.

In the T-NORM model, a norm activation can generate many different *deontic relations*. In other approaches, like for example in [1], a norm generates norm instances. We prefer to use the term deontic relation because it can also be used to denote obligations and prohibitions that are not created by activating a norm, but for example by making a promise or accepting an agreement.

In the `ON ?event WHERE` and in the `BEFORE ?event WHERE` components, the norm designer has to describe the *conditions* that a real event has to satisfy to match a norm. In our model all the relevant events and actions are represented in the *State Knowledge Base*. The data for managing the evolution of the state of norms, for example the deontic relation objects, are stored in the *Deontic Knowledge Base*. Obviously, the formalism chosen for representing the data in the *State KB* and the *Deontic KB* determines the syntax for expressing: the *conditions*, which are evaluated on the *State KB*, and the *actions* (after `THEN`), which are performed on the *Deontic KB*. Differently from other approaches, where the context or state of the interaction is represented by using propositional formulae [1,9], we decided to formalize the *State KB* and the *Deontic KB* by using semantic web technologies, in particular the W3C Web Ontology Language (OWL). This choice has the following advantages:

- events and actions are represented with a more expressive language, indeed OWL is a practical realization of a Description Logic known as *SROIQ(D)*, which is more expressive than propositional logic;
- in the definition of the conceptual model of the State KB it is possible to reuse existing OWL ontologies making the various systems involved in norm monitoring interoperable;
- it is possible to perform automatic reasoning (OWL can be regarded as a decidable fragment of First-Order Logic) on the *State KB* and deducing knowledge from the asserted one. In particular, this is important when the execution of an action logically implies another one. For example, the reproduction of an audio file implies its use, therefore if the use is forbidden so is its reproduction. This is a crucial advantage because instead of creating special properties that allow you to express which actions imply other ones (like for example it has been done in ODRL with the `implies` property[4]) it is sufficient to reason on the actions performed by using OWL reasoners.

In the specification of *conditions*, OWL classes are represented using unary predicates starting with a capital letter and OWL properties are represented using binary predicates starting with a lowercase letter. If an event is described with more conditions, they are evaluated conjunctively, variables (starting with ?) are bound to a value, and a negated condition is satisfied if there is no element in the KB that matches it. In the example reported in this paper, the conceptual model of the events represented in the *State KB* is formalized with the *Event Ontology* in OWL [4,6], which imports the *Time Ontology* in OWL[5] used for connecting events to instants or intervals of time, and the *Action Ontology* for representing domain-specific actions, like the PayAction class. The conceptual model of the *Deontic KB* is formalized with the *T-Norm Ontology* in OWL[6].

---

[4] https://www.w3.org/TR/odrl-model/#action.

[5] https://www.w3.org/TR/owl-time/.

[6] https://raw.githubusercontent.com/fornaran/T-Norm-Model/main/tnorm.owl.

In the second component of norms, the BEFORE condition and the ELSE branch are optional. The BEFORE part is mainly used for expressing deadlines for obligations. Although an obligation without a deadline cannot be violated and therefore it is not an incentive to perform the obligatory action, the BEFORE part is not compulsory. The ELSE branch is followed when the regulated action cannot happen anymore in the future, for example if it has to happen before a given deadline (in this case event3 is a time event) and the deadline expires without event2 being performed. In principle other conditions, beside BEFORE, can be used to express other temporal operators but they are not introduced in this version of our model. In the consequent (THEN) parts of a norm, it is possible to specify that:

- (COMPUTE) the value of some variables (for example the deadline that depends on the activation time) are computed using arithmetic operations and the value of variables obtained when matching the antecedent;
- (CREATE) new individuals belonging to a certain class and having certain properties have to be created in the *Deontic KB* for making the monitoring of norms feasible. Each conditional norm, when activated, can generate several deontic relations;
- (ASSERT) the value of certain properties of existing individuals created by the norm may be set.

The *debtor* of a deontic relation is the agent that is responsible for its violation or fulfilment; usually it is the actor of the regulated action. In legal systems there are exceptions to this general rule (for example for actions performed by minors or people with mental impairment or in cases of strict liability), but we leave this aspect for future works. Specifying the debtor is important because it is the agent to whom sanctions will apply (this aspect is not addressed in the current paper).

The *creditor* of a deontic relation is the agent to whom the debtor owns the performance or non-performance of the regulated action. In certain cases it may be difficult to establish the creditor of a deontic relation (for example who is the creditor of the prohibition of running a red light?); we leave for future works the analysis of this aspect.

3.1 Expressive Power of the Model

By using the T-NORM model we are able to express different types of norms. First of all it is possible to formalize conditional and direct (or un-conditional) obligations and conditional and direct prohibitions. Moreover, every conditional norm (whether it is an obligation or a prohibition) when activated will bring to the creation of *specific deontic relations* or to the creation of *general deontic relations*. Every specific deontic relation regulates the performance of an action by a specific agent, differently every general deontic relation regulates the performance of a class of actions that can be concretely realized by different agents, and therefore can generate many violations or fulfilments.

There exist models, which are not focused on regulating time-constrained actions, where (coherently with deontic logics) prohibitions are merely formalized as obligations to not perform the regulated action. However, when the regulated actions are time constrained it is crucial to react to their performance but also to their non-performance in due time. Think for example to the prohibition expressed by Norm02: *"Italian libraries cannot lend DVDs until 2 years are passed from the distribution of the DVD"*. This prohibition cannot be expressed as an obligation to not lend certain DVDs in a specific time interval, because while an obligation is fulfilled by the performance of a single instance of an action, a prohibition is not fulfilled by a single instance of refraining from the performance of an action. In the T-NORM model the main difference between obligations and prohibitions is that the performance of the regulated action brings about a fulfilment in the case of obligations and a violation in the case of prohibitions.

To illustrate the flexibility of our model, we shall now present examples of different types of norms. Due to space limitation we will not formalize them all. Norm01 is an example of *conditional obligation* and each one of its activations creates one *specific* deontic relation to pay 6 euros for the owner of every vehicle that entered in the limited-traffic area. Norm01 may be formalized with the T-NORM model in following way:

```
NORM Norm01
ON ?e1
    WHERE RestrictedTrafficAreaAccess(?e1) AND vehicle(?e1,?v) AND
    owner(?v,?agent) AND atTime(?e1,?inst1) AND
    inXSDDateTimeStamp(?inst1,?t1) AND ?t1.hour>7 a.m. AND ?t1.hour<7p.m
THEN
    COMPUTE ?t_end.hour=?t1.hour+24
    CREATE  DeonticRelation(?dr01_n);TimeEvent(?tev_end_n);
            Instant(?inst_end_n);
    ASSERT  isGenerated(?dr01_n,Norm01);activated(?dr01_n,?e1);
            debtor(?dr01_n,?agent);end(?dr01_n,?tev_end_n);
            atTime(?tev_end_n,?inst_end_n);
            inXSDDateTimeStamp(?inst_end_n,?t_end);
    ON ?e2  BEFORE ?tev_end_n
        WHERE PayAction(?e2) AND reason(?e2,?e1) AND recipient(?e2,Milan)
        AND price(?e2,6) AND priceCurrency(?e2,euro) AND actor(?e2,?agent).
    THEN ASSERT fulfills(?agent,?dr01_n); fulfilled(?dr01_n,?e2)
    ELSE ASSERT violates(?agent,?dr01_n); violated(?dr01_n,?tev_end_n)
```

where a counter n is incremented each time the norm is activated, so that each activation creates a different deontic relation.

Norm02 (*"Italian libraries cannot lend DVDs until 2 years are passed from the distribution of the DVD"*) is an example of *conditional prohibition*, its activation creates a *general* deontic relation every time a new DVD is distributed. The general deontic relation created for each specific DVD regulates the actions of all the agents registered in Italian libraries.

The third type of norms is a *conditional prohibition* that generates *specific* deontic relations, an example of this type of norm is Norm03: *"a person who has a positive swab to Covid-19 cannot leave the house for the next 15 days"*. The fourth type of norm is a *conditional obligation* that generates *general* deontic relations, like for example in Norm04: *"when the school bell rings, students have 5'min to enter their classroom"*.

An example of *unconditional prohibition* is given by Norm05: *"when the red light is on it is prohibited to pass the traffic light"*. This prohibition is unconditional because there is no need to react to its activation by performing specific actions. For enforcing this prohibition it is enough to check the state of the red light every time an agent pass the traffic light and if the red light is on there is directly a violation. Finally, the following Norm06: *"the lecturer of a course has to organize 2 exams per year"* is an example of *unconditional obligation*.

Finally, we present an example of conditional obligation where the obliged action should be performed before another event that is not a time event (there is not a deadline). Norm07 is: *"When an agent enters into a supermarket parking between 7 a.m. and 7 p.m., they have to pay 2 euros for every hour of the parking unless they did some shopping at the supermarket"*.

It is important to mention an important constraint for the use of the model: the regulated action must have an actor, this actor is the debtor of the deontic relation and is the agent who will fulfill or violate the deontic relation.

3.2   The Model of Exceptions

The meaning of having the *permission* to perform an action has been widely studied in the literature and different types of permission have been analyzed. In [8] the important distinction between *strong* and *weak* permission has been discussed. Having the weak permission to do an action is equivalent to the absence of the prohibition to do such an action. Differently, we have the strong permission to do an action when there is the explicit permission to do such an action; usually strong permissions are used to explicitly derogate to existing prohibitions. A similar notion is that of *exemption*, which is used to derogate obligations. In the T-Norm model we introduce one construct, the *exception*, that can be used for modelling both permission and exemption and can be iterated at any level of depth.

By using the T-Norm model we can specify different types of exceptions. The *first type* is represented by exceptions to norms activation. When some specific conditions on the event that activates the norm are met, the consequent deontic relation has not to be generated. An example of this type of exception to Norm01 is: *"ambulances do not have to pay for entering into the limited traffic area"*. In this case a check on the type of the vehicle inhibits the creation of the obligation to pay, thus creating an exemption.

The exceptions of the *second type* are those to deontic relations, i.e. when some specific conditions on the regulated event are satisfied the generation of violation/fulfilment is inhibited. An example of this type of exception to Norm02 is: *"school teachers can always borrow every DVD from the library"*. In this case, a check on the position of the borrower can be used to prevent the violation of the prohibition, that is, for creating a permission. This type of exception cannot be expressed by inhibiting the activation of the norm (using the first type of exception) because the condition (being a school teacher) is on the borrower, who is not part of the activating event of the prohibition.

Both these types of exceptions could be expressed by adding some specific conditions to the antecedent of a norm. However, this solution requires to modify an already enforced norm by adding further conditions. This is not a good solution because it implies changing a previously defined norm every time an exception is introduced. A better solution consists in expressing exceptions with a construct that is external to norms. Our idea is to introduce a construct that is able to inhibit the activation or the fulfilment/violation of a norm when the activating or the regulated event happens and some further conditions are met. Therefore, we formalize exceptions with a construct whose effects is to inhibit the activation of one of the components of a norm. Given that an exception is strictly related to a norm, we assume that it has access to all the variables introduced in the related norm, to which it simply adds some more conditions. An exception is expressed in one of the following ways on the basis of its type:

```
EXCEPTION TO Norm_n TYPE 1
ON  ?event1
WHERE conditions on event1
THEN  exceptionToNorm(Norm_n,?event1)
```

```
EXCEPTION TO Norm_n TYPE 2
ON  ?event2
WHERE conditions on event2 AND isGenerated(?dr,Norm_n)
THEN  exceptionToDR(?dr,?event2)
```

For example the formalization of an exception of the fist type to Norm01 for ambulances is:

```
EXCEPTION TO Norm01
ON   ?e1 WHERE Ambulance(?v)
THEN exceptionToNorm(Norm01,?e1)
```

These types of exceptions cannot be formalized by simply deleting a norm or a *general deontic relation*, because they suspend the effects of norms only in particular situations. For example, Norm01 applies to all vehicles except ambulances and Norm02 applies to all library subscribers except school teachers.

By analysing real cases of norms, we realized that there exists a *third type* of exceptions whose effect is to inhibit the fulfilment or violation of *specific deontic relations*. These exceptions are different from those of the second type because they are triggered by an event that is not the one regulated by the norm. For example an exception to the Covid-19 Norm03 is: *"if the house is on fire then everybody is allowed to leave it"*. This exception is activated by an event (the house is on fire) that is different from the action that is regulated by the norm (leaving the house). We model those exceptions in the following way:

```
EXCEPTION TO Norm_n TYPE 3
ON  ?event_n
WHERE conditions on event_n AND isGenerated(?dr, Norm_n) AND
      NOT fulfills(?agent,?dr) AND NOT violates(?agent,?dr)
THEN  exceptionToDR(?dr,?event_n)
```

For example the exception to Norm03 is formalized as[7]:

```
EXCEPTION TO Norm03 TYPE 3
ON  ?en
WHERE Fire(?en) AND place(?en,?house) AND residence(?house,?agent) AND
      isGenerated(?dr,Norm03) AND activated(?dr,?e1) AND
      affectedPerson(?e1,?agent) AND NOT fulfills(?agent,?dr) AND
      NOT violates(?agent,?dr)
THEN  exceptionToDR(?dr,?en)
```

It is also possible to have exceptions to exceptions that will inhibit the activation of the three types of exceptions described above.

4   Operational Semantics of the Model

In this section, we will show how the model of norms proposed so far can be used to monitor the temporal evolution of normative states on the basis of the events occurred in the interaction among agents. Our goal is to compute the violation or fulfilment of norms on the basis of actual events.

The operational semantics of the T-NORM model can be specified by providing an unambiguous procedure for translating the model into a target formalism that already has an operational semantics. As target formalism we choose production rules, because their structure and behavior make it fairly easy to translate norms into them. Production rules, often simply called productions or rules, have been investigated in computer science, and in particular in the AI literature related to knowledge representation and reasoning [2]. A production rule has the form:

IF *conditions* THEN *actions*.

It has two parts: an antecedent set of *conditions* that are tested on the current state of the *working memory* and a *consequent* set of *actions* that typically modify the *working memory*.

The operational semantics of a production rule system is given in the W3C Recommendation of the RIF Production Rule Dialect[8] by means of a labeled terminal transition system. Such an operational semantics depends on the adoption of a *conflict resolution strategy* for selecting the rule instance that must fire when more than one rule is applicable. Our conflict resolution strategy is

---

[7] Where **affectedPerson** is the property that connects the event of having a positive swab with the tested person and it is used for connecting the activation event of the norm with the activation of the exception.

[8] https://www.w3.org/TR/rif-prd/#Operational_semantics_of_rules_and_rule_sets.

as follows. Firstly, use the *priority* among rules (for example, as we will discuss later, production rules for representing exceptions have higher priority than production rules for expressing norms). Secondly, when two or more rules have the same priority, use the *order* conflict resolution strategy, i.e., pick the first applicable rule in order of presentation. This choice will not influence the final state reached by the working memory because the actions of the production rules used for expressing norms will never remove knowledge from the *State KB*, they have effects only on the *Deontic KB*.

We will now describe the procedure for translating every norm written using the T-Norm model into three production rules and every exception into one production rule. In particular, every norm (`Norm_n`) translates into three production rules according to the following procedure:

1. Create one production rule equal to the fist `ON...THEN` part in the norm. Add, among the *conditions* part of this production rule, the condition for managing exceptions of the first type (i.e. `NOT exceptionToNorm(Norm_n,?e1)`, this condition is satisfied if in the working memory there is not an exception to `Norm_n` that matches with the activation event.
2. Create one production rule equal to the second `ON...THEN` part in the norm. Add, among the *conditions* part of this production rule, the condition for managing the exception of the second and third type (i.e. `NOT exceptionToDR(?dr,?e2) AND NOT exceptionToDR(?dr,?en)`), the conditions for checking that the regulated action is performed before `event3` (that for obligations may represent a deadline) and after the activation of the norm, and the conditions for checking that the deontic relation, which can be matched with the rule, is generated by `Norm_n` and it is not already fulfilled or violated.
3. Create one production rule for expressing the `ON...ELSE` part in the norm. This rule is fired when the regulated action (represented in the norm with variable `event2`) can no longer be performed before the event represented with the variable `event3`. That is, when `event3` has occurred (e.g. the deadline has passed) and the regulated action (e.g. the payment) has not been executed. The procedure adds, among the *conditions* of this production rule, the condition for checking that `event3` is happened and that the deontic relation, generated by `Norm_n`, is not already fulfilled nor violated. As for the previous rule, the procedure adds also the conditions for managing the exception of the second and third type.

Every exception to a given norm (`Norm_n`) translates into one production rule thanks to another automatic procedure. Since each exception has access to all variables introduced in the related norm, the conditions in the norm are merged with the conditions of the exception during the creation of the production rule. In particular, conditions on `e1` (asserted in the corresponding norm) are added to the conditions of the production rule created from exception of the first type. Conditions on `e2` (asserted in the corresponding norm) are added to the conditions of the production rule created from exception of the second type.

Production rules that represent first-, second-, and third-type exceptions must fire before production rules that express norms, so they have a higher *priority* than the latter. Since production rules, used to formalise exceptions to norms, act before the production rules of the norms themselves, they are able to inhibit the norm for certain events.

Exceptions to exceptions are able to inhibit an exception to norm for certain events. They must fire fistly, thus production rules for representing *exceptions to exceptions* must have higher priority than the production rules for expressing exceptions to norms. In order for one exception to exception to inhibit the activation of one specific exception to Norm_n, it is required to add to the production rule of the latter a further condition for checking that does not exist an exception to exception for its activation event, i.e. NOT exceptionToException(Norm_n,?e).

The conditions of the production rules are evaluated on a *working memory*, which consists of: (i) the *State KB* where all the relevant events happened and the actions performed by the agents are recorded, those events are represented using the *OWL Event Ontology*; and (ii) the *Deontic KB*, where all the information for managing the evolution of the state of norms is stored.

Given that the *working memory* contains an OWL ontology, it is possible to use OWL reasoning on its content for computing for example that the performance of an action implies another one. This is a crucial aspect of the proposed normative model because without any further addition, it is possible to reason on the effects that the logical implication between actions has on norms fulfilment or violation. In fact, we obtain that the obligation to perform an action is fulfilled by any action that implies the regulated one. This is because we have the following chain of implications: action $a1$ implies action $a2$ and $a2$ produces a fulfilment, so the performance of $a1$ leads to a fulfilment. For example, since selling an object to someone involves a transfer of ownership, a sale will fulfill the obligation to transfer ownership of an object to someone. Similarly, the prohibition to perform an action is violated by the performance of any action that implies the regulated one. For example, since the reproduction of an audio file implies its use, if the use of a particular audio file is prohibited its reproduction will lead to an violation. Finally, the permission to perform a generic action implies the permission to perform all the more specific actions implied by the generic one. This is because the specific action implies the more generic one that will activate the exception that in turn inhibits the norm. For example, if an agent has permission to transfer the ownership of a product, through OWL reasoning it is possible to infer that she also has permission to sell or give someone else the product.

5   Architecture of the Framework and Its Implementation

The architecture of the framework designed to compute the fulfillment or violation of a set of norms (formalized with the T-NORM model) is depicted in Fig. 1. In the proposed framework, we take advantage of two types of computation: OWL reasoning on the *State KB* and forward chaining realized by means of production rules. OWL reasoning and forward chaining are combined in a safe manner because they alternate. In particular, the main steps of a software able to simulate the evolution of the norms state over time, is as follows:

1. Every time an event or an action occurs its representation is added to the *State KB*, then an OWL reasoner is executed on the working memory. We assume that only events that happen at the current instant of time can be inserted in the *State KB*;
2. Then run the forward chaining engine on the working memory resulting from the previous step using the production rules generated from the norms and from the exceptions and store the resulting *State KB* together with the *Deontic KB* in the working memory;
3. Updates the variable that keeps track of the current instant of time to the next *significant* time instant[9] and go back to point 1.

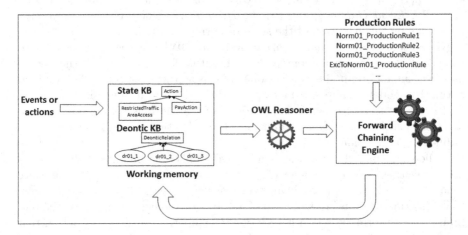

Fig. 1. Architecture of the framework designed to compute the fulfillment or violation of norms.

In our model we need to combine OWL reasoning and forward chaining because it is not possible to use only OWL reasoning for computing the violation or fulfilment of norms. In fact, when norms regulate time constrained actions, it is necessary to deduce that the non-performance of the regulated action before a deadline implies violation or a fulfilment. Given that OWL reasoning works on an open world assumption, inferences of this type cannot be drawn directly. One possible solution to this problem is computing the closure of specific classes using an external routine as proposed in [5]. The advantage of using production

---

[9] An instant of time is significant when its occurrence is significant for at least one norm, e.g. it is the time instant in which a deadline expires or the time instant at which an event or an action occurs.

rules is a clear separation of two different types of computation, each one used coherently with its nature, and having a more declarative solution where the semantics of norms is expressed with production rules instead of using Java code.

We tested the described framework by implementing a Java prototype that uses Pellet[10], an open-source Java based OWL reasoner, and the JENA general purpose rule engine[11] for realizing forward chaining on production rules. The reason why we chose to use the JENA framework is that, differently from other rule-based systems like DROOLS (used in [1]) or Jess (used in [7]), its rule engine natively supports rule-based computations over an OWL ontology serialized as an RDF graph. JENA provides forward chaining realized by means of an internal RETE-based interpreter.

To test the framework, the various type of norms discussed in Sect. 3.1 were manually translated into a set of production rules written using rule syntax and structure of the JENA rule-based reasoner. The translation is done following the procedure described in Sect. 4. Given that the JENA rule engine does not natively support the possibility to specify the *priority* among rules, we introduced a variable called `salience` whose value change from 0 to 2 and a new builtin called `isSalince(n)` that can be used in production rules for checking if the value of the `salience` variable is equal to `n`.

In order to simulate the evolution in time of the state of the norms, a set of real actions matching with the activation condition of the norms or with their regulated actions have been inserted in the *State KB*. As depicted in Fig. 2, in order to check the fulfillment or violation of the different deontic relations created by the various activation of `Norm01`, we entered three accesses to the restricted traffic zone in the *State KB*. For one of these accesses (`access3`) we have entered the corresponding payment and therefore the deontic relation that obliges the owner of the vehicle to pay becomes fulfilled. For another access (`access2`) we do not enter the corresponding payment and thus, when the deadline expires, the deontic relation that expressed the obligation to pay becomes violated. For the last of the accesses (`access1`), the vehicle is an ambulance, so thanks to the exception, the obligation to pay is not even created. The Java project developed for simulating the fulfillment or the violation of `Norm01`, the three production rules generated starting from `Norm01` and the production rule generated from the exception to `Norm01` (see Sect. 3.2) are available on GitHub[12].

6   Related Work

In the literature, there are various proposals where models of norms and policies are formalized using different languages and where different frameworks are investigated with the goal of providing various services. Useful services are: searching of policies having certain characteristics [11], anticipating conflicts

---

[10] https://github.com/stardog-union/pellet.
[11] https://jena.apache.org/documentation/inference/#rules.
[12] https://github.com/fornaran/tnorm.Norm01.

RestrictedTrafficAreaAccess	DeonticRelation	Violated	PayAction	Fulfilled
access1. atTime.inXSDDateTimeStamp: 2020.05.19T11:00:00 hasVehicle.type:Ambulance	a new deontic relationship is not created because there is an exception for vehicles of type Ambulance			
access2. atTime.inXSDDateTimeStamp: 2020.05.20T11:00:00 hasVehicle.type:Vehicle	dr01_1. end.atTime. inXSDDateTimeStamp: 2020.05.21T11:00:00	dr01_1 is violated at 2020.05.21T11:00:00 because the deadline is not met		
access3. atTime.inXSDDateTimeStamp: 2020.05.31T11:00:00 hasVehicle.type: Vehicle	dr01_2. end.atTime. inXSDDateTimeStamp: 2020.06:01T11:00:00		pay3. atTime.inXSDDateTimeStamp: 2020.05.31T13:00:00 reason: acess3	dr01_2 is fulfilled at 2020.05.31T13:00:00 with pay3

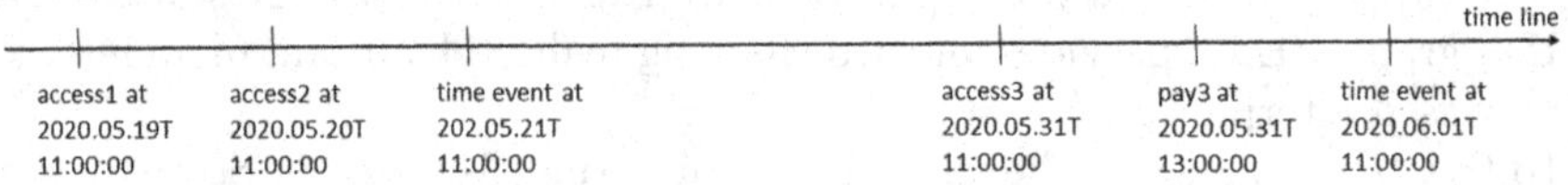

```
                                                                                              time line
  ┼──────────┼──────────────┼────────────────────────┼───────────┼──────────────┼
access1 at      access2 at        time event at          access3 at      pay3 at        time event at
2020.05.19T    2020.05.20T        202.05.21T             2020.05.31T    2020.05.31T    2020.06.01T
11:00:00       11:00:00           11:00:00               11:00:00       13:00:00       11:00:00
```

Fig. 2. Fulfillment/violation of the different deontic relations created by the activations of Norm01.

among policies [13], monitoring [6] or compliance checking [3], and simulation for performing a what-if reasoning [14].

One of the pioneer techniques for normative reasoning is deontic logic [17]. Despite deontic logic approaches present some limitations, for example the triggering and regulated actions are usually expressed with simple propositional formulae [9], some of their basic concepts and insights are still used in many recent approaches where other formal languages are used. In order to pursue interoperability among different normative systems, it is crucial to use a standard language for the formalization of norms. Today's there are two standards: the previously mentioned ODRL policy expression language, which is a W3C Recommendation and the OASIS standard LegalRuleML[13], which defines a rule interchange language for the legal domain and is formalized using RuleML. ODRL has many connections with the model proposed in this paper as it is a language for expressing obligations, prohibitions, and permissions. A great limitation of ODRL is not having an operational semantics that allows to compute the fulfillment or the violation of policies. In our previous work [6] we proposed to extend the ODRL information model to express its operational semantics using finite state machines implemented using production rules. In this work we have moved further away from ODRL, in order to overcome some limitations. Firstly, in ODRL it is not possible to specify generic policies applicable every time to a different agent. In ODRL the debtor of a policy can only be a specific agent. Differently, thanks to our abstract model for policies specification, it is possible to apply one policy to all the agents who will perform a certain action (for example having a positive swab) or who plays a certain role. Secondly, we do not consider exceptions (and in particular permissions) at the same level of obligations and prohibitions. From our perspective exceptions are derived concepts and they

---

[13] https://www.oasis-open.org/committees/legalruleml/.

exist only if there is a corresponding basic level construct that expresses obligations and prohibitions. Finally, while ODRL has a fixed set of deontic types, in our model we focus on specifying the sequence of events that bring to a violation or to a fulfillment. An important aspect that the T-NORM and the ODRL model have in common is the use of semantic web technologies. Although they use them for different purposes: ODRL uses the OWL language for the specification of the policy meta-model, while in the T-NORM model, as well as in the OWL-POLAR model [13], the OWL language is used for modeling the actions performed by agents and consequently to express the activation conditions and the actions regulated by the norms.

We now continue our comparison by focusing on models of norms that are expressed using semantic web languages and/or by using production rules, although none of them combines OWL reasoning and productions as we do. Two features that make our model innovative are: the formalization of the relation between norms and time constraints and the possibility to directly describe what sequence of events or actions would bring an agent to the violation or to the fulfillment of a norm. In the OWL-POLAR framework [13], similarly to our approach, the state of the world is represented using an OWL ontology. Differently, policies activation is computed by translating the conjunctive semantic formulae, used for describing what is prohibited, permitted or required by the policy, into SPARQL queries that are evaluated on the state of the world. In this work we propose a straighter approach where norms conditions are directly evaluated on the state of the world without the need of translations. An interesting aspect of the OWL-POLAR framework that we plan to investigate in our future works, is the mechanism for anticipating possible conflicts among policies, and for conflict avoidance and resolution.

In [1] one type of norm is defined as a tuple that can generate a norm instance that in turn can be fulfilled or violated. A norm specifies a target condition that describes the state that fulfills the norm and a maintenance condition used for defining the conditions that, when they no longer subsists, lead to a violation. In this approach count-as rules are used to introduce institutional facts, regulated by norms, starting from brute events. Differently from our model, where it is possible to model different type of deadlines, in this approach only a time-out property, i.e. a deadline for the reparation of the violation of a norm, is taken into account. In [1] an interesting violation handling norm is formalized that is activated when another norm is violated. Similarly to our approach the monitoring is realized using a production system that concretely is implemented using DROOLS, but no discussion is offered on the advantages of using OWL reasoning and on how to combine it with forward-chaining realized by means of production rules.

Another interesting proposal is the KAoS policy management framework [14]. In KAoS Semantic Web technologies are used for policy specification and management, in particular policy monitoring and enforcing is realized by a component that compiles OWL policies into an efficient format. In the literature there are other interesting approaches where norms are specified as rules but they are not taking advantage of the use of semantic web technologies. For example in [15] norms are generators of commitments for the agents playing a certain role in an artificial institution. In [7] norms have a type, they may have a deadline, and given that their form is: *preconditions* → *postconditions*, those norms are easily expressible with Jess rules[14]. Finally in [3] an extension of the ODRL language is proposed to capture the semantics of business policies thanks to their translation into Answer Set Programming for making it possible to realize compliance checking. An interesting aspect of this work is that the result of compliance checking can be positive or negative with an explanation of the aspects of the policy that caused the non-compliance.

In our future work, we plan to investigate the application of sanctions or rewards and to study the formalization of the notion of institutional power, and we plan to further investigate the expressive power of the model for specifying other types of deontic relations.

Acknowledgement. The research reported in this paper has been funded by the SNSF (Swiss National Science Foundation) grant no. 200021_175759/1. We acknowledge the contribution to this research by Mr Marco Sterpetti during his master thesis at Politecnico di Milano.

References

1. Alvarez-Napagao, S., Aldewereld, H., Vázquez-Salceda, J., Dignum, F.: Normative monitoring: semantics and implementation. In: De Vos, M., Fornara, N., Pitt, J.V., Vouros, G. (eds.) COIN -2010. LNCS (LNAI), vol. 6541, pp. 321–336. Springer, Heidelberg (2011). https://doi.org/10.1007/978-3-642-21268-0_18
2. Brachman, R., Levesque, H.: Knowledge Representation and Reasoning. Morgan Kaufmann Publishers Inc., San Francisco (2004)
3. De Vos, M., Kirrane, S., Padget, J., Satoh, K.: ODRL policy modelling and compliance checking. In: Fodor, P., Montali, M., Calvanese, D., Roman, D. (eds.) RuleML+RR 2019. LNCS, vol. 11784, pp. 36–51. Springer, Cham (2019). https://doi.org/10.1007/978-3-030-31095-0_3
4. Fornara, N.: Specifying and monitoring obligations in open multiagent systems using semantic web technology. In: Elci, A., Kone, M.T., Orgun, M.A. (eds.) Semantic Agent Systems. Studies in Computational Intelligence, vol. 344. Springer, Heidelberg (2011). https://doi.org/10.1007/978-3-642-18308-9_2
5. Fornara, N., Colombetti, M.: Representation and monitoring of commitments and norms using OWL. AI Commun. **23**(4), 341–356 (2010)
6. Fornara, N., Colombetti, M.: Using semantic web technologies and production rules for reasoning on obligations, permissions, and prohibitions. AI Commun. **32**(4), 319–334 (2019)
7. Garcia-Camino, A., Noriega, P., Rodriguez-Aguilar, J.P.: Implementing norms in electronic institutions. In: Proceedings of the Fourth International Joint Conference on Autonomous Agents and Multiagent Systems, AAMAS 2005, pp. 667–673, New York, NY, USA. ACM (2005)

---

[14] Jess is a rule engine for the Java platform.

8. Governatori, G., Olivieri, F., Rotolo, A., Scannapieco, S.: Computing strong and weak permissions in defeasible logic. J. Philos. Log. **42**(6), 799–829 (2013)
9. Governatori, G., Rotolo, A.: A conceptually rich model of business process compliance. In: Proceedings of the Seventh Asia-Pacific Conference on Conceptual Modelling - Vol. 110, pp. 3–12. Australian Computer Society Inc. (2010)
10. Horrocks, I.: OWL: A description logic based ontology language. In: van Beek, P. (ed.) CP 2005. LNCS, vol. 3709, pp. 5–8. Springer, Heidelberg (2005). https://doi.org/10.1007/11564751_2
11. Oltramari, A., et al.: PrivOnto: a semantic framework for the analysis of privacy policies. Seman. Web **9**(2), 185–203 (2018)
12. Panagiotidi, S., Alvarez-Napagao, S., Vázquez-Salceda, J.: Towards the norm-aware agent: bridging the gap between deontic specifications and practical mechanisms for norm monitoring and norm-aware planning. In: Balke, T., Dignum, F., van Riemsdijk, M.B., Chopra, A.K. (eds.) COIN 2013. LNCS (LNAI), vol. 8386, pp. 346–363. Springer, Cham (2014). https://doi.org/10.1007/978-3-319-07314-9_19
13. Sensoy, M., Norman, T.J., Vasconcelos, W.W., Sycara, K.P.: OWL-POLAR: a framework for semantic policy representation and reasoning. J. Web Sem. **12**, 148–160 (2012)
14. Uszok, A., et al.: New developments in ontology-based policy management: increasing the practicality and comprehensiveness of KAoS. In: POLICY 2008, 2–4 June 2008, Palisades, New York, USA, pp. 145–152. IEEE Computer Society (2008)
15. Viganò, F., Fornara, N., Colombetti, M.: An event driven approach to norms in artificial institutions. In: Boissier, Q., et al. (eds.) AAMAS 2005. LNCS (LNAI), vol. 3913, pp. 142–154. Springer, Heidelberg (2006). https://doi.org/10.1007/11775331_10
16. Villata, G.E.S. (Ed): Special Issue: Normative Multi-agent Systems, Volume 5 of Journal of Applied Logics - IfCoLog Journal. College Publications (2018)
17. von Wright, G.H.: Deontic logic. Mind, New Series **60**(237), 1–15 (1951)

Collaborative Human-Agent Planning
for Resilience

Ronal Singh[1(✉)], Tim Miller[1], and Darryn Reid[2]

[1] University of Melbourne, Melbourne, Australia
{singhrr,tmiller}@unimelb.edu.au
[2] Department of Defence Science, Adelaide, Australia
Darryn.Reid@dst.defence.gov.au

Abstract. Intelligent agents assist people in complex scenarios, such as managing teams of semi-autonomous vehicles. However, planning models may be incomplete, leading to plans that do not adequately meet the stated objectives, especially in unpredicted situations. Humans, who are apt at identifying and adapting to unusual situations, may be able to assist planning agents in these situations by encoding their knowledge into a planner at run-time. We investigate whether people can collaborate with agents by providing their knowledge to an agent using linear temporal logic (LTL) at run-time without changing the agent's domain model. We presented 24 participants with baseline plans for situations in which a planner had limitations and asked the participants for workarounds for these limitations. We encoded these workarounds as LTL constraints. Results show that participants' constraints improved the expected return of the plans by 10% ($p < 0.05$) relative to baseline plans, demonstrating that human insight can be used in collaborative planning for resilience. However, participants used more declarative than control constraints over time, but declarative constraints produced plans less similar to the participants' expectations, which could lead to potential trust issues.

1 Introduction

Intelligent agents assist human operators in complex scenarios, such as task planning to fulfil a set of objectives when supervising teams of semi-autonomous vehicles [32]. The models used by these agents are typically both incorrect and incomplete. They lack details of how to respond in unpredicted and unpredictable situations, such as when they encounter a situation for which they have no training data or have not been modelled explicitly [30].

Humans are far superior at recognising unusual situations and adapting robustly. The ability for a person to provide an intelligent agent with additional context and information at *runtime* that is not part of its model (i.e. not encoded by an expert at design-time) would increase the effectiveness and trustworthiness of the agent. Consider an example of a team of autonomous aerial vehicles (UAVs) searching for missing hikers in an area near a small airport. Due to aircrafts leaving and arriving at the airport, certain regions may be 'no-fly' zones. However, the underlying task planner has no concept of 'no-fly' zones at all. Thus, the question is: how can a human operator input the constraints required to the task planner to avoid the no-fly zones while still achieving its objectives? We call such knowledge *resilience* constraints, as they are constraints that improve the resilience of plans. Following [21], we define *resilience* as the ability to recover from the consequences of an unpredicted or adverse event for a given state of the system.

We define human-agent collaborative planning for resilient planning in Markov Decision Processes (MDPs). We investigate whether people can recognise the limitations of plans, identify how to work around the limitations, and provide resilience constraints to a planner to find plans that adhere to these workarounds. Our longer-term vision is to enable non-AI experts to input this type of knowledge at runtime without modifying the domain theory. The agent can then re-plan to improve the solution using this knowledge. We hypothesise that constraints represented in LTL are suited to encode resilience constraints, as these logics fit naturally with how people describe plan properties. To test this hypothesis, we presented 24 participants with 6 tasks in a scenario involving surveillance by a team of UAVs. In each task, a default plan was presented, and an 'intelligence update' provided to the participants outlined additional information not knowable by the planner. Participants were asked to provide resilience constraints without changing the underlying domain model. We encoded participants' responses as LTL constraints and measured the resilience of the resulting plans. Our results showed that participants could provide insight leading to more resilient plans, improving the expected returns by 10%.

2   Related Work

This section provides an overview of related literature in human-agent collaborative planning and encoding domain-control knowledge in planning.

2.1   Human-Agent Collaborative Planning

In this paper, we are interested in incorporating user input into planners at run time rather than being explicitly coded at design time by expert modellers.

While the idea of machine learning algorithms that learn from user demonstration is a well-studied topic (e.g. [2,31]), it is less so in human-agent planning. TRAINS [16] and TRIPS [17] systems for *mixed-initiative* planning allowed users to provide input into the planning system while other works include [1]. As far as we are aware, Anderson et al. [3] was the first to investigate the combination of human and computational expertise, aimed at avoiding search local optima rather than improving resilience. Hayes et al. [19] investigate how HTN-like constraints can be learnt from task graphs provided by experts. While it is possible to incorporate this into our work, we instead use linear temporal logic due to its expressiveness. Icarte et al. [22] had similar objectives to ours, but we are interested in how people represent knowledge (advice) that they have without introducing domain variables, something they did not investigate. De Giacomo et al. [12] use LTL to specify restraining specifications that could assess solutions using features unknown to the agent. They require external sensors to verify the restraining specifications, and they do not require agents to be aware of the constraints, while this is imperative for our agents. Similarly, they do not undertake user studies.

A complementary approach to ours is enabling humans to modify a reward function. Kelley et al. [23] proposed an interface that allows an operator to increase and decrease the agent's reward functions; e.g. put a high reward on visiting a desirable area, allowing the operator to create more resilient plans. While they did not perform controlled human behavioural experiments, their approach would be complementary to ours, allowing simple constraints that can be modelled as rewards. For managing large teams of agents, we believe that the approach of using concepts such as LTL constraints would scale better because LTL is a better representation of the way that people describe behaviour [25].

The work from Kim et al. [25] is the closest related work to ours, and their experimental setup inspired ours. In their study, participants provided strategies in natural language for solving planning problems. These strategies were encoded as preferences in LTL, and new plans were generated. In five out of the six domains, the collaborative plans were lower cost than the non-collaborative plans. Kim et al. [25] argue that LTL formulae are more suitable for representing how people instruct subordinates and are more succinct than explicitly enumerating the steps of a plan. The difference is the fundamental aim of the work: Kim et al. [25] aim for strategies over entire domains that improve the cost and solving time of plans – in other words, design-time knowledge from people who understand planning—while in this work, we aim to increase resilience in individual, unpredicted situations using knowledge from operators.

2.2 Encoding Domain-Control Knowledge in Planning

Domain-independent planners cope with the complexity of planning through domain-independent heuristics [20]. However, domain-independent heuristics are not always well informed; for example, they miss key knowledge when interactions between goals are strong [18].

Domain-specific Control knowledge (DCK) refers to knowledge for solving a particular problem, and is independent of the domain theory of a problem. It has been shown to increase the scalability of planners [4,27]. There are a wide range of formalisms for representing DCK, including macro-actions [10], abstracted state features for generalised planning [24], procedural domain-control knowledge [5], hierarchical planning [27], and temporally-extended goals [4,8,9]. In this paper, we use temporally-extended goals, specified as linear temporal logic (LTL) formula, [8,9] to encode human knowledge. LTL-based planning is discussed in Sect. 3.3. As far as we are aware, experiments and applications using such formalisms have been performed only by using domain-control knowledge hand-coded by planning experts at design time, with only a comparatively few experiments looking at how expert users could supply such knowledge [25].

3 Model of Collaborative Planning for Resilience

This section defines our model of resilient planning for MDPs and extends this to human-agent collaborative planning using temporal constraints.

3.1 Resilient Planning

Resilience is the ability to recover from the consequences of an unpredicted or unpredictable event for a given state of the system [21]. In this paper, we are interested in one type of resilient planning: when an automated planner cannot possibly derive a correct solution because it lacks the information and concepts necessary to do so. We assume that the information regarding the unpredicted event is known to a human operator, who can judge the resilience of the current plan. The challenge is that the model is *obsolete*; that is, it no longer represents the problem at hand, and an automated planner could only derive a correct solution by coincidence because it lacks the information and concepts necessary to represent the knowledge that is available to the operator directly. This is an important problem in many domains with incomplete models, and there will always be attributes for which automated planning tools cannot plan.

The challenge is that the planner has one model, but the resulting plan is executed in some environment that is unknown to the planner. This is, of course, a ubiquitous challenge in artificial intelligence: models used to make decisions are by definition incomplete simplifications of the world they model. A successful plan may work in one scenario while failing in another, but both correspond to the same scenario in the abstract model space.

To define this concept formally, we first define a conceptual model for planning. We adopt a common model of planning using *Markov Decision Processes* [29].

Definition 1 (Markov Decision Process (MDP) [29]). *A Markov Decision Processs (MDP) is a tuple $\Pi = (S, A, P, R, \gamma)$, in which S is a set of states, A is a set of actions, $P(s, a, s')$ is a transition function from $S \times A \to 2^S$, which defines the probability of action a going to state s' if executed in state s, $R(s, a, s')$ is the reward received for transitions from executing action a in state s and ending up in state s', and γ is the discount factor.*

Definition 2 (Planning Problem [29]). *A planning problem is a tuple (Π, I, O), in which $I \in S$ is the initial state and O is the objective to be achieved. In the simplest case, a goal-directed MDP [18], O is just a set of goal states, such as $O \subset S$, but a more common objective is simply to maximise the expected discounted reward [29]. or potentially satisfying preferences over plan trajectories [15].*

The task is to synthesise a policy $\pi : S \to A$ from states to actions that start in state I and achieve object O.

Definition 3 (Resilient Planning). *We define a* resilient planning *problem as a tuple* (Π, Π', I, O), *in which* $\Pi = (S, A, P, R, \lambda)$ *is the* base *MDP and* $\Pi' = (S', A', P', R', \lambda')$ *is the* augmented *MDP. Using* Π, *the automated planner synthesises a policy* $\pi : S \rightarrow A$ *that achieves the objective* O *from initial state* I *over the* augmented *model* Π'. *We assume that* $S \subseteq S'$ *and* $A \subseteq A'$.

For a reward-maximising MDP problem, the planner produces a policy π, with the aim of maximising $\Sigma_{t=0}^{\infty} \gamma'^t R'(s'_t, a'_t, s'_{t+1})$ over all trajectories possible from π. Note here that the reward function, transition function, etc., are given by the augmented problem Π', while the planner only has access to the base problem Π.

Clearly, the general task of resilient planning is not feasible, as Π and Π' could model completely different domains, e.g. a shipping port vs. a manufacturing line. However, given reasonable assumptions about the relationships between Π and Π', such as $S \subseteq S'$ and $A \subseteq A'$, the problem becomes more feasible. For example, an optimal policy on Π may still achieve high (but not maximal) rewards on problem Π' if the transition probabilities and rewards change only slightly.

3.2   Human-Agent Collaborative Planning for Resilient Planning

In our definition of resilient planning, Π is the planning model, and Π' is the actual environment. In *collaborative human-agent planning*, the model Π is known to the planner, and the base model Π and alternative model Π' are both partially known to the human. For example, the human represents the concepts and locations of no-fly zones in their mental model.

Definition 4 (Collaborative resilient planning). *We define a collaborative resilient planning problem as a resilient planning problem* (Π, Π', I, O). *The task of the human is to define an augmented initial state* I' *and objective* O' *for the automated planner to synthesise a policy* $\pi : S \rightarrow A$ *using* (Π, I', O'), *such that* π *solves the objective* O *from initial state* I *under problem* Π'.

Note that a human can modify objectives, but not the *domain* model (transitions). There are two main reasons for only modifying the objectives. First, it treats the planning agent as a black-box, making it easier to design interaction with such agents, as highlighted in [12]. Second, we believe that the cognitive demands of modifying action definitions and state spaces would be difficult and error-prone for operators under time pressure and require a level of knowledge that unduly restricts usability, while changing objectives may be more feasible [25].

3.3   Resilient Planning Using Temporal Constraints

A key to solving a collaborative resilient planning problem is how to structure O'. We claim that temporal constraints provide a suitable formalism to describe the 'shape' of solutions. That is, they propose a structure over the generated plans, rather than just goal states or rewards. In short, planners that support temporal constraints are *domain-configurable planners* in the taxonomy of Nau [26], different from domain-specific planners because they can generalise to other domains, but more flexible than domain-independent planners because they support domain-control knowledge. These claims align with recent works, e.g. [22].

Temporal constraints encode properties that hold over the whole sequence of states in a solution plan [4,8,9]. They are flexible enough to specify liveness constraints (some good thing eventually happens), safety constraints (some bad thing never happens), and fairness constraints (an outcome will happen infinitely often if attempted an infinite number of times). A standard way for expression temporal constraints is *linear temporal logic*.

Definition 5 (Linear Temporal Logic [28]**).** *Linear temporal logic (LTL) is an extension of propositional logic with modal operators to describe temporal relationships between states on a trajectory. Given a set of atomic propositions P, the grammar for LTL is defined as follows:*

$$\phi ::= p \mid \neg\phi \mid \phi \wedge \phi \mid \bigcirc\phi \mid \phi\mathcal{U}\phi,$$

in which $p \in P$, $\neg$ *and* $\wedge$ *are logical negation and conjunction respectively,* $\bigcirc\phi$ *specifies that* ϕ *will hold in the next state, and* $\mathcal{U}$ *is the 'until' operator, for which* $\psi\mathcal{U}\phi$ *states that* ψ *will hold until* ϕ *becomes true. New temporal operators can be derived from these basic definitions, such as always achieving a particular state, or achieving a particular state at some point in the future.*

Definition 6 (LTL Planning). *An LTL planning problem is a tuple* (Π, I, O, ϕ), *in which* Π *describes an MDP, I and O are the initial states and objectives, respectively, and* ϕ *is an LTL formula.*

A policy is valid iff it achieves the objectives and iff the trajectories generated from the policy satisfy the temporal constraint ϕ.

There exists several LTL solvers in classical planning [4,9], non-deterministic planning [8], and planning with MDPs [15]. Other works include [6,7,11,13,14]. Most of these solvers address the problem by encoding the LTL constraint as a finite state machine (FSM) and then derive a new planning problem that is the cross product of the FSM and the original planning problem. The underlying solver can solve this product problem. The accepting states are reached if a generated trajectory satisfies the LTL constraint. The method of solving is not the focus of this paper.

4   Evaluation

Our evaluation goals are: (1) to determine whether participants can identify invalid plans due to the incompleteness of the planning model; and (2) whether participants can improve plan resilience via insights encoded as temporal constraints.

4.1 Domain

We simulated an aerial surveillance scenario based on an application of interest to our industry partner. Participants played the role of an operator controlling multiple unmanned aerial vehicles (UAVs), with the objective of undertaking surveillance on assets and targets (unidentified sea vehicles) in the environment. The UAVs are capable of: (1) navigating between cells specified by coordinates; (2) picking up and dropping pallets; and (3) taking and communicating photos of the targets. The objectives are to take photos of all targets, visit each asset at least once, and deliver pallets to assets when required. An intelligent agent assists in achieving the default objectives of surveillance, but the planning model used by the planner makes some assumptions: 1) all targets are unknown; 2) the objectives of taking photos, visiting assets, or delivering pallets can be achieved in any order; 3) the targets and assets move at approximately the same speed; and 4) all UAVs are well resourced to complete their missions. While conceptually the task seems straightforward, the set of possible allocations is combinatorially large, and solving this is difficult without automated assistance for anything other than trivial problems.

4.2 Protocol

We asked 24 participants, from a variety of backgrounds such as computer science, management, defence science, physics, law, and government, to complete a series of six surveillance tasks. Over half had a qualification in computer science, and 5 were females. Each task had the same baseline objectives described above and additional 'Operator Preferences', which are ordered preferences that the plans should achieve for this specific task only, but not in general. For example, identifying particular targets before others. The models for each task were specified as a deterministic planning task using PDDL 3.0, and represent the base model Π from Definition 4.

Baseline Plan. The participants were presented with a *baseline plan* that achieves the baseline objectives, generated using state-of-the-art planning that models temporal preferences, LPRPG-P [9]. To help the participants visualise this task, the plans were visualised on simple maps that showed the assumed trajectory of targets (if they were non-stationary) and the proposed plan for the UAVs. One scenario is shown in Fig. 1.

Intelligence Updates. Participants received 'updates', which are new information derived from intelligence reports that may affect a plan. Importantly, updates contained some information that was not considered in the original model. For example, for the scenario in Fig. 1, participants were told that certain coordinates contained heavy fog, and thus taking a picture of the (moving) target in this fog may be unsuccessful. However, the planning model had no concept of 'fog', and as such, participants could not simply tell the planner to avoid fog.

Table 1. The six tasks completed by participants.

Scenario	Description
T1	Fog in a specific area, limiting visibility to take photos of targets
T2	One target identified as friendly, one identified as hostile, possessing missiles that could take out a drone
T3	One UAV facing heavy headwinds and will take longer than anticipated to reach its target
T4	One UAV out of service and one target is friendly
T5	Two UAVs low on fuel, with different estimates of their likelihood of reaching their targets
T6	Uncertainty about the location of a resource that must be delivered to an asset

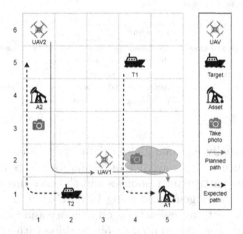

Intelligence update: Cells (4,2) and (5,2) contain fog. It is unlikely any photo taken in these regions will succeed.

Fig. 1. Example of one of the tasks used in the study.

Resilience Constraints. For each task, participants were asked to: 1) provide an alternate plan that satisfies the baseline requirements, operator preferences, and the intelligence update; and 2) to write, in natural language, what goals and preferences they would tell the intelligent agent to fulfil so that it would generate the plan provided in item (1). We note that the participant constraints were constraints on the UAV plans and not on the environment, that is, participants could only provide preferences for the UAVs. Table 1 gives an overview of the intelligence updates received for all six scenarios, that is, six participant tasks.

The complexity of the aerial surveillance scenario is that participants had to consider how state constraints affect the concurrent behaviour of multiple vehicles satisfying the baseline requirements, operator preferences, and the intelligence update. While the participants were required to specify manual plans, they were provided with baseline plans, to begin with. This means that they worked with an intelligent planner rather than solving the task from scratch.

4.3 Procedure

The experiment began with a training task using the same domain to ensure that the participants understood the task, and then participants were given six tasks of varying complexity. Participants typically took between 30–40 mins to complete the study, although they were not given any time limit.

Table 2. Examples of preference encodings, where UAV1 and UAV2 are unmanned aerial vehicles and T1 is a target.

Statement	Encoding
Move UAV1 to cell 4,3 and take picture of T1	(preference p1 (sometime-after (agentloc uav1 v4 v3) (have-photo t1 uav1)))
UAV1 to take all photos	(forall (?t - target) (preference p1 (sometime (have-photo?t uav1))))
D2 to deliver pallet R1	(preference p1 (sometime (carry-pallet r1 d2)))

The authors manually encoded the participants' resilience constraints into LTL constraints, which took an average of 30 min for all six tasks. Table 2 lists some examples of the participant responses and the encodings using PDDL 3.0. The augmented plans were generated using LPRPG-P [9] as planning problem (Π, I', O'). We did not set any restrictions on memory and time available to the planner; our problems were solved on a 64-bit machine with 8GB ram and an i7 processor.

4.4 Assessing Plans

While the planning tasks were specified as deterministic multi-agent plans, the second model, which we call the *assessment model*, was an MDP, which modelled the rewards for completing tasks and the uncertainties in the environment. Note that we did not provide the assessment model to the participants because we believe that giving all of the underlying MDP model does not reflect reality, and in most cases, this information is not available.

A deterministic baseline model formed the base of the MDP model, simply using all of the same variables, actions, preconditions, and effects. Then, the following modifications were made. For each goal/preference, a reward of 20 was given, while for each action in a plan, a cost of 1 was applied. For ordering between preferences (e.g. each preference A before preference B), a reward of 10 was given if this ordering was preserved. Any task containing quantified uncertainties (that is, where participants were given an uncertainty estimate), these uncertainties were used; while for unquantified uncertainties, we used 50% as the estimate. From this assessment model, the *expected return* of the baseline plan and participants' plans were calculated using a simple custom solver. As well as the baseline plan, participants' plans were compared against an optimal plan, which is a plan that maximises the expected return given the MDP assessment model.

5 Results

5.1 Automated Plans Encoded as LTL

Table 3 compares the baseline plans with the plans generated using the resilience constraints. The *Base Plan* is the expected return of the original plan generated without the intelligence update. The *Opt. Plan* is the maximum expected return with respect to the intelligence update, generated using a simple customised solver. The *Auto. Plan* shows the average and standard error of the expected return of 24 plans generated from using the automated planner (LPRPG-P) with the participants' constraints encoded as LTL. *Improvement* is the percentage improved between the baseline and manual plan, while *Optimality* is the percentage difference between the optimal and automated plans. The p-values are derived using a Mann-Whitney U test (ranked sum test) for unpaired samples.

Table 3. Comparing automated plans with baseline and optimal plans. Numbers in brackets represent the standard error.

Task	Base plan	Opt. plan	Auto. plan	Improvement		Optimality	
T1	72	83	80.9 (0.4)	12.3%	$(p < .01)$	−2.6%	$(p < .01)$
T2	65	87	70.7 (1.9)	8.8%	$(p < .01)$	−18.7%	$(p < .01)$
T3	76	92	85.8 (1.2)	12.9%	$(p < .01)$	−6.7%	$(p < .01)$
T4	63	68	67.3 (0.8)	6.7%	$(p < .01)$	−1.1%	$(p = .76)$
T5	53	70	58.7 (0.8)	10.8%	$(p < .01)$	−16.1%	$(p < .01)$
T6	70	80	76.9 (0.3)	9.9%	$(p < .01)$	−3.9%	$(p < .01)$
Ave.				10.2%		−8.2%	

Table 4. Execution times for automated plans. Numbers in brackets represent the standard error.

Task	Time (seconds)		
	Base plan	Opt. plan	Auto. plan
T1	0.32	0.40	0.7 (0.1)
T2	0.77	1.05	4.4 (0.4)
T3	0.24	460.50	317.9 (40.5)
T4	0.79	21.00	4.9 (1.7)
T5	0.25	27.26	1.1 (0.2)
T6	1.05	2.27	2.3 (0.7)
Ave.	0.57	85.41	55.2 (21.5)

The results support that LTL encodings are suitable for representing participants' plans. Across all tasks, participants were able to express preferences such that the resulting plans (generated by the planner) were significantly more resilient plans ($p < 0.05$). In only nine instances across all of the 144 tasks, participants did not generate an improved plan, and only one had a lower expected return. In this case, this was due to a misunderstanding of the intelligence update. On aggregate, the resilient plans were sub-optimal for five of the six tasks ($p < 0.05$). For task 4, most of the participants' preferences generated an optimal plan.

The results also demonstrate that participants successfully used the intelligence update to identify problems with the baseline plan and work around this. Over the six tasks, participants were consistently able to specify plans with an improved expected return over the baseline plan. Participants did not always specify the optimal plan. This could be due to the short training session and only six tasks not being enough to learn many subtleties of the domain. Further, participants were not given quantified uncertainties and rewards, so they could not optimally calculate the maximum expected reward. We did not provide the complete assessment model to the participants because this information is not available in reality. More importantly, our results show that even with incomplete information, participants could still have an impact.

Table 4 shows the execution times for generating plans. These results show that using resilience constraints (both our own and the participants') take longer to generate the plans than the baseline. This is because preferences are soft constraints that typically make the problem harder: plans need to satisfy both the baseline goals and the soft constraints, and soft constraints do not prune the search space. The results for task 3 particularly vary significantly between participants, with some plans generated in 1–2 s, while others ranged from 300–500 s. From our investigations, we believe this is a limitation of the planner rather than the participants' responses. Table 5 provides some examples of the encodings and the execution times for some of the responses for task 3.

Table 5. Examples of task 3 encodings and execution times.

Statement	Encoding	Planning time (s)

Assign D1 to take photo of T2 and D2 to take photo of T1 to intercept targets at minimum time	(preference intercept-t1
	   (sometime (have-photo t1 d2)))
	(preference intercept-t2
	   (sometime (have-photo t2 d1)))
		1.11

I want to turn D1 off so that D2 takes all photos and visits all assets	(preference not-move-d1
	   (always (agentloc d1 v0 v7)))
	(preference not-d1-to-t1
	   (always (not (have-photo t1 d1))))
	(preference not-d1-to-t2
	   (always (not (have-photo t2 d1))))
		460.5

I want D2 to photos of both targets, T1 and T2	(forall (?t - targets)
	   (preference d2-to-targets
	     (sometime (have-photo?t d2))))
		184.8 s

5.2 Comparison of Manual and Automated Plans

Table 6 shows the absolute and relative differences of expected return between manual and automated plans. There was no significant difference for tasks 3–6 ($p < 0.05$). This is further evidence that the LTL formula is a suitable representation for capturing resilience constraints. For task 1, the automated plans had a higher expected return than the manual plans ($p < 0.05$). This is the fog scenario from Fig. 1. In this case, many participants' manual plans moved UAV1 to cell (4,3), then moved three cells to asset A1. However, for most, their resilience constraints stated UAV1 to NOT take a photo in cells (4,2) or (4,3), which allowed the planner to find the more efficient path of taking the photo at cell (4,1), then moving just one cell to asset A1. This demonstrates one advantage of declarative constraints: the planner can find the best way to achieve the constraint. We believe that we would see this more often for more complex scenarios because specifying a complete control plan would be infeasible. For task 2, we see the inverse: the manual plans have a higher return than the automated plans. The LTL constraints did not control the UAVs in an intended way. However, we believe that had the participants been able to see the generated plans, they would have corrected the constraints.

5.3 Control vs. Declarative Preferences

We analysed the participant responses and classified the resilience constraints as either *control* or *declarative*. Control constraints provide explicit control commands, such as manoeuvring a particular UAV to a particular location, then

Table 6. Difference between expected return of manual and automated plans. Numbers in brackets represent the standard error.

Task	Manual plan	Auto plan	Average diff	Ave. Relative diff	
T1	79.7 (0.3)	80.9 (0.4)	1.2 (0.5)	1.4%	$(p < .010)$
T2	73.8 (2.1)	70.7 (1.9)	−3.1 (1.6)	−4.8%	$(p = .013)$
T3	85.4 (0.9)	85.8 (1.2)	0.4 (0.9)	0.2%	$(p = .497)$
T4	67.5 (0.4)	67.3 (0.8)	−0.3 (0.4)	−0.6%	$(p = .192)$
T5	58.8 (0.8)	58.7 (0.8)	0.0 (0.6)	−0.2%	$(p = .153)$
T6	77.0 (0.2)	76.9 (0.3)	0.0 (0.3)	−0.1%	$(p = .841)$
Ave.			−0.3 (0.2)	−0.7%	

taking a photo, then going to an asset; while declarative constraints specify a property, such as that the UAV could take a photo of a particular target. There were 32 and 112 *control* and *declarative* types respectively.

Figure 2 shows that participants used declarative preferences more as they completed more tasks, which could relate to either experience, task complexity, or both. We compared the differences between manual and automated plans, defined as the number of actions present in the manual plan but not in the auto-

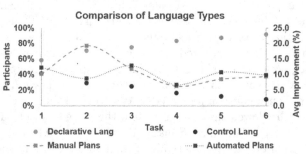

Fig. 2. Control vs. declarative information and plan similarity

mated plan. No significant difference was noted in plan differences overall between the preferences types. We compared the plan differences between the first and last three tasks, that is, $T1−T3$ (M = 5.5, SD = 3.2) & $T4−T6$ (M = 6.5, SD = 2.9); increased use of declarative preferences leads to significant differences between plans. This is not surprising because the planner has more control over the solution with declarative preferences. While this is only over six tasks, we expect this result to hold more generally. Such differences raise potential issues of trust and transparency. If not understood and accepted by the operator, such differences could decrease the operator's trust in intelligent agents and ultimately result in disuse.

6 Conclusions

We investigated whether people could recognise the limitations of automatically-generated plans and specify constraints on new plans that are more resilient. Twenty-four participants specified constraints for improving baseline plans that had limitations. Our results show that participants' constraints expressed using LTL improved the expected return of the plans, demonstrating the potential to include human insight into collaborative planning for resilience. In future work, we aim to perform experiments with participants in the loop, enabling them to specify preferences using a restricted language that can be automatically encoded as LTL constraints and refine the solution iteratively. We will investigate more intuitive and natural methods for eliciting resilience constraints to enable automatic encoding in LTL. We also aim to explore tasks of varying complexity levels in different domains. Regarding presenting the tasks to the participants, we will explore different approaches, such as randomly presenting the tasks of varying complexity.

Acknowledgements. The research was funded by a Sponsored Research Collaboration grant from the Commonwealth of Australia Defence Science and Technology Group and the Defence Science Institute, an initiative of the State Government of Victoria.

References

1. Ai-Chang, M., et al.: Mapgen: mixed-initiative planning and scheduling for the mars exploration rover mission. IEEE Intell. Syst. **19**(1), 8–12 (2004)
2. Amershi, S., Cakmak, M., Knox, W.B., Kulesza, T.: Power to the people: The role of humans in interactive machine learning. AI Mag. **35**(4), 105–120 (2014)
3. Anderson, D., et al.: Human-guided simple search. In: Proceedings of the Seventeenth National Conference on Artificial Intelligence and Twelfth Conference on Innovative Applications of Artificial Intelligence, pp. 209–216 (2000)
4. Bacchus, F., Kabanza, F.: Using temporal logics to express search control knowledge for planning. Artif. Intell. **116**(1), 123–191 (2000)
5. Baier, J.A., Fritz, C., McIlraith, S.A.: Exploiting procedural domain control knowledge in state-of-the-art planners. In: ICAPS, pp. 26–33 (2007)
6. Camacho, A., Baier, J.A., Muise, C., McIlraith, S.A.: Finite LTL synthesis as planning. In: Twenty-Eighth International Conference on Automated Planning and Scheduling (2018)
7. Camacho, A., Muise, C.J., Baier, J.A., McIlraith, S.A.: LTL realizability via safety and reachability games. In: IJCAI. pp. 4683–4691 (2018)
8. Camacho, A., Triantafillou, E., Muise, C., Baier, J.A., McIlraith, S.A.: Non-deterministic planning with temporally extended goals: LTL over finite and infinite traces. In: AAAI (2017)

9. Coles, A.J., Coles, A.: LPRPG-P: Relaxed plan heuristics for planning with preferences. In: Proceeedings of the 21st International Conference on Automated Planning and Scheduling, pp. 26–33. AAAI Press (2011)

10. Coles, A., Smith, A.: Marvin: a heuristic search planner with online macro-action learning. J. Artif. Intell. Res. (JAIR) **28**, 119–156 (2007)

11. De Giacomo, G., De Masellis, R., Montali, M.: Reasoning on LTL on finite traces: Insensitivity to infiniteness. In: Twenty-Eighth AAAI Conference on Artificial Intelligence (2014)

12. De Giacomo, G., Iocchi, L., Favorito, M., Patrizi, F.: Foundations for restraining bolts: Reinforcement learning with ltlf/ldlf restraining specifications. In: Proceedings of the International Conference on Automated Planning and Scheduling, vol. 29, pp. 128–136 (2019)

13. De Giacomo, G., Rubin, S.: Automata-theoretic foundations of fond planning for LTLf and LDLf goals. In: IJCAI, pp. 4729–4735 (2018)

14. De Giacomo, G., Vardi, M.Y.: Linear temporal logic and linear dynamic logic on finite traces. In: Twenty-Third International Joint Conference on Artificial Intelligence (2013)

15. Faruq, F., Lacerda, B., Hawes, N., Parker, D.: Simultaneous task allocation and planning under uncertainty. In: 2018 IEEE/RSJ International Conference on Intelligent Robots and Systems, IROS 2018, pp. 3559–3564 (2018)

16. Ferguson, G., Allen, J.F., Miller, B.W., et al.: TRAINS-95: Towards a mixed-initiative planning assistant. In: AIPS, pp. 70–77 (1996)

17. Ferguson, G., Allen, J.F., et al.: TRIPS: An integrated intelligent problem-solving assistant. In: AAAI/IAAI, pp. 567–572 (1998)

18. Geffner, H., Bonet, B.: A concise introduction to models and methods for automated planning. Synth. Lect. Artif. Intell. Mach. Learn. **8**(1), 1–141 (2013)

19. Hayes, B., Scassellati, B.: Autonomously constructing hierarchical task networks for planning and human-robot collaboration. In: IEEE International Conference on Robotics and Automation, pp. 5469–5476. IEEE (2016)

20. Helmert, M.: The fast downward planning system. J. Artif. Intell. Res. **26**, 191–246 (2006)

21. Ibanez, E., et al.: Resilience and robustness in long-term planning of the national energy and transportation system. Int. J. Crit. Infrastruct. **12**(1–2), 82 (2016)

22. Toro Icarte, R., Klassen, T.Q., Valenzano, R.A., McIlraith, S.A.: Advice-based exploration in model-based reinforcement learning. In: Bagheri, E., Cheung, J.C.K. (eds.) Canadian AI 2018. LNCS (LNAI), vol. 10832, pp. 72–83. Springer, Cham (2018). https://doi.org/10.1007/978-3-319-89656-4_6

23. Kelley, L., Ouimet, M., Croft, B., Gustafson, E., Martinez, L.: An approach to integrating human knowledge into agent-based planning. In: Workshop on Impedance Matching in Cognitive Partnerships at IJCAI-17 (2017). https://people.eng.unimelb.edu.au/adrianrp/COGPARTNER-17/COGPARTNER-Kelly.pdf

24. Khardon, R.: Learning action strategies for planning domains. Artif. Intell. **113**(1), 125–148 (1999)

25. Kim, J., Banks, C.J., Shah, J.A.: Collaborative planning with encoding of users high-level strategies. In: Proceedings of AAAI (2017)

26. Nau, D.S.: Current trends in automated planning. AI Mag. **28**(4), 43 (2007)

27. Nau, D.S., et al.: Shop2: An HTN planning system. J. Artif. Intell. Res. (JAIR) **20**, 379–404 (2003)

28. Pnueli, A.: The temporal logic of programs. In: Foundations of Computer Science, 1977, 18th Annual Symposium on, pp. 46–57. IEEE (1977)

29. Puterman, M.L.: Markov decision processes: discrete stochastic dynamic programming. John Wiley & Sons (2014)
30. Reid, D.J.: An autonomy interrogative. In: Abbass, H.A., Scholz, J., Reid, D.J. (eds.) Foundations of Trusted Autonomy. SSDC, vol. 117, pp. 365–391. Springer, Cham (2018). https://doi.org/10.1007/978-3-319-64816-3_21
31. Rosenfeld, A., Agmon, N., Maksimov, O., Azaria, A., Kraus, S.: Intelligent agent supporting human-multi-robot team collaboration. In: Proceedings of the 24th International Conference on Artificial Intelligence, pp. 1902–1908. AAAI Press (2015)
32. Rosenfeld, A., Agmon, N., Maksimov, O., Kraus, S.: Intelligent agent supporting human-multi-robot team collaboration. Artif. Intell. **252**, 211–231 (2017)

Environmental Consequences of Institutional Facts in Artificial Institutions

Rafhael R. Cunha[1,2]([✉]) [iD], Jomi F. Hübner[2] [iD], and Maiquel de Brito[3] [iD]

[1] Federal Institute of Education, Science and Technology of Rio Grande do Sul
(IFRS), Campus Vacaria, Vacaria, Brazil
[2] Automation and Systems Department, Federal University of Santa Catarina,
Florianópolis, Brazil
rafhael.cunha@posgrad.ufsc.br, jomi.hubner@ufsc.br
[3] Control, Automation, and Computation Engineering Department, Federal
University of Santa Catarina, Blumenau, Brazil
maiquel.b@ufsc.br

Abstract. In multi-agent systems, the agents may have goals that
depend on the common interpretation of actions and other agents acting
in the system. These goals are thus social goals. Artificial institutions
are used to provide such a social interpretation by assigning statuses to
the concrete elements that compose the system. These statuses are sup-
posed to enable the assignee element to perform functions that are not
exclusively inherent to their design features. However, the consequences
in the environment of the enabled functions are not explicit in the existing models of artificial institutions. As a consequence, (i) agents may
have difficulties reasoning about the achievement of their social goals
and (ii) these institutions are not well instrumented to receive incoming agents in the case of open systems. Considering these problems, this
paper proposes the addition of *purposes* in artificial institution models
to express the consequences in the environment of the constitution of
status-functions helping the agents to reason about the fulfillment of
their social goals. We evaluate the proposal in some scenarios, showing how the agents can use purposes to reason about the satisfaction of
their social goals in institutional contexts and how the institution can be
flexible enough to support new agents operating in the system.

Keywords: Purposes · Status-functions · Artificial institutions ·
Multi-agent systems

1   Introduction

Multi-agent systems (MAS) are systems composed of autonomous computational
entities, henceforth referred to as *agents*, that can interact with each other within

This study was supported by the Federal Institute of Education, Science and Technology of Rio Grande do Sul (IFRS).

A. Theodorou et al. (Eds.): COINE 2021, LNAI 13239, pp. 44–61, 2022.
https://doi.org/10.1007/978-3-031-16617-4_4

a dynamic environment to achieve their common and individual goals [39]. The interaction among the agents is at the very core of MAS, making it a useful approach to handling computational problems involving social aspects [37]. One of these aspects is the shared interpretation of the facts occurring in the system. For example, consider a scenario where the agent Bob has the goal of holding a book. To satisfy this goal, Bob can buy a book owned by Tom. To this end, Bob needs to execute an action that means *giving a value in exchange for a good* and waits for the agent Tom to understand this action before handing him the book. In this scenario, Bob's goal is a *social goal* because it depends on the common interpretation of action and other agents acting in the system.

Inspired by human societies, some authors propose models and tools to provide this common interpretation for computer systems and, in particular, for MAS [20]. They usually consider that some concrete facts occurring in the environment *constitute* (or *count as*) institutional facts [6,7,9,16]). The attribution of status to concrete elements happens through the enabling of the constitutive rules in a process called constitution [31,32]. For example, agents acting in an e-commerce scenario may constitute (or count as) *buyers*, while some of their actions may count as *payments*. Artificial Institutions are the component of the MAS that is in charge of defining the conditions for function assignment to the concrete elements (e.g., an agent to become a *buyer* or an action to become a *payment*).

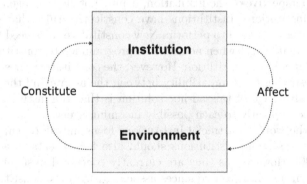

Fig. 1. Relations between institution and environment.

The existing works on Artificial Institutions are mainly concerned with specifying and managing the constitution, which is the institutional consequence of facts occurring in the environment (shown on the left side of Fig. 1). However, the constitution may enable new facts in the system that potentially lead to environmental changes. For instance, the constitution of *payment* might activate a norm obliging the agent that counts as a *seller* to deliver a book to the agent that counts as a *buyer*. If the norms are fulfilled, the environment moves to a state where the agent that counts as the *buyer* holds a book. These environmental consequences of the constitution of status-functions remain unexplored (shown on the right side of Fig. 1). As far as we know, proposals described in the literature do not provide the means for the institution to explicitly express the consequences in the environment of the constitutions associated with the status-functions. While the status-functions are explicit, *the environmental consequences of constitutions are implicit.*

The disadvantages of not expressing the consequences in the environment of the constitution of status-functions can be observed from the perspective of both the agents and the institution. From the perspective of the agents, they may not exploit the constitution of status-functions to achieve goals that match the environmental consequences of such a constitution. For example, consider that *Bob* is coded to achieve its goal of holding a book by performing an action called *transfer*, available in the environment and acknowledged by the institution as a *payment*. *The agent* needs to be reprogrammed if, for instance, the action *transfer* becomes unavailable, if the institution changes so that *transfer* no longer counts as a *payment*, or if it needs to exploit the constitution of new status functions (possibly in different institutions) that produce the same effect of *payment*. The constitutive rules are not enough to make it explicit that constitution of the status-functions can lead to a state of the world where some agent has achieved its social goals. The connection between the execution of an action that constitutes a status function and its consequences in the environment is implicit in the system developer's mind.

From the perspective of the institution, it may not support agents coded for other similar institutions. Institutions have constitutive rules that match with the actions that agents need to perform. New constitutive rules need to be added to preserve compatibility[1] when new agents, programmed to constitute different status functions, join the institution. However, the constitutive rules do not have the role of preserving the compatibility between the agents and the institution. The main disadvantage of this ad-hoc solution is that the institutions need to be programmed explicitly to each possibly incoming agent.

Although the work on artificial institutions focus mostly on supporting the regulation of the system, institutions should also help agents to achieve their social goals [30]. However, as they are currently conceived, institutions do not specify the environmental consequences associated with the constitution of the status-functions. They could better support the reasoning of agents [30] concerning the satisfaction of their own social goals and be more prepared to receive agents designed by different developers. Thus, the main contribution of this paper is a model based on the notion of *purpose* that explicitly represents the environmental consequences of the constitution of the status-functions and their relation

---

[1] Compatibility in this work refers to the situation in which the vocabulary used in the specification of the agents works appropriately with the vocabulary of the institutional specification. Compatibility can occur in several ways, including (i) if the vocabulary present in the agent's specification is identical to the institutional vocabulary or (ii) if the programmer encodes compatibility with the institutional specification within the agent.

with agents' goals. It is inspired by the "Construction of the Social Reality" by John Searle [31,32] theory that seems to be fundamental for comprehending the social reality.

This paper is organized as follows: Sect. 2 introduces the main background concepts necessary to understand our proposal and its position in the literature. It includes philosophical theory and related works. Section 3 presents the proposed model and its required interfaces. Section 4 implements the proposal based on some examples that allow us to identify some limitations and advantages that the model offers on the agent and institutional perspective. Finally, Sect. 5 presents some conclusions about this work and suggests future works.

2 Background

This section presents the essential concepts which base our contribution. Subsection 2.1 presents the philosophical concepts that support our contribution. Subsection 2.2 briefly describes state the art in artificial institutions concerning the explicit representation of the consequences associated with the institutional concepts.

2.1 Philosophical Background on Institutions

Institutions are composed of institutional facts based on status functions and constitutive rules [31,32]. Status-functions are statuses that have associated functions. These statuses enable concrete elements to perform functions (associated with the statuses) that cannot be explained through their physical virtues. Constitutive rules specify the assignment of status-functions to concrete elements with the following formula: X count-as Y in C. For example, a piece of paper count-as money in a bank, where X represents the concrete element, Y the status-function and C the context where that attribute is valid.

Some functions are called *agentive functions* because they are assigned from *practical interests of the agents* [32, p.20]. These practical interests of agents are called *Purposes*. The purposes are associated with the consequences in the environment of the constitution of status-functions that are aligned with the agents' interests. For example, an agent has a goal of *holding a book* when it delivers a paper note that institutionally is considered as *payment*. In MAS, *hold a book* represents a state of the world that is associated with a purpose. This purpose is achieved when the status-function *payment* is constituted. That is, the agent satisfies its goal of *holding a book* when it constitutes the status-function *payment*. The consequences may differ if the agent delivers a paper note in a different context. This is because the purposes must always reflect the interest of all agents involved in that context. Moreover, the agents involved in the interaction must have the same understanding of these facts (i.e., about the purposes) [32, p.22]. Otherwise, none of them achieve their social goal.

From that theory, it is possible to conclude that a similar system can be applied to MAS to make explicit the environmental consequences of the constitution of the status-functions (i.e., the purposes) that compose the institutions.

It will permit to improve the agents' reasoning about the satisfaction of their social goals and overcome the difficulties that motivate the realization of this work.

2.2 Institutions in MAS

In MAS, several works propose artificial institutions as a counterpart of human institutions. In different ways, these works use the *count-as* relationship, established through the constitutive rules proposed by Searle, to support the regulation of the system [5]. Activation of a constitutive rule (i.e., its constitution) usually activates a regulative rule in the system, inflicts a regulative rule, etc. However, in this work, we believe that the status-functions, when constituted, can bring environmental effects to the system, in addition to altering the dynamics of regulative rules. The agents can exploit these effects to achieve their social goals. For example, in the bookstore example, the constitution of *payment* leads the environment to a state where an agent *holds a book*. This section reviews state of the art on artificial institutions concerning the explicit representation of the effects of the constitutions of the status-functions.

Works on Artificial Institutions are usually inspired by the theory of John Searle [31,32]. Some works present functional approaches, relating brute facts to normative states (e.g., a given action counts as a violation of a norm). These works do not address ontological issues, and, therefore, it becomes even more difficult to support the meaning of abstract concepts present in the institutional reality. Other works have ontological approaches, where brute facts are related to concepts used in the specification of norms (e.g., sending a message counts as a bid in an auction). However, these works have some limitations that are discussed below (see a detailed analysis of works that implement Searle's theory in [11]).

Some approaches allow the agents to reason about the constitutive rules [1, 6,7,10,16,36]. However, the status-function Y is usually just a label assigned to the concrete element (X) and used in the specification of the regulative norms. Therefore, Y does not seem to have any other purpose than to serve as a basis for the specification of stable regulative norms [1,35]. Some exceptions are (i) in the works of [16–19] where Y represents a class formed with some properties as roles responsible for executing actions, time to execute them, condition for execution, etc.; (ii) in [35] where Y is a general concept, and X is a sub-concept that can be used to explain Y. Although the exceptions contain more information than just a label in the Y element, these data are somehow associated with regulative norms.

There are no models that make explicit what the constituted elements (i.e., the status-functions) perform in the institution. Thus, the agents may not understand that the actions performed can also satisfy their social goals. For example, the agent's goal of *holding a book* can be a state of the world pointed to by a purpose that is associated with *payment* status-function. Considering the previously described example of selling books, there is currently no way for *Bob* to understand that the action performed, if interpreted through its *purpose*, can also satisfy its social goal. It occurs because there is not work that makes explicit the purposes of the status-functions. If the purposes of status-functions were made explicit, the status-functions' name would be less relevant to the system's correct functioning. Also, new agents could enter the system and understand the purposes of carrying out some functions that have institutional interpretation and thus resolve themselves to satisfy their goals.

The limitation discussed above indicates the need to develop a model that explains the purposes of status-functions belonging to institutional reality. Aguilar et al. [29] corroborate this conclusion by stating that institutions have not yet considered how to help agents in decision-making, helping them to achieve their own goals. The modeling of purposes of status-functions, described in the next section, is a step to fill this open gap.

3   The Purpose of Status-Functions

Inspired by Searle's Theory (cf. Sect. 2.1), this section describes a model to specify the purposes associated with the status-functions in artificial institutions. The focus is on the main concepts and their relations. The mathematical formalization of the model described below can be found in [12].

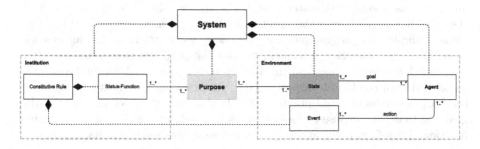

Fig. 2. Overview of the model.

The essential elements of the model used in this work are *agents*, *goals*, *institutions*, and *purposes*, depicted in the Fig. 2. *Agents* are autonomous entities that can interact within a dynamic environment composed of non-autonomous elements to achieve their goals [39]. The literature presents several definitions of *goal* that are different but complementary to each other (see more in [3,21,22,24,27,38]). In this work, *goals* are states of the environment that agents aim to achieve. Agents can perform actions that trigger events in the MAS. *States* are formed by one or more properties that describe the characteristics of the system at some point of its execution [8].

Institutions provide the social interpretation of the environmental elements of the MAS as usually proposed in the literature. This occurs through the interpretation of constitutive rules that assign status to environmental elements, as described in Sect. 2. It is beyond the scope of this paper to propose a model of artificial institutions. Instead, it considers this general notion of the institution as the entity that constitutes status-functions, adopted by several models in the field of MAS.

While *agents* and *institutions* are known concepts, *purposes* are introduced in the proposed model. The functions associated with status-functions can satisfy the practical interests of agents [32, p.20]. From the institution's perspective, we call these interests as *Purposes*. From the agents' perspective, these interests are their goals. Then, we claim that (i) *goals match with the purposes of status-functions* and (ii) *goals and purposes point to environmental states related to the status-functions*. For example, when an agent performs an action that constitutes *payment*, this makes possible the execution of other intermediate actions that bring the system to states such as *hold a book* (i.e., the agent goal). The intermediate actions (e.g., deliver the book to the agent who made the payment) between the constitution of the status-functions and the environmental states being reached are ignored in our proposal, since we consider that the agent is not interested in these intermediate steps.

Shortly, this model provides two relationships: (i) between purposes and status-functions and (ii) between purposes and the goals of the agents. Thus, if (i) there is a constitutive rule specifying which action constitutes a status-function, (ii) there is a purpose associated with that status-functions, and (iii) an agent has a goal that matches with the states pointed to by the purpose, then (iv) it is explicit how the agent should act to achieve its goal. In the previous example, the programmer can use these two relations in the agent code to program two queries: (i) a query to find the purposes that point to states that match the agent goals and (ii) a query to find out which status-function is associated with the found purposes. Thus, for example, the agent can find that the purpose of *books trade* points to the *hold a book* state which matches the goal and that the purpose of *books trade* is associated with the *payment* status-function. Therefore, if the agent constitutes *payment*, it achieves its goal in this system.

3.1 Ontology of the Model

We specify the proposed model in an OWL 2 ontology (see Fig. 3). The three main classes of the model are *Status-Function*, *Purpose* and *State*. The first represents status-functions that may exist in the institution. For example, the assertion *payment* ∈ Status-Function indicates an individual identified by *payment* that belongs to the *Status-Function* class. The second class (*Purpose*) represents the purposes that may come to exist in the system if the constitution of the status-function is performed. These purposes represent a social combination that expresses the interests of agents through the states that are pointed out from the purposes. For example, *books trade* is an individual of class *Purpose* that represents a social combination of consequences that may exist in the system after the constitution of a status function that matches the interests of agents. The third class (*State*) represents states that may take effect in the system after the constitution of status-functions is performed. For example, *holdAbook* is an individual of class *state* that represents a potential state that may take effect in the system. Furthermore, to add new purposes to the system, it is enough to create new individuals to represent them. In this way, the taxonomy of classes and relations are reused. If necessary, the institution's ontology can be related to the ontology of the application domain.

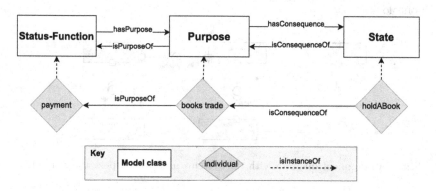

Fig. 3. Ontology for the model.

The relations *isConsequenceOf* and *isPurposeOf* (shown in Fig. 3) are the inverse of the relations *hasConsequence* and *hasPurpose* respectively. These relationships are necessary when someone wants to find out the status-functions associated with a particular state (i.e., someone does not know the status-function name, but someone already knows the state). For example, if one wants the *holdAbook* state, through the relations, one can find out the purpose that points to that state (i.e., *books trade*) and the status-function associated with the purpose (i.e., *payment*). The model allows us to explicitly define the states pointed to by purposes and the relationships between these purposes and the status-functions. At this point, it is important to make it clear that the choice to implement the model through an ontology is a design decision aiming at the reuse of existing ontologies. However, the model can be implemented in any other data structure that makes it possible to specify states, purposes and status-functions.

4   Implementing a MAS with and Without Purpose

This section describes the advances provided by the proposed model in the design of open MAS. To this end, consider an open MAS where the agents Bob, Alice, François, and João aim to "hold a book". However, the agents are coded by different programmers and therefore have different plans composed of different actions to achieve their goals.

The example is implemented through the components depicted in Fig. 4. Agents are programmed in Jason [4] and the environment in CArtAgO [26]. A

CArtAgO artifact encloses specific APIs and provides actions for the agents to act. For the artificial institution, we use an implementation of the Situated Artificial Institution (SAI) model [13]. It provides means to specify status-functions and constitutive rules and manage the constitution process. The purpose model is implemented through an ontology encapsulated in a CArtAgO artifact which is accessible to the agents. The query and persistence of data in the ontology are enabled by the MasOntology[2], a set of tools developed in CArtAgO to interact with ontologies[3]

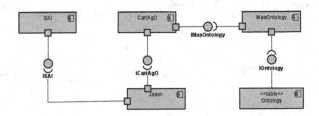

Fig. 4. Component diagram with the systems used to compose the example.

This section is organized as follows: Subsect. 4.1 describes the limitations of not using the model from the perspective of the agents. Subsection 4.2 shows how the model overcomes the limitations described in the previous section. The Subsect. 4.3 describes the limitations of not using the model from the institution's perspective. Finally, the Subsect. 4.4 discusses the advantages that the model offers when used from an institutional perspective.

4.1   Limitations of a MAS Without a Purpose Model—Agent Perspective

This section considers a scenario where all agents described in the introduction are located in a bookstore. The Listings 1.1 to 1.4 depict the agents program. Moreover, this system is instrumented with an institution that contains a constitutive rule stating that the concrete action *transfer* count-as *payment*. Such a system could include other status-functions and constitutive rules , but, for simplicity, we focus only on this case to illustrate the main features of the proposed model (cf. Sect. 3).

```
1   !holdBook.   // Bob's code
2
3   +!holdBook
4      <- ?constitutive_rule(Action,payment,_,_);
5         Action.
```
Listing 1.1. Plan of the agent Bob

---

[2] https://github.com/smart-pucrs/MasOntology.
[3] An initial implementation of this platform can be found in https://github.com/rafhaelrc/psf_model.

```
1  !holdBook.   // Alice's code
2
3  +!holdBook
4     <- ?constitutive_rule(Action,afford,_,_);
5        Action.
```

Listing 1.2. Plan of the agent Alice

```
1  !holdBook.   // Francois' code
2
3  +!holdBook
4     <- ?constitutive_rule(Action,repay,_,_);
5        Action.
```

Listing 1.3. Plan of the agent François

```
1  !holdBook.   // Joao's code
2
3  +!holdBook
4     <- ?constitutive_rule(Action,remit,_,_);
5        Action.
```

Listing 1.4. Plan of the agent João

The main limitation is *the agents may not exploit the constitution of status-functions to achieve goals that match the environmental consequences of such a constitution.* For example, consider the fragment in Listing 1.1. This fragment describes Bob's goal (i.e., holdBook, in line 1) and the plan to reach its goal (lines 3–5). When executing the plan, Bob consults the institutional specification (line 4) to find out what concrete action might constitute payment, and in line 5, it executes that action. Bob is coded to achieve its goal by constituting the status-function payment. However, the problem occurs when other agents are coded to achieve their goals through the constitution of status-functions other than payment (e.g., afford, repay, and remit). For example, consider fragment in Listing 1.2. This fragment describes Alice's goal (i.e., holdBook, in line 1) and the plan to reach its goal (lines 3–5). The way of execution is similar to Bob's code. However, there is no constitutive rule stating that a given concrete action count-as afford, and thus Alice cannot achieve its goal through this plan.

This problem can be summarized in the fact that the actions instrumentalized in the plans of Alice, François and João are not foreseen in the institutional specification. This is because the *agents are coded to act considering the action or its constitution itself and not the effects that the constitution of status-functions can bring to the system.* If the status-functions used in the agent's plans (e.g. afford, repay and remit) are different from the status-functions described in the institutional specification, agents cannot resolve which are the appropriate actions to perform.

The agents could overcome the aforementioned limitation if they could choose the status-functions to constitute based on the effects that their constitution produces in the environment. However, without an explicit representation of purposes, this might not be possible. The agents may not be able to exploit the constitution. For example, the constitutive rule *transfer count-as payment* does not make it explicit that the consequence of constitution of the status-function payment can lead to a state of the world where the agents have achieved their goals. Moreover, if new status-functions produce similar effects in the environment when constituted, the agent may have difficulties in using them to satisfy its goals. As they are currently conceived, institutions do not provide instruments for agents to reason about the consequences of actions that affect the institution and, therefore, conclude which actions satisfy their goals.

4.2   Advantages of Purpose—Agent Perspective

To illustrate how the proposed model solves the limitations from the agents' perspective, consider again the example involving the agents Bob, Alice, François, and João, that keep their goals of *holding a book*. However, the purposes related to the status-function payment are now explicit (i.e., the model illustrated in Fig. 3 is available for the agents to query).

All the agents can act in the same way to achieve their goals, according to the code depicted in Listing 1.5. At this point it is important to be clear that the actions from lines 2 to 4 are available by the institutional infrastructures of the system in which the agents interact. The institution has a CArtAgO artifact that allows the agents to access information related to institutional specification and purposes. The system also has a CARtAgO artifact developed by us that allows the agent to perform the concrete action provided for in the constitutive rule of the institutional specification. Since the agents have access to the institutional and constitutive specifications of the system, the programmer of agents can implement them with a generic plan that helps them to achieve their goal on the system. Thus, the code of both agents can be the same.

The agent code runs as follows: In line 2, the agent queries the purpose that points to the desired state. The name of the found purpose is *books trade*. In line 3, the agent queries which status-function is associated with the *books trade* purpose. The status-functions name is *payment*. In line 4, the agent queries which concrete action can constitute the *payment* status-function. The action name is transfer. Finally, the agent performs this action.

```
1    . . .
2    getPurposesOfState(holdAbook,NamePurposes);
3    getStatusFunctionsFromPurposes(NamePurposes,
         NameStatusFunction);
4    ?constitutive_rule(Action,NameStatusFunction,_,_);
5    Action.
```

Listing 1.5. Plan of the agents

We can notice the possibility of agents exploiting the constitution of status-functions to achieve their goals that combine them with the environmental consequences. By adding purposes related to status-functions, agents can reason about the purposes (i.e., the consequences) of carrying out actions that constitute status-functions. From this, the agents can check which actions are aligned with their social goals and, if performed, these actions can satisfy them. For example, the status-functions `payment` has the purpose of `books trade` associated. This purpose points to the `holdABook` state that matches the agents' goal. From this, the agent can infer that the status-function `payment` can help it achieves its goal. This solution allows the agent itself to check if its social goal can be satisfied. This solution seems to be appropriate because it prevents the agent from following unnecessary regulative rules (e.g., a regulative rule stating that it is obligated to make a payment) or performing actions it does not know the consequences (e.g., respect the regulative rule and make the payment, however, payment does not produce the practical effect in the environment that is consistent with it goal of holding a book).

4.3 Limitations of a MAS Without Purpose—Institution Perspective

Consider that agents Bob, Alice, François and João have the same goal of holding a book and can enter different systems, that are a bookstore, a library, a friend's house, and a hostel house. These systems provide, respectively, the environmental actions *transfer, signLoan, receiveABook,* and *putBookOnShelf.* Each system has its own institution that assigns institutional meaning to these actions. To help the agents to act in the system, each institution includes the status-functions known by the different agents. The institutional specifications are shown in Listings 1.6 to 1.9. The first institution contains a constitutive rule stating that the action *transfer count-as payment, rent, donation and replace.* The second institution contains a constitutive rule stating that *signing a loan count-as payment, rent, donation and replace.* The third institution contains a constitutive rule stating that *receiving the book from a friend count-as payment, rent, donation and replace.* Finally, the fourth institution contains a constitutive rule stating that *putting a book on a shelf count-as payment, rent, donation and replace.*

```
status_functions: payment, rent, donation, replace.

Constitutive_rules: 1: transfer count-as payment. 2: transfer
count-as rent. 3: transfer count-as donation. 4: transfer
    count-as
replace.
```

Listing 1.6. Bookstore Institutional Specification

```
status_functions: payment, rent, donation, replace.

Constitutive_rules: 1: signLoan count-as payment. 2: signLoan
```

```
count-as rent. 3: signLoan count-as donation. 4: signLoan
   count-as
replace.
```

Listing 1.7. Library Institutional Specification

```
status_functions: payment, rent, donation, replace.

Constitutive_rules: 1: receiveABook count-as payment. 2:
receiveABook count-as rent. 3: receiveABook count-as donation
   . 4:
receiveABook count-as replace.
```

Listing 1.8. Friend's House Institutional Specification

```
status_functions: payment, rent, donation, replace.

Constitutive_rules: 1: putBookOnShelf count-as payment. 2:
putBookOnShelf count-as rent. 3: putBookOnShelf count-as
   donation.
4: putBookOnShelf count-as replace.
```

Listing 1.9. Hostel House Institutional Specification

The problem from an institutional perspective is that the vocabulary used in specifying agents needs to be compatible with the vocabulary used in specifying institutions. Four constitutive rules are required in the example, one for each potential incoming agent. For every new different agent, a new constitutive rule has to be added in each institution to keep it compatible with the agent. The institutional specification is thus quite dependent on how agents are programmed. The institutional developer must be worried about the agents' internals instead of specifying a good institution (independent of the incoming agents). As it is currently conceived, the institution is not open enough to support the performance of different agents designed with different (but similar) plans and goals.

4.4   Advantages of Purpose—Institution Perspective

Consider again the example involving the agents Bob, Alice, François, and João that still have the same goal but can move through four systems containing four different institutional specifications. Each institution contains its own institutional specification that is extended by adding purposes related to the status-functions. The institutional and purpose specification for the bookstore scenario is depicted in Listing 1.10. The institutional and purpose specification for the library scenario is depicted in Listing 1.11. The institutional and purpose specification for the friend's house scenario is depicted in Listing 1.12. Finally, the institutional and purpose specification for the hostel scenario is depicted in Listing 1.13. These purposes point to states of the world that match the agents' goals.

```
status_functions: payment payment has purpose of: holdABook

Constitutive_rules: 1: transfer count-as payment.
```
Listing 1.10. Bookstore Institutional and Purpose Specification

```
status_functions: rent. rent has purpose of: holdAbook

Constitutive_rules: 1: signLoan count-as rent.
```
Listing 1.11. Library Institutional and Purpose Specification

```
status_functions: donation. donation has purpose of:
    holdAbook

Constitutive_rules: 1: receiveABook count-as donation.
```
Listing 1.12. Friend's House Institutional and Purpose Specification

```
status_functions: replace. replace has purpose of: holdAbook

Constitutive_rules: 1: putBookOnShelf count-as replace.
```
Listing 1.13. Hostel House Institutional and Purpose Specification

We can notice that the institutional specification, particularly the constitutive rules, is not taylored for the different possible incoming agents. The compatibility between the agents' vocabulary and the institution is no longer handled by the constitutive rules. The link between the status-functions and agents' goals is done in a new space conceived adequately for that. If a new agent is considered a participant of the institution, only this space has to be adapted. The constitution is kept unchanged. For example, the *bookstore* specification contains an associated space that describe the purpose of the **payment** status-function. In this case, **payment** is related to the purpose of books trade that points to states that match with the goals of Bob, Alice, François and João.

5   Results and Discussions

The problems motivating this paper are (i) agents not exploiting the environmental consequences of the constitution of status-functions to achieve their goals and (ii) the incompatibility between the vocabulary used while specifying the agents and the institution. These problems are partially solved by computational models that implement artificial institutions. However, these models do not represent the purpose of status-functions. Agents have to be hard-coded to know which status-functions can be useful for them to achieve their social goals, and institutions must be recoded to include new agents specified by different parties. Considering these problems, we propose a model to express the purposes associated with the status-functions that compose the artificial institutions. The conception of our model is an adaptation, from a particular point of view, of Searle's theory [31,32] which claims that the purposes are the practical interests of the individuals that can be satisfied by the constitution of the status-functions (cf. Sect. 2.1). In this computational adaptation of this conception, purposes are associated with status-functions in the institutional specification, i.e., they are external to the agents and explicit in the institution. Even being external, they are connected to the goals of the agents. This connection between status-functions and goals through the purposes captures the Searle's conception of institutional elements (status-functions in this case) that satisfy the practical interests (goals, in this case) of the agents.

There are some advantages of such a conception. The first one is the *flexibility* of the agents to act in different institutions, even without knowing their status-functions. The model presented in this work allows that agents' plans can be specified considering the purposes related to the status-functions rather than the status nomenclature. The advantages are (a) the agents can reason about the consequences of the constitution of the status-functions and adapt to different scenarios, and (b) by reasoning about the consequences of the constitution of the status-functions, an agent can perceive that these consequences are similar to its interests and therefore useful to reach its goals. The agent's capability to reason about the consequences of the constitution of the status-functions and adapt to different scenarios is an important advance especially in open systems [2,40]. The agent's understanding about what makes its social goal satisfied is also an important advance in its autonomy [29]. In this case, the agent can reason about the actions in the plans and the regulative rules that govern the system. In both cases, the agent has more autonomy and flexibility while deciding whether a particular action will help it reach its social goal. The second advantage is related to the *institution's flexibility* as being prepared to receive different agents designed by different developers. The model allows the explicit declaration of a link between status-functions and purposes. The institution requires that new incoming agents know only their goals, the particular status-functions and actions managed by the institution can be discovered at run-time.

According to [14], humans usually have a representation (i) internal of the social reality, i.e., the individuals do not necessarily reason in terms of status-functions, norms, purposes, etc. and (ii) implicit, as it is built on top of people's mental states (that believe, for instance, that a certain man is the king). In the proposed model, purposes are (i) explicit, as it is properly specified through institutional concepts and (ii) external, as it is persisted outside the agent's mind. Dignum, et.al. [15] discuss the different approaches for modeling and implementing organizational concepts, showing the disadvantages of leaving concepts internal and implicit and the benefits of making them external and explicit. Although the work discusses these issues from an organizational point of view, the observed advantages can also be applied to institutions. Such conception is in agreement with some authors that point that institutions can (or even should) be used for reasons that are beyond the normative ones [16,23,25,28,29,33,34].

As future work, we plan to explore additional theoretical aspects related to the proposal, such as (i) investigations about how other proposed institutional abstractions fit on the model, (ii) the verification of the consistency among status-functions' purposes and agents' social goals, and (iii) check if the functions related to status must be further detailed. We plan to also address more practical points such as (i) the modeling of a status-functions' purposes based on a real scenario, (ii) the implementation of the proposal in a computer system and (iii) its integration in an computational model that implements the constitution of status-functions in an MAS platform.

References

1. Aldewereld, H., Álvarez-Napagao, S., Dignum, F., Vázquez-Salceda, J.: Making norms concrete. In: Proceedings of the 9th International Conference on Autonomous Agents and Multiagent Systems: vol. 1. pp. 807–814. International Foundation for Autonomous Agents and Multiagent Systems (2010)
2. Aldewereld, H., Dignum, V.: OperettA: organization-oriented development environment. In: Dastani, M., El Fallah Seghrouchni, A., Hübner, J., Leite, J. (eds.) LADS 2010. LNCS (LNAI), vol. 6822, pp. 1–18. Springer, Heidelberg (2011). https://doi.org/10.1007/978-3-642-22723-3_1
3. Boissier, O., Bordini, R.H., Hubner, J., Ricci, A.: Multi-agent oriented programming: programming multi-agent systems using JaCaMo. MIT Press (2020)
4. Bordini, R.H., Hübner, J.F., Wooldridge, M.: Programming multi-agent systems in AgentSpeak using Jason, vol. 8. John Wiley & Sons (2007)
5. Brito, M.D.E., Thévin, L., Garbay, C., Boissier, O., Hübner, J.F.: Supporting flexible regulation of crisis management by means of situated artificial institution 17(4), 309–324 (2016)
6. Brito, M.d, et al.: A model of institucional reality supporting the regulation in artificial institutions. Ph.D. thesis, Universidade Federal de Santa Catarina (2016)
7. Cardoso, H.L., Oliveira, E.: Institutional reality and norms: specifying and monitoring agent organizations. Int. J. Coop. Inf. Syst. 16(01), 67–95 (2007). https://doi.org/10.1142/s0218843007001573
8. Cassandras, C.G., Lafortune, S.: Introduction to Discrete Event Systems. Springer, Cham (2021). https://doi.org/10.1007/978-3-030-72274-6
9. Cliffe, O., De Vos, M., Padget, J.: Answer set programming for representing and reasoning about virtual institutions. In: Inoue, K., Satoh, K., Toni, F. (eds.) CLIMA 2006. LNCS (LNAI), vol. 4371, pp. 60–79. Springer, Heidelberg (2007). https://doi.org/10.1007/978-3-540-69619-3_4
10. Cliffe, O., De Vos, M., Padget, J.: Specifying and reasoning about multiple institutions. In: Noriega, P., Vázquez-Salceda, J., Boella, G., Boissier, O., Dignum, V., Fornara, N., Matson, E. (eds.) COIN -2006. LNCS (LNAI), vol. 4386, pp. 67–85. Springer, Heidelberg (2007). https://doi.org/10.1007/978-3-540-74459-7_5

11. Cunha, R.R., Hübner, J.F., de Brito, M.: Instituições em sistemas multiagentes a luz da teoria da construção da realidade social. Workshop Escola de Sistemas de Agentes, seus Ambientes e Aplicações XIII, 71–81 (2019)
12. Cunha, R.R., Hübner, J.F., de Brito, M.: A conceptual model for situating purposes in artificial institutions. Revista de Informática Teórica e Aplicada **29**(1), 68–80 (2022)
13. De Brito, M., Hübner, J.F., Boissier, O.: Situated artificial institutions: stability, consistency, and flexibility in the regulation of agent societies. Auton. Agent. Multi-Agent Syst. **32**(2), 219–251 (2018)
14. Bulling, N., van der Torre, L., Villata, S., Jamroga, W., Vasconcelos, W. (eds.): CLIMA 2014. LNCS (LNAI), vol. 8624. Springer, Cham (2014). https://doi.org/ 10.1007/978-3-319-09764-0
15. Dignum, V., Aldewereld, H., Dignum, F.: On the engineering of multi agent organizations. In: Proceedings of the 12th International Workshop on Agent-Oriented Software Engineering, pp. 53–65 (2011)
16. Fornara, N.: Specifying and monitoring obligations in open multiagent systems using semantic web technology. In: In: Semantic Agent Systems, pp. 25–45. Springer (2011). https://doi.org/10.1007/978-3-642-18308-9_2
17. Fornara, N., Colombetti, M.: Ontology and time evolution of obligations and prohibitions using semantic web technology. In: Baldoni, M., Bentahar, J., van Riemsdijk, M.B., Lloyd, J. (eds.) DALT 2009. LNCS (LNAI), vol. 5948, pp. 101–118. Springer, Heidelberg (2010). https://doi.org/10.1007/978-3-642-11355-0_7
18. Fornara, N., Colombetti, M.: Representation and monitoring of commitments and norms using owl. AI Commun. **23**(4), 341–356 (2010)
19. Fornara, N., Tampitsikas, C.: Using owl artificial institutions for dynamically creating open spaces of interaction. In: AT, pp. 281–295 (2012)
20. Fornara, N., Viganò, F., Colombetti, M.: Agent communication and artificial institutions. Auton. Agent. Multi-Agent Syst. **14**(2), 121–142 (2007). https://doi.org/ 10.1007/s10458-006-0017-8
21. Hindriks, K.V., de Boer, F.S., van der Hoek, W., Meyer, J.-J.C.: Agent programming with declarative goals. In: Castelfranchi, C., Lespérance, Y. (eds.) ATAL 2000. LNCS (LNAI), vol. 1986, pp. 228–243. Springer, Heidelberg (2001). https:// doi.org/10.1007/3-540-44631-1_16
22. Hübner, J.F., Bordini, R.H., Wooldridge, M.: Declarative goal patterns for agents-peak. In: Proceedings of the Fifth International Joint Conference on Autonomous Agents and Multiagent Systems (AAMAS'06) (2006)
23. Murray-Rust, D., Papapanagiotou, P., Robertson, D.: Softening electronic institutions to support natural interaction. In: Human Computation, vol. 2(2) (2015). 10.15346/hc.v2i2.3
24. Nigam, V., Leite, J.: A dynamic logic programming based system for agents with declarative goals. In: Baldoni, M., Endriss, U. (eds.) DALT 2006. LNCS (LNAI), vol. 4327, pp. 174–190. Springer, Heidelberg (2006). https://doi.org/10. 1007/11961536_12
25. Padget, J., De Vos, M., Page, C.A.: Deontic sensors. In: IJCAI International Joint Conference on Artificial Intelligence 2018-July (section 5), pp. 475–481 (2018)
26. Ricci, A., Piunti, M., Viroli, M.: Environment programming in multi-agent systems: an artifact-based perspective. Auton. Agent. Multi-Agent Syst. **23**(2), 158–192 (2011)
27. van Riemsdijk, B., van der Hoek, W., Meyer, J. J. C.: Agent programming in dribble: from beliefs to goals using plans. In: Proceedings of the second interna-

tional joint conference on Autonomous agents and multiagent systems, pp. 393–400 (2003)
28. Rocha, C.A.C.: Symbolic environments of agent societies. Workshop Escola de Sistemas de Agentes, seus Ambientes e Aplicações XIV (2020)
29. Rodriguez-Aguilar, J.A., Sierra, C., Arcos, J.L., Lopez-Sanchez, M., Rodriguez, I.: Towards next generation coordination infrastructures. Knowl. Eng. Rev. **30**(4), 435–453 (2015). https://doi.org/10.1017/S0269888915000090
30. Rodriguez-Aguilar, J.A., Sierra, C., Arcos, J.L., López Sánchez, M., Rodríguez Santiago, I.: Towards next generation coordination infrastructures. Knowledge Engineering Review, 2015, vol. 30(4), p. 1–19 (2015)
31. Searle, J.: Making the social world: The structure of human civilization. Oxford University Press (2010)
32. Searle, J.R.: The construction of social reality. Simon and Schuster (1995)
33. Telang, P.R., Singh, M.P., Yorke-Smith, N.: A coupled operational semantics for goals and commitments. J. Artif. Intell. Res. **65**, 31–85 (2019)
34. Tomic, S., Pecora, F., Saffiotti, A.: Norms, Institutions, and Robots 14(8), 1–14 (2018). https://arxiv.org/abs/1807.11456
35. Vázquez-Salceda, J., Aldewereld, H., Grossi, D., Dignum, F.: From human regulations to regulated software agents' behavior. Artif. Intell. Law **16**(1), 73–87 (2008)
36. Viganò, F., Colombetti, M.: Model Checking Norms and Sanctions in Institutions (ii), 316–329 (2008)
37. Winikoff, M.: Challenges and directions for engineering multi-agent systems. arXiv preprint arXiv:1209.1428 (2012)
38. Winikoff, M., Padgham, L., Harland, J., Thangarajah, J.: Declarative and procedural goals in intelligent agent systems. In: International Conference on Principles of Knowledge Representation and Reasoning. Morgan Kaufman (2002)
39. Wooldridge, M.: An introduction to multiagent systems. John Wiley & Sons (2009)
40. Zambonelli, F., Jennings, N.R., Wooldridge, M.: Organisational abstractions for the analysis and design of multi-agent systems. In: Ciancarini, P., Wooldridge, M.J. (eds.) AOSE 2000. LNCS, vol. 1957, pp. 235–251. Springer, Heidelberg (2001). https://doi.org/10.1007/3-540-44564-1_16

Noe: Norm Emergence and Robustness Based on Emotions in Multiagent Systems

Sz-Ting Tzeng[1]([⊠]), Nirav Ajmeri[2]([⊠]), and Munindar P. Singh[1]([⊠])

[1] North Carolina State University, Raleigh, NC 27695, USA
{stzeng,mpsingh}@ncsu.edu
[2] University of Bristol, Bristol BS8 1UB, UK
nirav.ajmeri@bristol.ac.uk

Abstract. Social norms characterize collective and acceptable group conducts in human society. Furthermore, some social norms emerge from interactions of agents or humans. To achieve agent autonomy and make norm satisfaction explainable, we include emotions into the normative reasoning process, which evaluates whether to comply or violate a norm. Specifically, before selecting an action to execute, an agent observes the environment and infers the state and consequences with its internal states after norm satisfaction or violation of a social norm. Both norm satisfaction and violation provoke further emotions, and the subsequent emotions affect norm enforcement. This paper investigates how modeling emotions affect the emergence and robustness of social norms via social simulation experiments. We find that an ability in agents to consider emotional responses to the outcomes of norm satisfaction and violation (1) promotes norm compliance; and (2) improves societal welfare.

1 Introduction

Humans, in daily life, face many choices at many moments, and each selection brings positive and negative payoffs. In psychology, decision-making [33] is a cognitive process that selects a belief or a series of actions based on values, preferences, and beliefs to achieve specific goals. Emotions, the responses to internal or external events or objects, can involve the decision-making process and provide extra information in communication [17,32]. Social norms describe societal principles between agents in a multiagent system. While social norms regulate behaviors in society [15,30,35], humans and agents have the capacity to deviate from norms in certain contexts. For instance, people shake hands normally but deviate from this social norm during a pandemic. Chopra and Singh [8] describe how social protocols rely on a foundation of norms though they do not discuss how the appropriate norms emerge.

An agent that models the emotions of its users and other humans can potentially behave in a more realistic and trustworthy manner. The decision-making process for humans or agents involves evaluating possible consequences of available actions and choosing the action that maximizes the expected utility [11]. Herbert Simon, one of the founders of AI, emphasized that general thinking and problem-solving must incorporate the influence of emotions [34]. Without considering emotions or other affective characteristics, such as personality or mood, some compliance seems irrational [4]. Humans'

© Springer Nature Switzerland AG 2022
A. Theodorou et al. (Eds.): COINE 2021, LNAI 13239, pp. 62–77, 2022.
https://doi.org/10.1007/978-3-031-16617-4_5

compliance shows hints on rational planning over their objectives [17]. Including emotion or personality in normative reasoning makes these compliance behaviors explainable. Norms either are defined in a top-down manner or emerge in a bottom-up manner [25,30]. Works on norms include norm emergence based on the prior outcome of norms, automated run-time revision of sanctions [10], or considering various aspects during reasoning [1,2]. However, sanctions in the real world are often subtle instead of harsh punishments. For instance, sanctions could be trust updates or emotional expression and might change one's behavior [6,27]. Kalia et al. [16] considered norm outcome with respect to emotions and trust and goals. Modeling and reasoning about emotions and other affective characteristics in an agent then become important in decision making and would help the agent enforce and internalize norms.

Accordingly, we propose *Noe*, an agent architecture that integrates decision-making with normative reasoning and emotions. We investigate the following research question.

RQ$_{emotion}$. How does modeling the emotional responses of agents to the outcomes of interactions affect norm emergence and social welfare in an agent society?

To address RQ$_{emotion}$, we refine the abstract normative emotional agent architecture [4] and investigate the interplay of norms and emotions. We propose a framework *Noe* based on BDI architecture [29], norm life-cycle [4,12,30], and emotion life-cycle [3, pp. 62–64] [21]. To evaluate *Noe*, we design a simulation experiment with various agent societies. We investigate how norms emerge and how emotions in normative agents influence social welfare.

To make the problem tractable, we apply one social norm in our simulation and simplify the emotional expression to reduce the complexity. Specifically, our *Noe* agents process emotions by appraising norm outcomes. For the emotion model, we adopt the OCC model of emotions [28] in which we consider both emotional valence and intensity and assume violation of norms yields negative emotions.

Organization. The rest of the paper is structured as follows. Section 2 discusses the relevant related works. Section 3 describes *Noe*, including the symbolic representation and the decision-making in *Noe*. Section 4 details the simulation experiments we conduct to evaluate *Noe* and describes the experimental results. Section 5 presents the conclusions and the future directions.

2   Related Works

Ortony et al. [28] model emotions based on events, action, and objects. Marsella and Gratch [21] proposed a computational model of emotion to model appraisal in perceptual, cognitive, and behavioral processes. Moerland et al. [24] surveyed emotions in relation to reinforcement learning. Keltner and Haidt [17] differentiate the functional approaches and research of emotions by four-level analysis: individual, dyadic, groups, and cultural. Briefly, emotions provide some information for agents or people to coordinate social interactions. We take inspiration from these works.

Savarimuthu and Cranefield [30] proposed a life-cycles model for norms and discussed varied mechanisms of norm study. Broersen et al. [7] introduced the so-called

Beliefs-Obligations-Intentions-Desires (BOID) architecture on top of the Beliefs-Intentions-Desires (BDI) architecture [29], which further include obligation and conflict resolution. Lima et al. [18] developed Gavel, an adaptive sanctioning enforcement framework, to choose appropriate sanctions based on different contexts. However, these works do not consider emotions in the decision-making process.

Argente et al. [4] propose an abstract normative emotional agent architecture, which combines emotion model, normative model, and Belief-Desire-Intention (BDI) architecture. Argente et al. defined four types of relationships between emotions and norms: (1) emotion in the process of normative reasoning, (2) emotion generation with norm satisfaction or violation, (3) emotions as a way to enforce norms, (4) anticipation of emotions promotes internalization and compliance of social norms. Yet, Argente et al. do not validate the interplay between emotions and norms with their proposed architecture.

Bourgais et al. [6] present an agent architecture that integrates cognition, emotions, emotion contagion, personality, norms, and social relations to simulate humans and ensure explainable behaviors. However, emotions are predefined and not generated via appraisal in this work.

Von Scheve et al. [31] consider emotion generation with norm satisfaction or violation. Specifically, an observer agent perceives the transgression of a norm of another, its strong negative emotions (e.g., contempt, disdain, detestation, or disgust) constitute negative sanctioning of the violator. The negative sanctioning then leads to negative emotions (e.g., shame, guilt, or embarrassment) in the violator. Besides, compliance with the social norms can stem from the fear of emotional-driven sanctions, which would lead to negative emotions in the violator. Such fear enforces social norms. Yet, emotions are not part of the decision-making process in this work.

3   Noe

We now describe the architecture, norm formal model, and decision-making.

3.1   Architecture

Noe integrates the BDI architecture [29] with a normative model [4,12,30] and an emotional model [3,21]. A *Noe* agent assesses the environment, including other agents' expressed emotions, its cognitive mental states, and infer possible outcomes to make a decision. Figure 1 shows the three components of *Noe*.

The normative component of *Noe* includes the following processes:

- Identification: the agent recognize norms from its norm base based on its beliefs
- Instantiation: activate norms related to the agent
- Normative reasoning process: the reasoning process makes decisions based on the beliefs, current intention, self-directed emotions, other-directed emotions received from others, active norms, and how the norm satisfaction or violation influences the world and itself The *Noe* agents then update the intention based on the results of normative reasoning

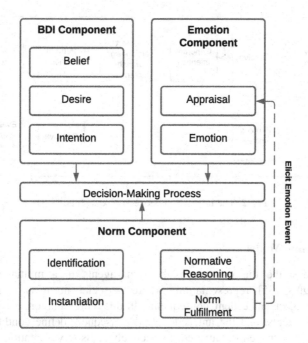

Fig. 1. *Noe* architecture, representing and reasoning over beliefs, desires, intentions, emotions, and norms.

- Norm fulfillment process: check if a norm has been fulfilled or violated based on the selected action. The compliance or violation of a norm will then trigger an elicit emotion event that will be appraised at the emotion component.

The BDI component includes the following parts:

- Beliefs: form beliefs based on perceptions
- Desires: generate desires based on the beliefs
- Intention: the highest priority of desires to achieve based on the beliefs
- Action: select action based on the current intention, emotions, possible outcomes, and the evaluation of violating or complying with norms, if any
The beliefs, desires, and intentions are mental states of *Noe* agents.

The emotional component includes the following processes:

- Appraisal: calculate the appraisal value based on the beliefs, desires, and norm satisfaction or norm violation. In this work, we consider only norm satisfaction or norm violation
- Emotion: generate emotion based on the appraisal values [21].

Figure 2 illustrates the interactions between agents in our simulation scenario.

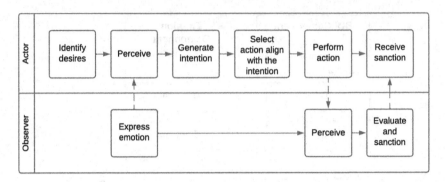

Fig. 2. The interaction between *Noe* agents.

3.2   Norm Formal Model

Social norms describe the interactions between agents in a multiagent system. We adopt Singh's [35] representation, where a social norm is formalized as $Norm$(subject, object, antecedent, consequent). In this representation, the subject and object represent agents, and the antecedent and consequent define conditions under which the norm is activated or satisfied, respectively. This representation describes a norm activated by the subject towards the object when the antecedent holds, and the consequent indicates if the norm was satisfied or violated.

Following Singh [35], we consider three types of norms in *Noe*.

- Commitment (C): the subject commits to the object to bring out the consequence if the antecedent holds. Consider Alice and Bob are queuing up in a grocery store. Alice and Bob commit to keeping social distance during the pandemic, represented as C(Alice, Bob, $during$ = pandemic, social distance).
- Prohibition (P): the object prohibits the subject from the consequence if the antecedent holds. Caleb, the grocery store manager, prohibits Bob from jumping the queue while lining up in that store, represented as P(Bob, Caleb, $when$ = line up; at = grocery store, jump).
- Sanction (S): same as commitment or prohibition, yet the consequence would be the sanctions. Sanctions could be positive, negative, or neutral reactions to any norm satisfaction or violation [27]. If Bob breaks the queue, he receives negative sanctions from Alice, represented as S(Bob, Alice, jump, negative sanctions). Negative sanctions could be physical actions, e.g., scolding someone, or emotional expression, e.g., expressions of disdain, annoyance, or disgust.

To simulate the norm emergence and enforcement in human society, we include emotions into the decision-making process since, by nature, humans do not always act rationally in terms of utility theory. Here we formalize emotions with $E_i(target, intensity, decay)$ indicating agent a_i has emotion e toward the target with intensity and decay value. An example of the prohibition case would be, Bob would not jump the queue if Alice is angry, represented as P(Bob, Alice, Bob $\succ$ Alice $\wedge$ E_{Alice} = angry, jump).

We model the emotional response of agents with triggered emotions from norm satisfaction, or violation [4]. Here we represent the elicited emotions with $Elem_{name}(A_{expect}, A_{real}, Em_1, Em_2)|Em_1, Em_2 \in E; A_{expect}, A_{real} \in A$ where A is a set of actions. E is a set of emotions, and Em_1 and Em_2 are the emotions triggered by norm satisfaction and violation accordingly. If the A_{expect} is equal to the A_{real}, a norm has been fulfilled, and Em_1 was elicited. $Ap(beliefs, desires, Elem)$ represents the appraisal function.

3.3 Decision-Making

Schwarz [32] addresses the influence of moods and emotions at decision making and discusses the interplay of emotion, cognition, and decision making. Specifically, the aspects include pre-decision affect, post-decision affect, anticipated affect, and memories of past affect. In our model, we include the pre-decision affect into the decision-making process. With pre-decision affect, people recall information from memories that match their current affect [32]. For instance, people in a sad emotion or interacting with hostile people tend to overestimate adverse outcomes and events.

In our model, emotions serve as mental objects and an approach to sanctioning. We consider emotions as intrinsic rewards from agents' internal state in contrast to physical rewards from the environment. We adopt the OCC model of emotions [28], in which we consider emotional valence and intensity. We formulate emotions with simple values where positive values indicate positive emotions and larger values indicate higher intensity. A mood is a general feeling and not a response to a specific event or stimulus compared to emotions. Therefore, we consider emotions but not mood. Noe agents' appraisal function considers norm satisfaction and violation only. The agents are aware of other agents' expressed emotions in the same place. In this work, we assume that agents express true and honest emotions and can correctly perceive the expressed emotions. In other words, felt emotions are equal to expressed emotions. Another assumption is that emotions are consistent with the notions of rational behavior.

Algorithm 1 displays the decision loop of our model. At the beginning of the simulation, all agents are initialized with certain desires, and during the run, an intention would be generated by prioritizing desires with the agent's beliefs. When choosing the next move with line 5 in Algorithm 1, the agent chooses the one with maximum utility from all available actions. Algorithm 2 details the action selection. The decision takes the agent's beliefs, current intention, and possible consequences into accounts. While norms are activated with the beliefs, the agent would further consider emotions and cost and possible consequences with norms at line 9 in Algorithm 2. For instance, if people violate some social norms, they may be isolated from society. Regarding the influence of emotions, people may overestimate the negative outcomes when they are in the negative emotion and tend to comply with the norms.

4 Evaluation

We evaluate Noe via a line-up environment where agents form queues to receive service. We detail the environment in Sect. 4.1.

Algorithm 1: Decision loop of a *Noe* agent

---

1 Initialize one agent with its desires D;
2 **for** *t=1,T* **do**
3   Observe the environment (including the expressed emotions from others E_{around}) and form beliefs b_t;
4   Generate intention I based on b_t and D;
5   a_t = ActionSelection(b_t, I, D);
6   Execute action a_t;
7   Elicit self-directed emotions E_{self} from agent itself based on if action a_t fulfills a norm;
8   Self-sanction with E_{self};
9   Observe the environment (including the performed actions a_{t_other} of other agents) and form beliefs b_{t+1};
10   Elicit other-directed emotions E_{other} for observer agents based on if action a_{t_other} fulfills a norm;
11   Sanction others with E_{other};
12 **end**

Algorithm 2: Action selection

Input: beliefs b_t, intention I, desires D
Output: Action a_t
1 **Function** Action Selection:
2      $E_{around} \subset b_t$;
3   **for** *each a in ACTIONS(b_t)* **do**
4   Activate norms N with beliefs b_t and a;
5   **if** $N = \varnothing$ **then**
6   a_t = MAX$_a$(RESULT(b_t, intention, a))
7   **else**
8   a_t = MAX$_a$(RESULT(b_t, intention, a, N) $\times$ amplifier(E_{around}))
9   **end**
10   **end**
11   **return** a_t
12 **return**

4.1 Line-Up Environment

Figure 3 shows the line-up environment. We build this line-up environment using Mesa [22], a Python-based framework for building, analyzing, and visualizing agent-based models.

The line-up environment includes two shared locations—home and grocery stores. The agents move between home and grocery stores to get food. We consider one social norm in the line-up environment: agents are expected to line up to enter the grocery store. To simulate real human reactions to norm violations, we refer to a social psychology experiment [23]. In the line-up environment, we model defensive reactions of people in the queue as negative emotions toward those who jump the queue by barging

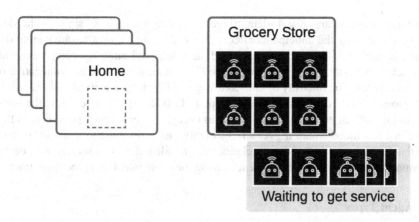

Fig. 3. Simulation details. Agents move between their homes and the grocery store. The store has a capacity limit of eight customers at one time. As a result, other agents must line up outside the store to get service.

in ahead of someone already in the queue. Conversely, people show positive emotions toward those who stay in the queue.

We initialize the agents with the following parameter values:

- Health (Integer value from 0–100): When the health value reaches zero, the agent is marked as *deceased* and unable to act. The health value decreases by 1 unit at each step.
- Deceased (Boolean: True or False): set as True when an agent runs out of health.
- Emotion (Integer value): simplified with numerical values where positive values indicate positive emotions and negative indicate negative emotions. The emotions come along with a duration. Default at 0.
- Number of food packets owned (Integer value from 0–15): once obtained food from the stores, agents would be able to restore its health value via consuming food anywhere.
- Food expiration day (Integer value from 0–15): once the agent gets food packets, we update the expiration day with 15. The expiration day decreases by 1 unit at each step. Food expires once the expiration day reaches 0. Default at 0.
- Beliefs: the perceived and processed information from the world, including other agents' expressed emotions.
- Desires: desired states, including *have food* and *wandering*.
- Intention: the highest priority of desires to achieve at a specific time. When the agent's health is lower than the threshold, 80% of the health, the agent sets its intention as *get food*; otherwise, the agent sets its intention as *wandering*.

When an agent runs low on stock, it has a higher probability of moving to a grocery store. The grocery store can provide food packets to eight agents in one time step. While waiting in line to get food, the agent could either stay in the line or jump ahead in the line to get food in less time. Jumping the line may increase other agents' delay in getting food packets. Those who witness the violation would then cast negative emotions, further interpreted as anger or disdain, triggered by that behavior. To simplify the simulation, we presume the anticipated affects [32] with: (1) receiving negative emotions triggers negative self-directed emotions such as shame and guilt; (2) complying with norms leads to positive or neutral emotions; (3) violating norms leads to negative or neutral emotions. The intensity of emotions triggered each time is fixed, but the values of emotions can add up. Each triggered emotion lasts 2 steps. At each step, the duration and intensity of emotion decrease by 1 as decay. A simple assumption here is that people in a bad mood would trigger stronger emotions in response to a non-ideal state. Note that at the beginning of the simulation, we initialize the agent society with health in normal distribution to avoid all agents having the same intention at the same time.

4.2 Agent Types

To answer our research question and evaluate *Noe*, we define three agent societies as baselines. We describe the agents societies below:

Obedient society. Agents in an obedient society always follow norms.

Anarchy society. Agents in an anarchy society jump lines when they cannot get food.

Sanctioning society. Agents in the sanctioning society jump lines considering the previous experience of satisfying or violating a norm. Agents sanction positively or negatively based on norm satisfaction or violations directly and comply with enforced norms.

***Noe* society.** Agents in the *Noe* society jump lines considering the previous experiences of satisfying or violating a norm, current emotional state of the other agents, current self emotional state, and estimated outcome of satisfying or violating a norm. *Noe* agents who observe norm satisfaction or violations would appraise the norm outcomes and trigger emotions to sanction the actor agent.

Table 1 summarizes the characteristics of the agents in the four societies.

Table 1. Characteristics of the various agent societies.

Agent type	Violation allowed	Sanctioning	Emotions involved
Obedient society	✗	✗	✗
Anarchy society	✔	✗	✗
Sanctioning society	✔	✔	✗
Noe society	✔	✔	✔

4.3 Hypotheses and Metrics

To address our research question $RQ_{emotion}$ on emotions and norm emergence, we propose three hypotheses:

H_1 (**Norm satisfaction**): Norm satisfaction in *Noe* agent society is higher compared to the baseline agent societies.

H_2 (**Social welfare**): *Noe* agent society yields better social welfare compared to the baseline agent societies.

H_3 (**Social experience**): *Noe* agent society yields a better social experience compared to the baseline agent societies.

To evaluate H_1 on norm satisfaction, we compute one metric, M_1 (Cohesion): Percentage of norm satisfaction.

To evaluate H_2 on social welfare, we compute two metrics: (1) M_2 (Deceased): Cumulative number of agents deceased; (2) M_3 (Health): Average health of the agents.

To evaluate H_3 on social experience, we compute one metric, M_4 (Waiting time): Average waiting time of agents in the queues.

To test the statistical significance of H_1, H_2, and H_3, we conduct the independent t-test and measure effect size with Glass's Δ for unrelated societies [13, 14]. We adopt Cohen's [9, pp. 24–27] descriptors to interpret effect size where above 0.2, 0.5, 0.8 indicate small, medium, and large.

4.4 Experimental Setup

We run each simulation with 400 agents and queue size 80 for 3,000 steps. We choose a relatively small number of agents to reduce the simulation time while our results are stable for a more significant number of agents. The simulation stabilizes at about 1,500 steps, but we keep extended simulation steps to have more promising results. Table 2 lists the payoffs applied in our simulation.

We present the results with a moving average of 100 steps. We choose this size of running window to show the temporal behavior change in a small sequence of time. With a larger size, the running window may alleviate the behavior change. To minimize deviation from coincidence, we run each simulation with 10 iterations and compute the mean values.

Table 2. Payoff table.

Component	Type	Reward
Deceased	Extrinsic	−500
Norm compliance & Positive emotion	Intrinsic	1
Norm violation & Negative emotion	Intrinsic	−1

4.5 Experimental Results

In this section, we describe the simulation results comparing the three baselines and *Noe* agents. Table 3 summarizes these results. Table 4 lists the value of Glass's Δ and p-values from the independent t-test.

According to Table 3 and Table 4, we see that *Noe* generate better cohesion and fewer deceased agents than baselines (p < 0.01; Glass's Δ > 0.8). The null hypothesis corresponding to H_1 is rejected. Note that we do not consider the cohesion metric for the obedient agent society here since agents in the obedient society are always compliant. However, *Noe* also yields the worst social experience where the low waiting time is a desirable state (p < 0.01; Glass's Δ > 0.8).

Table 3. Comparing *Noe* agent society with baseline agent societies on various metrics.

Agent society	Cohesion	Deceased	Health	Waiting time
Obedient	–	55.30	79.27	8.95
Anarchy	0.22	81.60	79.50	5.45
Sanctioning	0.88	169.30	86.26	2.55
Noe	**0.99**	**54.00**	79.00	8.95

Table 4. Statistical analysis.

Agent society	Glass's Δ				p-value			
	Cohesion	Deceased	Waiting time	Health	Cohesion	Deceased	Waiting time	Health
Obedient	0.19	0.65	0.01	0.18	0.32	<0.01	0.98	0.52
Anarchy	102.43	3.10	40.82	0.21	<0.01	<0.01	<0.01	0.46
Sanctioning	13.67	15.53	76.68	3.34	<0.01	<0.01	<0.01	8.45
Noe	–	–	–	–	–	–	–	–

H_1 Norm Satisfaction. Figure 4 displays the cohesion, the percentage of norm satisfaction, in the baseline agent societies and the *Noe* agent society. We find that the percentage of norm satisfaction in the *Noe* agent society, average at 99% and p-value < 0.01, is constantly higher than the sanctioning agent society, average at 88% and p-value < 0.01 and Glass's Δ > 0.8. The sanctioning agent society learns to comply with the norm as time goes by. The *Noe* agent society does sanction as well. Yet, considering emotions and the possible outcome makes *Noe* agent society enforce the norm faster than the sanctioning agent society. Specifically, *Noe* agent society enforces the norm at about 100 steps while sanctioning agent society at 1,500 steps.

H_2 Social Welfare. Figure 5 compares the average number of deceased in the obedient, anarchy, sanctioning, and *Noe* agent societies. Refer to Fig. 4, sanctioning agent society learns the norm via positive and negative sanctioning from norm satisfaction and violation. However, the agents in that society do not consider the possible severe consequences and cause compliant agents to die in the queue. When the number of deceased reaches the threshold, the simulation stabilizes. Therefore, no more agent from the sanctioning agent society dies after the threshold. On the contrary, *Noe* agent society sanctions and considers possible outcomes of norm satisfaction and violation, therefore learning the norm and avoiding unacceptable consequences.

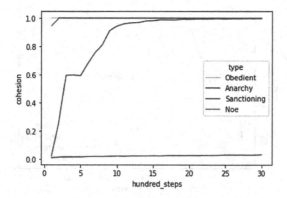

Fig. 4. Simulation result: average cohesion. Comparing average cohesion (M_1) yielded by *Noe* and baseline agent societies.

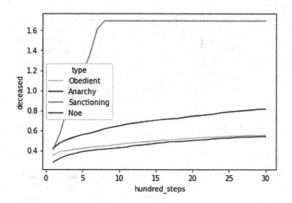

Fig. 5. Simulation result: average number of deceased. Comparing average number of deceased (M_2) in *Noe* and baseline agent societies.

Figure 6 compares the average health of the agents in the obedient, anarchy, sanctioning, and *Noe* agent societies. The sanctioning agent society yields higher health State, with a mean at 86.26, but at the expense of more deaths. The rest of the agents then be able to remain in high health.

H₃ Social Experience. Figure 7 compares the average waiting time the agents spend in a queue at the grocery store in the obedient, anarchy, sanctioning, and *Noe* agent societies. The *Noe* agent society learns the norm fast and remains the same waiting time in the queue. However, some agents in the sanctioning agent society take advantage of those who learn norms faster than themselves. Therefore, many agents die during the learning process, and the simulation stabilizes. In Fig. 7, the obedient agent society shares the same trend with *Noe* agent society since emotions enforce the line-up norm.

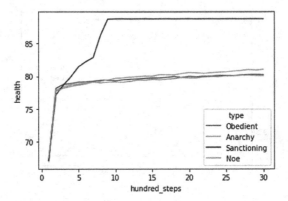

Fig. 6. Simulation result: average health value. Comparing average health value (M_3) in *Noe* and baseline agent societies.

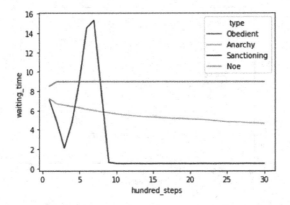

Fig. 7. Simulation result: average waiting time of agents in queues. Comparing average waiting time (M_4) in *Noe* and baseline agent societies.

Combining the results for H_1 and H_2 and H_3, we note that while sanctioning enforces norms, a combination of sanctioning and emotions enforce norms better. Specifically, having emotions as amplifiers of outcomes yield higher norm satisfaction compared to our baselines. The results also indicate that, first, sanctioning agents that consider only norm violation or norm satisfaction may bring out worse social welfare compared to *Noe* that considers both norms and their consequences. Second, although *Noe* agents remain relatively high waiting time in the queues, the number of deceased is lower than the baselines. Note that the sudden drop of deceased number or increase of health value for sanctioning agents resulted from the stabilization of that society. Third, *Noe* agents stay in positive emotions during the simulation while sanctioning agents start from negative emotions and eventually achieve the expected behaviors.

5   Discussion and Conclusion

We present an agent architecture inspired by the norm life-cycle [4], BDI architecture [29], and emotion life-cycle [3,21] to investigate how emotions influence norm emergence and social welfare. We evaluate the proposed architecture via simulation experiments in an environment where agents queue up to receive service. Our simulations consider two characteristics of an agent society: sanctioning and emotions that participate in action selection and arise from evaluating selected action. The experiments show that incorporating emotions enables agents to cooperate better than those who do not.

In our agent architecture, we make an assumption that agents can recognize others' emotions. However, we acknowledge that emotion recognition is a challenging task [5]. Whereas recent works in AI have focused on emotion recognition through facial expressions and emotion recognition using wearables, it is worth noting that there is no agreement in modeling emotions in the psychology community [5,19,20].

Murukannaiah et al. [26] address many shortcomings of current approaches for AI ethics, including taking the value preferences of an agent's stakeholder and other agents' users, learning value preferences by observing the responses of other agents' users, and value-based negotiation. Incorporating these aspects in Noe is an interesting future direction.

As a future extension of current work, we plan to differentiate emotions in Noe instead of modeling emotions with emotion valences to provide more information for value preferences. We also consider including a mix of personalities in future research to have different appraisal results. In this work, Noe agents are assumed to express true and honest emotions. However, emotions can also serve as a tool to influence, persuade, or deceive others in an adversarial context. It would be crucial to identify and model these contradictions while humans are in the loop.

Acknowledgments. STT and MPS thank the NSF for partial support under grant IIS-1908374.

References

1. Ajmeri, N., Guo, H., Murukannaiah, P.K., Singh, M.P.: Robust norm emergence by revealing and reasoning about context: socially intelligent agents for enhancing privacy. In: Proceedings of the 27th International Joint Conference on Artificial Intelligence (IJCAI), pp. 28–34. IJCAI, Stockholm, July 2018. https://doi.org/10.24963/ijcai.2018/4
2. Ajmeri, N., Guo, H., Murukannaiah, P.K., Singh, M.P.: Elessar: ethics in norm-aware agents. In: Proceedings of the 19th International Conference on Autonomous Agents and MultiAgent Systems (AAMAS), pp. 16–24. IFAAMAS, Auckland, May 2020. https://doi.org/10.5555/3398761.3398769
3. Alfonso Espinosa, B.: Agents with Affective Traits for Decision-Making in Complex Environments. Ph.D. thesis, Universitat Politècnica de València (2017). https://doi.org/10.4995/Thesis/10251/90497
4. Argente, E., Del Val, E., Perez-Garcia, D., Botti, V.: Normative emotional agents: a viewpoint paper. IEEE Trans. Affect. Comput. (2020). https://doi.org/10.1109/TAFFC.2020.3028512
5. Barrett, L.F., Adolphs, R., Marsella, S., Martinez, A.M., Pollak, S.D.: Emotional expressions reconsidered: challenges to inferring emotion from human facial movements. Psychol. Sci. Public Interest **20**(1), 1–68 (2019)

6. Bourgais, M., Taillandier, P., Vercouter, L.: BEN: an agent architecture for explainable and expressive behavior in social simulation. In: Calvaresi, D., Najjar, A., Schumacher, M., Främling, K. (eds.) EXTRAAMAS 2019. LNCS (LNAI), vol. 11763, pp. 147–163. Springer, Cham (2019). https://doi.org/10.1007/978-3-030-30391-4_9

7. Broersen, J., Dastani, M., Hulstijn, J., Huang, Z., van der Torre, L.: The BOID architecture: conflicts between beliefs, obligations, intentions and desires. In: Proceedings of the 5th International Conference on Autonomous Agents, pp. 9–16 (2001). https://doi.org/10.1145/375735.375766

8. Chopra, A.K., Singh, M.P.: From social machines to social protocols: software engineering foundations for sociotechnical systems. In: Proceedings of the 25th International World Wide Web Conference, pp. 903–914. ACM, Montréal, April 2016. https://doi.org/10.1145/2872427.2883018

9. Cohen, J.: Statistical Power Analysis for the Behavioral Sciences, 2nd edn. Lawrence Erlbaum Associates, Hillsdale (1988)

10. Dell'Anna, D., Dastani, M., Dalpiaz, F.: Runtime revision of sanctions in normative multi-agent systems. Autonom. Agents Multi-Agent Syst. **34**(2), 1–54 (2020). https://doi.org/10.1007/s10458-020-09465-8

11. Edwards, W.: The theory of decision making. Psychol. Bull. **51**(4), 380 (1954). https://doi.org/10.1037/h0053870

12. Frantz, C., Pigozzi, G.: Modeling norm dynamics in multiagent systems. J. Appl. Log. - IfCoLoG J. Log. App. **5**(2), 491–564 (2018)

13. Glass, G.V.: Primary, secondary, and meta-analysis of research. Educ. Res. **5**(10), 3–8 (1976). https://doi.org/10.3102/0013189X005010003

14. Grissom, R.J., Kim, J.J.: Effect Sizes for Research: Univariate and Multivariate Applications. Routledge, Abingdon-on-Thames (2012). https://doi.org/10.4324/9780203803233

15. Kafalı, Ö., Ajmeri, N., Singh, M.P.: DESEN: specification of sociotechnical systems via patterns of regulation and control. ACM Trans. Softw. Eng. Methodol. (TOSEM). **29**(1), 7:1–7:50 (2020). https://doi.org/10.1145/3365664

16. Kalia, A.K., Ajmeri, N., Chan, K., Cho, J.H., Adalı, S., Singh, M.P.: The interplay of emotions and norms in multiagent systems. In: Proceedings of the 28th International Joint Conference on Artificial Intelligence (IJCAI), pp. 371–377. IJCAI, Macau, August 2019. https://doi.org/10.24963/ijcai.2019/53

17. Keltner, D., Haidt, J.: Social functions of emotions at four levels of analysis. Cogn. Emotion **13**(5), 505–521 (1999). https://doi.org/10.1080/026999399379168

18. de Lima, I.C.A., Nardin, L.G., Sichman, J.S.: Gavel: a sanctioning enforcement framework. In: Weyns, D., Mascardi, V., Ricci, A. (eds.) EMAS 2018. LNCS (LNAI), vol. 11375, pp. 225–241. Springer, Cham (2019). https://doi.org/10.1007/978-3-030-25693-7_12

19. Marín-Morales, J., et al.: Affective computing in virtual reality: emotion recognition from brain and heartbeat dynamics using wearable sensors. Sci. Rep. **8**(1), 1–15 (2018). https://doi.org/10.1038/s41598-018-32063-4

20. Marsella, S., Gratch, J., Petta, P.: Computational models of emotion. In: Scherer, K.R., Banziger, T., Roesch, E. (eds.) A Blueprint for Affective Computing: A Sourcebook and Manual, chap. 1.2, pp. 21–46. Oxford University Press (2010)

21. Marsella, S.C., Gratch, J.: EMA: a process model of appraisal dynamics. Cogn. Syst. Res. **10**(1), 70–90 (2009). https://doi.org/10.1016/j.cogsys.2008.03.005

22. Masad, D., Kazil, J.: MESA: an agent-based modeling framework. In: Proceedings of the 14th PYTHON in Science Conference, pp. 53–60 (2015)

23. Milgram, S., Liberty, H.J., Toledo, R., Wackenhut, J.: Response to intrusion into waiting lines. J. Personal. Soc. Psychol. **51**(4), 683 (1986). https://doi.org/10.1037/0022-3514.51.4.683

24. Moerland, T.M., Broekens, J., Jonker, C.M.: Emotion in reinforcement learning agents and robots: a survey. Mach. Learn. **107**(2), 443–480 (2017). https://doi.org/10.1007/s10994-017-5666-0

25. Morris-Martin, A., De Vos, M., Padget, J.: Norm emergence in multiagent systems: a viewpoint paper. Autonom. Agents Multi-Agent Syst. **33**(6), 706–749 (2019). https://doi.org/10.1007/s10458-019-09422-0

26. Murukannaiah, P.K., Ajmeri, N., Jonker, C.M., Singh, M.P.: New foundations of ethical multiagent systems. In: Proceedings of the 19th International Conference on Autonomous Agents and MultiAgent Systems (AAMAS), pp. 1706–1710. IFAAMAS, Auckland, May 2020. https://doi.org/10.5555/3398761.3398958

27. Nardin, L.G., et al.: Classifying sanctions and designing a conceptual sanctioning process model for socio-technical systems. Knowl. Eng. Rev. (KER) **31**(2), 142–166 (2016). https://doi.org/10.1017/S0269888916000023

28. Ortony, A., Clore, G.L., Collins, A.: The Cognitive Structure of Emotions. Cambridge University Press, New York (1988). https://doi.org/10.1017/CBO9780511571299

29. Rao, A.S., Georgeff, M.P.: Modeling rational agents within a BDI-architecture. In: Proceedings of the 2nd International Conference on Principles of Knowledge Representation and Reasoning, pp. 473–484 (1991). https://doi.org/10.5555/3087158.3087205

30. Savarimuthu, B.T.R., Cranefield, S.: Norm creation, spreading and emergence: a survey of simulation models of norms in multi-agent systems. Multiagent Grid Syst. **7**(1), 21–54 (2011)

31. von Scheve, C., Moldt, D., Fix, J., von Luede, R.: My agents love to conform: norms and emotion in the micro-macro link. Comput. Math. Organ. Theory **12**(2–3), 81–100 (2006). https://doi.org/10.1007/s10588-006-9538-6

32. Schwarz, N.: Emotion, cognition, and decision making. Cogn. Emotion **14**(4), 433–440 (2000). https://doi.org/10.1080/026999300402745

33. Simon, H.A.: The new science of management decision. Harper Brothers (1960). https://doi.org/10.1037/13978-000

34. Simon, H.A.: Motivational and emotional controls of cognition. Psychol. Rev. **74**(1), 29–39 (1967). https://doi.org/10.1037/h0024127

35. Singh, M.P.: Norms as a basis for governing sociotechnical systems. ACM Trans. Intell. Syst. Technol. (TIST). **5**(1), 21:1–21:23 (2013). https://doi.org/10.1145/2542182.2542203

Run-Time Norms Synthesis in Multi-objective Multi-agent Systems

Maha Riad[(✉)] and Fatemeh Golpayegani

School of Computer Science, University College Dublin, Dublin, Ireland
maha.riad@ucdconnect.ie, fatemeh.golpayegani@ucd.ie

Abstract. Norms represent behavioural aspects that are encouraged by a social group of agents or the majority of agents in a system. Normative systems enable coordinating synthesised norms of heterogeneous agents in complex multi-agent systems autonomously. In real applications, agents have multiple objectives that may contradict each other or contradict the synthesised norms. Therefore, agents need a mechanism to understand the impact of a suggested norm on their objectives and decide whether or not to adopt it. To address these challenges, a utility-based norm synthesis (UNS) model is proposed which allows the agents to coordinate their behaviour while achieving their conflicting objectives. UNS proposes a utility-based case-based reasoning technique, using case-based reasoning for run-time norm synthesising in a centralised approach, and a utility function derived from the objectives of the system and its operating agents to decide whether or not to adopt a norm. The model is evaluated using a traffic junction scenario and the results show its efficacy to optimise multiple objectives while adopting synthesised norms.

Keywords: Norms synthesis · Multi-objective · Heterogeneous multi-agent systems

1 Introduction

Multi-agent systems (MAS) are complex systems consisting of agents which are autonomous entities with their own objectives, and can act dynamically. Agents' objectives can be represented by tasks they want to achieve, these tasks can be unintentionally supportive to other agents' objectives or incompatible with them [8]. Aside from the ability of the agents to have multiple objectives, agents may have heterogeneous types, in which each type has its own characteristics, preferences or category [7]. Moreover, agents can operate in open system settings where they can move freely inside and outside of the system. MAS is applied in many real world applications such as traffic systems [1,7], computer networks [4], smart energy grids [9] and the internet of things systems [13]. However, in such systems, it is not only crucial to model the heterogeneity, openness and autonomy of the agents, but also it is essential to consider the agents' behaviour coordination.

A. Theodorou et al. (Eds.): COINE 2021, LNAI 13239, pp. 78–93, 2022.
https://doi.org/10.1007/978-3-031-16617-4_6

Norms are behaviour guidelines imposed by a society or social group to regulate agents' actions. For example, in a traffic system, one norm is to slow down when seeing a senior driver because he might be more cautious than other drivers and drive slowly. Another example is represented in the norm of leaving the right (fast) lane empty when there is an ambulance. Accordingly, norms representation helps agents to achieve their objectives in an acceptable manner within their social groups without compromising their autonomy. This would facilitate group decision making, cooperation, and coordination between agents [12].

Multi-agent systems that encapsulate norms concepts such as prohibitions, obligations and permissions are called Normative Multi-Agent Systems (NorMAS) [2]. NorMAS rely on norms for regulating the behaviour of agents while reserving their autonomy property [2]. Norms have dynamic nature, and so each norm's life cycle begins with norm synthesis (which relies on creating and composing a set of norms [11]) and ends with norm disappearance [6].

Various efforts of researchers were directed to proposing a reliable norm synthesising mechanisms that can be used to synthesise norms at run-time and/or in an open system. The challenge of an open environment is that agents can enter and leave the system freely, and so a special technique is needed for aligning all of the agents with the system norms, particularly for the new agents entering the system. Moreover, synthesising norms at run-time would demand an online strategy for triggering new norms creation and update according to the changing environment. IRON [11], a state-of-the-artwork, was one of the most prominent mechanisms that showed its efficacy in synthesising norms at run-time in an open NorMAS. However, it has two main limitations. First, the synthesising strategy used may produce biased norms. For example, in a traffic junction scenario, IRON can synthesise a norm that obligates the driver to stop when he is at an intersection and there is another vehicle to his right trying to cross at the same time. Although this norm will ensure avoiding the collision of the vehicles, this will cause the left lane to have higher congestion and traffic density than the right lane because vehicles in the right lane would have higher priority to pass. Second, IRON does not consider whether the synthesised norms contradict the objectives of the system or other norms or not. If the norm synthesised in the previous traffic junction example is applied while having an emergency vehicle (ambulance) in the left lane, it will be against the system' objectives; if it aims to minimise the total waiting time of emergency vehicles. An example of contradicting norms is seen when it is a norm that a driver drives at an average or slow speed when having a child on board, and also the same car might drive too fast when the child has an emergency. So, in this case, two different unmatchable norms appear: (i) a car drives slowly if a child is on board, and (ii) a car drives too fast in case of having an emergency case.

In this paper, we overcome the limitations of IRON and the other related work by proposing UNS, a utility-based norm synthesise model. UNS coordinates norms and objectives, handle unmatchable norms, and support fairer technique of norm synthesising. In UNS, a utility-based case-based reasoning technique is proposed to facilitate the coordination of norms and objectives of agents and the system. UNS uses the case-based reasoning algorithm to syn-thesise norms. The utility function determines the necessity of norms adoption and elicits the suitable norm when there are unmatchable norms. Two norms are called unmatchable norms, when only one of them should be applied at the same time and context. For example, consider norm n_a, which suggests to stop if there is a car on the left side of a junction, and norm n_b, recommending to stop if there is a car on the right side of a junction. Although by applying these two norms a collision would be avoided, a deadlock situation will be created as well. The utility function is constructed based on the objectives of the system to ensure that they are considered in the process of norms reasoning. UNS is eval-uated using a simulated traffic scenario in SUMO and results show the system's capability of synthesising and reasoning norms at run-time while reaching the system's objectives.

The remainder of this paper is as follows: Sect. 2 covers the related work and the essential state-of-the-art work (IRON) needed to understand our model. The problem statement is defined and formulated in Sect. 3. In Sect. 4, the proposed model (UNS) is illustrated, and then it is empirically evaluated in Sect. 5. Finally, in Sect. 6, the conclusion and future work are elaborated.

2   Related Work

Synthesising norms is more challenging in open and run-time NorMAS. In open systems, the challenge is to transfer norms to new agents entering the system and make use of the norms adopted by other agents before leaving the system. Mah-moud *et al.* [10] address this challenge by proposing a potential norms detection technique (PNDT) for norms detection by visitor agents in open MAS. They implemented an imitating mechanism which is triggered if the visitor agents, who are monitoring the norms of the host agents, discovered that their norms are in-compliant with the norms of the other host agents. However, PNDT tech-nique used a fixed set of norms, which are commonly practised by the domain, ignoring the dynamic nature of norms.

In run-time NorMAS, it is challenging to define a dynamic set of norms and initiate it. Moreover, real run-time applications would not only demand synthesising new norms but would also require handling the whole norms life-cycle including norms refinement and disappearance. One of the efforts directed towards run-time norms revision was carried out in [3], in which a supervision mechanism for run-time norms revision was proposed, addressing the challenge of norms modification when weather changes or when accidents happen. How-ever, the norms revision mechanism is developed using a primary defined pool of norms and situations. In the revision process, the model just substitutes the norms depending on the situation; limiting the norms to a static set of norms. Accordingly, the dynamism is in altering the chosen norms set depending on an optimisation mechanism constructed based on the system's objectives and does not handle the changes and evolution of the norms. In [5], Edenhofer *et al.*. present a mechanism for dynamic online norm adaption in a heterogeneous dis-tributed multi-agent system for handling colluding attacks from agents with bad behaviour. The agents interact together and build a trust metric to represent the reputation of the other agents. The main focus of this paper is identifying the bad agents and showing that using norms improves the system's robustness. Although this work is based on an open, heterogeneous and distributed environment, it does not identify how norms can be revised and updated in this context.

IRON machine was developed by Morales *et al.* and presented in [11]. It addresses the limitations of the other previously mentioned works, as the main aim of IRON is to synthesise norms online using an effective mechanism that not only synthesises norms in run-time but also revises these synthesised norms according to their effectiveness and necessity and further dismisses the inefficient norms. IRON simulates multi-agent systems, in which norms are synthesised for coordinating the behaviour of agents, and handles conflicting situations that can occur, such as collisions of vehicles in a traffic scenario. As presented in [11], IRON is capable of run-time norm synthesising and addressing the issues of using static norms, however, the idea of coordinating norms and objectives is not addressed.

Accordingly in this paper, we will propose UNS which is not only responsible for online-norm synthesis in open multi-agent systems but also guarantees objective consideration in the process of norm reasoning by the aid of utility-based technique.

As this work represents a series of the closest and comprehensive efforts exerted towards online norm synthesis for MAS, in the following sub-section an extended elaboration for IRON strategy and algorithm will take place and will be further used as the baseline of our model.

2.1   Intelligent Robust On-line Norm Synthesis Machine (IRON)

IRON machine is composed of a central unit that is responsible for detection of conflicts, synthesises of new norms to avoid conflicts, evaluation of the synthesised norms, refinement of norms, and announcement of the norm set to the agents. To simplify the illustration of the responsibilities of IRON, we will use a traffic junction example with two orthogonal roads scenario. The vehicles represent the agents, each occupying a single cell and moving in a specific direction per time-step.

- In **conflicts detection**, conflicts are detected when a collision occurs between two or more vehicles. The occurrence of a collision will trigger IRON to synthesise new norm to avoid future collisions of similar cases. As for **norms synthesising**, norms are created based on a case-based reasoning algorithm. In the algorithm, the conflicting situation at time t is compared to the conflicting vehicles' context at time $t - 1$. Then a norm is created using the conflicting views as a precondition for applying the norm and prohibiting the 'Go' action in this context. The synthesised norm is then added to a norms set and communicated to the agents (vehicles) of the system. For example, in Fig. 2, if vehicle A and B collided at the intersection (grey cell) then the context and action of

A or B is chosen randomly by the system to create a new norm. If A is chosen the new norm will be $n = if(left(<), front(-), right(<)) \longrightarrow proh('Go')$. The left() attribute in the precondition of the norm stores the direction of the left neighbour vehicle of vehicle A. While the right() attribute stores the direction of the right vehicle to vehicle A, which is in this case vehicle B. Similarly, the front() attribute would store the direction of the front vehicle, however, because there is nothing in front of the vehicle the symbol $(-)$ is used.

- **Norms Evaluation** is carried out by measuring necessity and effectiveness of a norm and comparing it to a threshold. Necessity is measured according to the ratio of harmful violated norms, which are norms that resulted in conflicts when violated, compared to the total number of violated norms. The methodology used in the calculations is akin of reinforcement learning, in which the norm's necessity reward NNR is calculated by:

$$NNR = \frac{m_{V_C}(n) \times w_{V_C}}{m_{V_C}(n) \times w_{V_C} + m_{V_{\bar{C}}}(n) \times w_{V_{\bar{C}}}} \tag{1}$$

$m_{V_C}(n)$: Number of violations which led to conflicts
w_{V_C}: Weight that measure the importance of harmful applications
$m_{V_{\bar{C}}}(n)$: Number of violations which did not led to conflicts
$w_{V_{\bar{C}}}$: Weight that measure the importance of harmless applications
The effectiveness of norms is measured based on the extent to which the norm is successful (i.e. which resulted in the minimum number of conflicts). The norm's effectiveness reward NER is calculated by:

$$NER = \frac{m_{A_C}(n) \times w_{A_C}}{m_{A_C}(n) \times w_{A_C} + m_{A_{\bar{C}}}(n) \times w_{A_{\bar{C}}}} \tag{2}$$

$m_{A_C}(n)$: Number of applied norms which led to conflicts
w_{A_C}: Weight that measure the importance of unsuccessful applications
$m_{A_{\bar{C}}}(n)$: Number of applied norms which did not led to conflicts
$w_{A_{\bar{C}}}$: Weight that measure the importance of successful applications

- **Norms refinement** is carried out by generalisation or specialisation of norms. Norms are mapped in a connected graph that expresses the relationships between them. In other words, the graph shows the child and parent norms and their links. Norms generalisation is applied when two or more norms have acceptable necessity and effectiveness results compared to a threshold, which is primarily specified before the system run, for time-interval T. Specialisation or deactivation of norms is conducted when the effectiveness and necessity of the norm or its children have been below the threshold for time-interval T.
- **Norms communication** is the final step, in which the norms are communicated to the agents.

The main flow of activities that are carried out in the scenario of the traffic junction (similar to Fig. 2), is as follows. Vehicles (agents) movements take place per time-step, however, prior to these movements, the vehicles check the norms set for applicable norms. Applicable norms are norms with preconditions that matches the context (local view) of the agents. When a new collision is detected, a random agent/vehicle is chosen and then its context is added as a precondition of a new norm that prohibits the 'GO' action. Afterwards, this norm is added to the norms set (initially empty). In addition, norms evaluation and refinement are carried out per time-step, in which all the views at time-step t are revised to determine the set of applicable norms for each of the views. The retrieved set of applicable norms is divided into four subsequent sets: (i) applied norms that led to conflicts (ii) applied norms that did not lead to conflicts (iii) violated norms that led to conflicts (iv) violated norms that did not lead to conflicts. Then set (i) and (ii) are used to calculate the effectiveness of each of the norms, while set (iii) and set (iv) represent the main inputs for the necessity calculation. Finally, norms refinement is conducted.

3   Problem Statement

Let us consider a norm-aware multi-objective multi-agent system that is composed of a finite set of mobile agents as $Ag = \{ag_1, ag_2, ..., ag_n\}$. Each agent ag_i has a type t_{ag_i}, set of properties P_{ag_i}, set of objectives O_{ag_i} and set of adopted norms N_{ag_i}. In addition, the system itself has its own set of objectives O_s and set of norms N_s, where $O_{ag_i} \subseteq O_s$ and $N_{ag_i} \subseteq N_s$.

The norms are created by a centralised unit in the system in the form of a pair $(\alpha, \theta(ac))$ and then messaged to the agents. α represents a precondition for triggering the norm applicability. This precondition reflects a specific context of the agent co_{ag_i}, which is the local view of the agent ag_i that defines its direct neighbours $Ng_{ag_i} = \{ag_1, ag_2, ..., ag_k\}$ and their properties such as their moving direction in the traffic scenario example. So, $co_{ag_i} = \{P_{ag_k} : ag_k \subseteq Ng_{ag_i}\}$. θ symbolises a deontic operator (obligation, prohibition or permission) with a specific action ac_{ag_i} of agent ag_i which will apply the norm. For example, if an action is beneficial for an agent then it is obligated and if an action is harmful it is prohibited.

The central unit synthesises new norms after a conflicting state c arises between agents and uses the synthesised norm in future similar cases to avoid conflicts. Conflicting state c belongs to set of conflicts C, a conflict is considered detected when two agents or more carry out actions that result in a problem. The norm is synthesised by comparing the view at conflicting situation at time-step t, V_t to the view before the conflict occurrence V_{t-1}. The series of views that represent different situations at each time-step are added in a ViewTransition V set (i.e. $V_t \in V$ and $V_{t-1} \in V$).

In such a system, there are three main problems to be tackled. First, the process of synthesising norms should ensure fairness (i.e. created norms cannot be biased towards specific agents' situation). For example, if there is a norm created to coordinate the behaviour of two vehicles ag_1 and ag_2 in an intersection, this norm cannot always give priority to the vehicles on the right, because this will make the vehicles in the left lane always delayed. Second, when there is more than one applicable norm in the same context, often unmatchable ones, only one should be applied to avoid a deadlock situation. For example, in a scenario of vehicles crossing a junction, if there were two norms created: n_1 for stopping if there was a vehicle on the right, and $\acute{n}_1$ for stopping if there is a vehicle on the left, a decision should be made to apply one of these unmatchable norms only. Third, the agent's norms N_{ag_i} and objectives O_{ag_i} should be coordinated to ensure that the norms' compliance does not contradict reaching the objectives.

4   UNS: Utility-Based Norm Synthesis Model

UNS is a utility-based norm synthesis mechanism implemented in a normative, open, run-time, multi-objective, multi-agent system. UNS aims at reaching three main goals. First, to synthesise norms while supporting fairness during norm creation. Second, to handle unmatchable synthesised norms. Finally, to coordinate the objectives of agents with the synthesised norms. Figure 1 shows the architecture of UNS. It shows the five main responsibilities of UNS that take place per time-step at run-time: conflicts detection, norms synthesising, norms reasoning, norms evaluation and refinement.

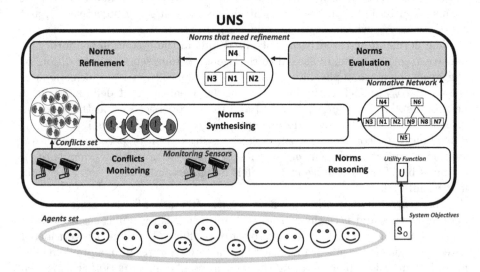

Fig. 1. Utility-based norm synthesis model architecture (components coloured in grey are inherited from IRON) (Color figure online)

Conflicts detection, norms evaluation and refinement are inherited from IRON and integrated in UNS. The details of the steps carried out by UNS are as follows:

4.1   Conflicts Detection

At each time-step t as agents take actions, a set of monitors (e.g. traffic cameras) $M = \{m_1, m_2, ..., m_n\}$ monitor these actions to detect any conflicts. A conflict c is detected when more than one agent actions contradict at the same view v_i, where $v_i \in V$. For example, in a traffic system, if vehicles standing before a junction in opposite directions decided to move (do a 'Go action') towards the same position, a collision will occur and so a conflict will arise. To detect conflicts, views V are sent as a parameter to the *ConflictDection* function (see Algorithm 1, line 6). A conflict object definition is composed of responsible agents $Ag^r \subseteq Ag$, context of these agents (which is the local views of each of these agents), and the views transition of a state s between time-step t and $t-1$, $(v_{s_{t-1}}^i, v_{s_t}^i)$.

4.2   Norms Synthesising

Case-based reasoning technique is used for norm synthesising. When a new conflict arises, a new case is created and then compared to similar cases and the best solution is chosen accordingly. In case that no similar case is found a new random solution is created for this case and added to the set of cases. In this manner, after conflicts are detected, UNS carries out the norms synthesising steps for each of these conflicts (see Algorithm 1, line 7 to line 17). All the agents responsible for the conflict are retrieved in Ag^r (e.g. all the vehicles that collided in the same intersection are considered as responsible agents). For each of these agents' context at $t-1$ if an applicable norm was not found (applicable norms are norms that have the same context as a pre-condition of the norm and the same agent action prohibited in the norm), a new norm creation process takes place (line 13). A new norm is composed of agents' context co_{ag_i} and prohibited action θac_{ag_i}. Getting the context of the agent at the previous time-step as a precondition of a norm and prohibiting the action that resulted in a conflict avoids future conflicts that might rise in similar situations. After the norm is created it is added to the system's norms set Ω (line 14).

UNS Supporting Fairness: In IRON norms synthesising was carried out by creating norms as a solution for only one randomly chosen agent from the agents involved in a conflict. However, in UNS we have proposed a norm synthesising process, which considers all the contexts of the agents involved in a conflict. For example, in IRON if two vehicles had a conflict in an intersection, the norm will be created based on prohibiting a Go action of only one of the two vehicles. Although this will decrease the probability of creating unmatchable norms, it will not ensure fairness as one side will always have priority of moving over the other side.

4.3   Norms Reasoning

The norm reasoning process must meet systems' objectives and handle unmatchable norms simultaneously. This is reached through defining a utility function U

Algorithm 1. UNS Strategy

```
1: for each t do
2:     Input: Ω, V
3:     Output: Ω
4: /*Conflicts Detection*/
5: //Inherited from IRON
6:     conflicts ← ConflictDetection(V)
7: /*Norms Synthesis*/
8:     for each c ∈ conflicts do
9:         Ag^r ← AgentsInConflictContexts(c)
10:        for each ag_i ∈ Ag^r do
11:            co_{ag_i} ← GetAgentContext(ag_i)
12:            if hasApplicableNorm(co_{ag_i}) == false then
13:                n ← CreateNorm(co_{ag_i}, θ(ac_{ag_i}))
14:                Ω ← Ω ∪ n
15:            end if
16:        end for
17:    end for
18: /*Norms Reasoning*/
19:    for each V_{t+1} ∈ V do
20:        N_a ← GetApplicableNorms(V)
21:        if N_a.size > 1 then
22:            Utilities[] ← null //comment:Utilities[k] = (ag_i, n, U_i)
23:            for each n ∈ N_a do
24:                Utilities.add(calculateUtility(n), n)
25:            end for
26:            ag_x ← getAgent(max(Utilities))
27:            ag_x.applyApplicableNorm()
28:        end if
29:    end for
30: /*Norms Evaluation*/
31: //Inherited from IRON
32: /*Norms Refinement*/
33: //Inherited from IRON
34: end for
```

that is constructed based on the system's objectives O_s and is used during the norm selection.

Utility Function Construction: In this paper, the utility function is constructed by adding the objectives with a maximisation function and subtracting the objectives with a minimisation function. For example, if O_s include two objectives $O_s = \{o_1, o_2\}$ and o_1 is to minimise all vehicles' average waiting time and o_2 is to minimise the average waiting time of emergency vehicles specifically, then the system utility function U will be defined as:

$$U = -o_1 - o_2 = -1 * (o_1 + o_2) \tag{3}$$

The utility function introduced can be considered as a type of unweighted additive utility function. In which using an additive approach is supported by the indifference property assumed between the objectives as all objectives need to be reached. Moreover, due to the equal preference to satisfying all of the objectives and eliminating any prioritisation no weights are needed. The general format of the defined utility function is:

$$U = \sum_{i=1}^{|X|} u(x_i) - \sum_{j=1}^{|M|} u(m_j) \qquad (4)$$

The $|X|$ is the number of the system objectives that needs to be maximised, and $|M|$ is the number of the system objectives that needs to be minimised. $u(x_i)$ reflects the sub-utility gained from the maximisation of objective x_i, while $u(m_j)$ presents the sub-utility gained from the minimisation of objective m_j.

Accumulated Utility Calculation: At each time-step before the agents start moving (taking actions) UNS determines the set of applicable norms N_a in each view V_t (see Algorithm 1, line 20). If more than one norm is applicable for the same view V_t, then UNS carries out the steps in Algorithm 1 (from line 22 to line 27) to choose the norm with the highest utility and dismisses the rest of the norms. For example, if we have a traffic scenario as seen in Fig. 2, where vehicle A, ag_1, and vehicle B, ag_2, are willing to move to the same junction (coloured in grey) at time t, the stored view at time t will be represent by (V_t). UNS will retrieve the set of applicable norms $N_a = \{n1, ń1\}$, where $n1$: is to stop if there is a vehicle on the right and $ń1$ is to stop if there is a vehicle on the left. $n1$ is suggested for vehicle A and $ń1$ is suggested for vehicle B. If both vehicles apply the norms then none of them will move, which result in a deadlock state. So, a decision must be made to choose only one of the two unmatchable norms. Accordingly, an empty array of struct is initialised (in line 21). The struct is composed of ag_i (which is the responsible agent), n (which is the applicable norm for this agent ag_i situation), and U_i (which is the calculated utility gained by the system if this norm n is applied). For each of the applicable norms in N_a, the utility function is calculated (line 23). However, in our utility calculation strategy, we calculate an accumulated utility function, which does not only consider the utility gained by the agent applying the norm, but also considers all the agents that are indirectly affected by the norm adoption decision. For example, in Fig. 2, if vehicle A will be the agent that will apply the norm and will stop if there is a vehicle on the right, it will force vehicles C, D, E and F to stop as well. While if vehicle B decides to apply the norm $ń1$ and to stop, vehicle G will be forced to stop as well. Based on this justification, to ensure gaining the actual maximum utility, UNS aggregates the utility of all the agents that are affected directly and indirectly with the norms adoption or dismissal. Then, the norm that gives the maximum utility is applied (lines 26 and 27), and the rest of the norms are dismissed.

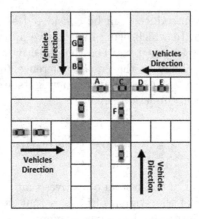

Fig. 2. A traffic junction composed of two orthogonal roads

4.4   Norms Evaluation and Refinement

The norm evaluation and refinement processes are inherited from IRON (illustrated in Sect. 2.1). These processes are used to evaluate norms at run-time using efficiency and necessity equations (Eqs. 1 and 2). If a norm's efficiency and necessity does not reach a certain threshold its refinement takes place and it is specialised or deactivated. Also, if a norm's efficiency and necessity exceeds a specified threshold it can be generalised.

5   Empirical Evaluation

In this section we show UNS capability to synthesise norms that support fairness, to handle unmatchable norms and to coordinate norms and objectives.

5.1   Empirical Settings

We simulate a traffic-based scenario, with a 19 × 19 grid as a road network with a junction of two orthogonal roads (see Fig. 2). Each road has two lanes; one for each direction. In Fig. 2, the cells coloured in grey show the four cells that represent the intersections. Vehicles are the agents and they have two main types: ordinary vehicles and high priority vehicles to represent heterogeneity. The ratio of generating priority vehicles to ordinary vehicles is 12:100 respectively. Also, as it is an open MAS, vehicles can enter and leave the road network freely. Vehicles move per time-step aiming to reach their final destination which was randomly generated by the simulator at the beginning of the trip of the vehicle. In each time-step, the system randomly chooses the number of new vehicles (between 2 to 8 vehicles) to be emitted to start their trip. The system aims at avoiding conflicts (i.e., the collisions between vehicles) through the synthesised norms. Norms are defined as a pair that includes the agent context and the prohibited action. The agent context is the local view of the vehicle describing the direction of vehicles on its left, front, and right, which we call neighbouring vehicles. For example, in Fig. 2 the vehicles in the local context of vehicle F are vehicles A, C and D. The action prohibited is a 'Go action' to avoid vehicle movement in future similar contexts. UNS synthesises norms and adds them to a norm set that is initially empty at the beginning of the simulation. When a stable normative system is reached the system converges. The system has two main objectives, minimising the average waiting time for all vehicles and minimising the total waiting time of priority vehicles. The utility function used in the norm reasoning is constructed based on the previous two objectives as follows:

$$- 1 * (\frac{X_{wt} + Y_{wt}}{X + Y} + Y_{wt}) \tag{5}$$

X_{wt}: Total waiting time of ordinary vehicles
Y_{wt}: Total waiting time of priority vehicles
X: Number of ordinary vehicles
Y: Number of priority vehicles

5.2   Experiment Results

To evaluate UNS's performance, three main scenarios are tested with the settings illustrated in the previous sub-section with varying violation rate of norms, which represents the ratio of agents obeying the adoption of the norms. UNS will be compared to IRON machine (explained in Sect. 2.1). The average waiting time for all vehicles and the total waiting time of priority vehicles are reported to show the performance of UNS and IRON. Moreover, the number of collisions is used to reflect the efficiency of the synthesised norms in avoiding conflicts. We present the moving average of the results at every 50 time-steps obtained from 10 runs of simulation as plotted in Fig. 3, 4, and 5.

5.3   Scenario A (Violation Rate 10%)

Figure 3(a) shows the average waiting time of all vehicles in UNS compared to the average waiting time of all vehicles in IRON. The average waiting time is decreased in UNS, particularly from time-step 322. Moreover, it can be noted that from time-step 322 almost the average waiting time in UNS is constant with an average value of 1.5 time-steps. As results show, UNS has minimised the average waiting time of the vehicles and so fulfilling the first objective of the system.

Figure 3(b) shows the total time taken by priority vehicles per time-step in UNS compared to IRON. The average total waiting time of priority vehicles using UNS is 8.09 time-steps, while the average total waiting time of priority vehicles reached in IRON is 12 time-steps. Moreover, Fig. 3(a) and (b) do not only emphasise how UNS can coordinate objectives and norms, but the noticed stability and uniformity of the results show the reliability of UNS which is necessary in real-applications.

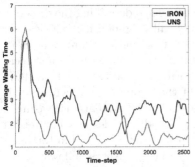
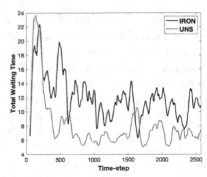

(a) Average waiting time for all vehicle types

(b) Total waiting time of priority vehicles

Fig. 3. Scenario A

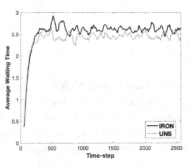
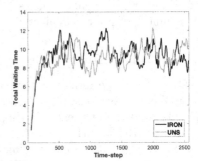

(a) Average waiting time for all vehicle types

(b) Total waiting time of priority vehicles

Fig. 4. Scenario B

Figure 5(a) presents the total number of collisions per time-step, which shows UNS is able to successfully synthesise norms at run-time to handle collisions. The results show UNS outperforms the synthesised norms set in IRON. Furthermore, observations showed that in a lot of time-steps UNS reached zero collisions, unlike IRON. The average number of collisions in UNS is 0.08 while the average number of collisions in IRON is 0.17. Also, comparing the total number of collisions, the total number of collisions in UNS is 51% lower than IRON, which shows the efficacy of the norm synthesis process.

5.4 Scenario B (Violation Rate 70%)

Figure 4(a) shows the average waiting time of all vehicles in UNS compared to IRON. The average waiting time in this scenario is increased to 2.45 time-steps compared to scenario A. However, UNS still outperforms IRON, in which its average waiting time per time-step decreased from 2.75 to 2.53 time-steps. This unexplained decrease in IRON shows the essence of the primary definition of the system objectives and its incorporation in the model. Moreover, the results show that even with a high violation rate the system objectives can be achieved using UNS.

Figure 4(b) shows that UNS and IRON have quite similar range of total waiting time for priority vehicles. However, UNS outperforms IRON as the average of the total waiting time of priority vehicles is 8.92 time-steps using UNS and 9.24 time-step using IRON.

The results also show that although the violation rate has increased by 60% compared to scenario A, the average total waiting time of priority vehicles in UNS has only increased by 9.30%. Furthermore, the number of collisions occurred in this scenario using UNS is 4.66% fewer compared to IRON as seen in Fig. 5(b).

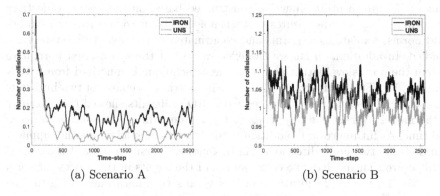

(a) Scenario A   (b) Scenario B

Fig. 5. Total number of collisions

5.5 Scenario C (Violation Rate 0%)

When using 0% violation rate with IRON simulation, IRON is not able to converge and continue the simulation. The reason behind this is that the system reaches a deadlock when all vehicles obey to the norms. Although, IRON strategy in synthesising norms relies on creating only one norm at a time, it might synthesises two unmatchable norms at different instances that when applied in the same conflict causes a deadlock. For example, if one norm is to stop if there is a vehicle on the right hand side and the second norm is to stop when there is a vehicle on the left, two lanes of the vehicles standing at the beginning of a junction will stop endlessly, when there is no violation. However, this situation does not arise in UNS because it handles unmatchable norms and if more than one norm is applicable, the utility for both norms is calculated and only one norm is applied (i.e. in the previous example, one vehicle will 'Stop' and the other will 'Go').

In all scenarios, UNS synthesises more norms than IRON. This is due to synthesising all the norms that would contribute in avoiding collision in a specific situation, supporting the idea of fairness. For example, in one of the runs IRON synthesised 15 norms, while UNS synthesised 17 norms. For example, UNS synthesises norm n_a, $n_a = (left(-), front(-), right(<), Proh(Go))$ and norm n_b, $n_b = (left(>), front(-), right(-), Proh(Go))$, both contributing in avoiding a collision. However, IRON only synthesises n_b which will always give priority to vehicles on the right side of the intersection, and consequently cannot support fairness.

6   Conclusion and Future Work

In this paper, we proposed a centralised utility-based norm synthesis (UNS) model which aims at coordinating objectives of the system with the synthesised norms in real-time. Norms in UNS are created to resolve conflicts that occur between agents and they are synthesised using case-based reasoning technique. UNS uses a utility function constructed based on the system objectives for norm reasoning. This ensures that when agents come to applying the synthesised norms, unmatchable norms and coordinated objectives of the system are handled. In addition, to ensure the effectiveness of the synthesised normative system the norms evaluation and refinement technique is inherited from IRON strategy [11]. The model was evaluated using a traffic scenario of two intersecting roads and results were compared with IRON. Results showed the efficiency of the model to meet the objectives of the system while synthesising norms in real-time. As future work, in addition to applying the model on another application domains two main directions will be followed. First, to use a decentralised architecture that involves the coordination of the agents in the process of norm synthesis. This would facilitate building several sets of norms according to each agent group's learning and objectives. Second, to transfer the norm reasoning process to be carried out in the level of agents rather than the system to ensure the agent's autonomy in the decision-making process.

References

1. Bailey, J.M., Golpayegani, F., Clarke, S.: CoMASig: a collaborative multi-agent signal control to support senior drivers. In: 2019 IEEE Intelligent Transportation Systems Conference (ITSC), pp. 1239–1244. IEEE (2019)
2. Dastani, M., Dix, J., Verhagen, H., Villata, S.: Normative multi-agent systems (Dagstuhl seminar 18171). Dagstuhl Rep. **8**(4), 72–103 (2018)
3. Dell'Anna, D., Dastani, M., Dalpiaz, F.: Runtime norm revision using Bayesian networks. In: Miller, T., Oren, N., Sakurai, Y., Noda, I., Savarimuthu, B.T.R., Cao Son, T. (eds.) PRIMA 2018. LNCS (LNAI), vol. 11224, pp. 279–295. Springer, Cham (2018). https://doi.org/10.1007/978-3-030-03098-8_17
4. Dorri, A., Kanhere, S.S., Jurdak, R.: Multi-agent systems: a survey. IEEE Access **6**, 28573–28593 (2018)
5. Edenhofer, S., et al.: Bottom-up norm adjustment in open, heterogeneous agent societies. In: 2016 IEEE 1st International Workshops on Foundations and Applications of Self* Systems (FAS* W), pp. 36–41. IEEE (2016)

6. Frantz, C., Pigozzi, G.: Modeling norm dynamics in multiagent systems. FLAP **5**(2), 491–564 (2018)
7. Ghanadbashi, S., Golpayegani, F.: Using ontology to guide reinforcement learning agents in unseen situations. Appl. Intell. **52**(2), 1808–1824 (2021). https://doi.org/10.1007/s10489-021-02449-5
8. Golpayegani, F., Dusparic, I., Clarke, S.: Using social dependence to enable neighbourly behaviour in open multi-agent systems. ACM Trans. Intell. Syst. Technol. (TIST) **10**(3), 1–31 (2019)
9. Golpayegani, F., Dusparic, I., Taylor, A., Clarke, S.: Multi-agent collaboration for conflict management in residential demand response. Comput. Commun. **96**, 63–72 (2016)
10. Mahmoud, M., Ahmad, M.S., Mohd Yusoff, M.Z.: Development and implementation of a technique for norms-adaptable agents in open multi-agent communities. J. Syst. Sci. Complex. **29**(6), 1519–1537 (2016). https://doi.org/10.1007/s11424-016-5036-1
11. Morales, J., Lopez-Sanchez, M., Rodriguez-Aguilar, J.A., Wooldridge, M.J., Vasconcelos, W.W.: Automated synthesis of normative systems. In: AAMAS, vol. 13, pp. 483–490 (2013)
12. Oliveira, A., Girardi, R.: An analysis of norm processes in normative multi-agent systems. In: 2016 IEEE/WIC/ACM International Conference on Web Intelligence Workshops (WIW), pp. 68–71. IEEE (2016)
13. Singh, M.P., Chopra, A.K.: The internet of things and multiagent systems: decentralized intelligence in distributed computing. In: 2017 IEEE 37th International Conference on Distributed Computing Systems (ICDCS), pp. 1738–1747. IEEE (2017)

Modeling and Understanding Social Behavior Using COINE Technologies

A Bayesian Model of Information Cascades

Sriashalya Srivathsan[1]([✉]), Stephen Cranefield[1]([✉]), and Jeremy Pitt[2]

[1] University of Otago, Dunedin, New Zealand
ashal.srivathsan@postgrad.otago.ac.nz, stephen.cranefield@otago.ac.nz
[2] Imperial College London, London, UK
j.pitt@imperial.ac.uk

Abstract. An information cascade is a circumstance where agents make decisions in a sequential fashion by following other agents. Bikhchandani et al., predict that once a cascade starts it continues, even if it is wrong, until agents receive an external input such as public information. In an information cascade, even if an agent has its own personal choice, it is always overridden by observation of previous agents' actions. This could mean agents end up in a situation where they may act without valuing their own information. As information cascades can have serious social consequences, it is important to have a good understanding of what causes them. We present a detailed Bayesian model of the information gained by agents when observing the choices of other agents and their own private information. Compared to prior work, we remove the high impact of the first observed agent's action by incorporating a prior probability distribution over the information of unobserved agents and investigate an alternative model of choice to that considered in prior work: weighted random choice. Our results show that, in contrast to Bikhchandani's results, cascades will not necessarily occur and adding prior agents' information will delay the effects of cascades.

Keywords: Information cascade · Coordination · Probabilistic graphical model · Bayesian inference

1 Introduction

Propagation of opinions in society has a significant impact. In daily life it is clear that people are affected by others' views. For example, in electoral and financial campaigns, the spreading of news, opinion and rumours can have an enormous effect on the behaviour of the crowd. When people look at others' actions, or listen to others, they update their assessment of the value of those actions and imitate accordingly.

Information cascades are a social phenomenon in which all individuals from some point in a sequence onwards make the same decision. It occurs when other people's prior choices can strongly impact the choices of those who follow and it is the result of solely following others while discounting their own opinion.

© Springer Nature Switzerland AG 2022
A. Theodorou et al. (Eds.): COINE 2021, LNAI 13239, pp. 97–110, 2022.
https://doi.org/10.1007/978-3-031-16617-4_7

Bikhchandani et al., [3] say that, "An informational cascade occurs when it is optimal for an individual, having observed the actions of those ahead of him, to follow the behavior of the preceding individual without regard to his own information". This phenomenon can be observed, for example, when people choose a restaurant or school [2].

People are more attracted when they see that someone already adopted a trend or chosen a specific fashion. New communication technology such as social media has become a habit, helping to share new trends, fashion and ideas [6]. It passes very quickly across web technologies when someone shares a particular fashion he or she likes, and this is subsequently shared by friends [12,17]. Resharing posts develops an information cascade in social media and leads others to choose a product, movie, or a specific fashion. Furthermore, recent studies [8,15] have shown that e-marketing is driven by information cascades. Customer ratings and reviews make a huge impact in online shopping. Thus, often people become more aware of and start to follow other's opinions when they need to shop online, rather than following their own preferences. It is evident that when shopping in Amazon or Ebay, people rely heavily on others' choices since the quality of the goods is still an issue [22].

In addition, an information cascade can aid society to unite its members for environmental collective action such as minimising emission of carbon and global warming as well as social and political collective action. Lohmann [16] notes that cascades are observed in society when individuals join and protest against a regime to address their political concerns.

It is obvious that people often avoid their own preference or personal signals and choose to pursue others' choices as soon as a cascade begins. However, even though they have strong qualities, people's own preferences are concealed once the cascade starts. For instance, the algorithm for discovering the real rating of an Amazon product was proposed by Wang et al., [22] as people demand plausible and accurate online reviews. Wang et al., attempted as much as possible to eliminate the herding effect occurring through online purchasing using their algorithm. But the actual rating was very difficult to obtain.

Bikhchandani et al., [3] have presented a probabilistic model to explain how an information cascade comes about, in the context of uptake of a fashion or fad. Their model predicts that cascades are inevitable, once they start. It is assumed that there is a true value of the fashion (0 or 1), which may be perceived correctly (with some probability $p >= 0.5$) or incorrectly. A cascade can be either a *correct* cascade, where eventually all individuals make the choice that aligns with the true value, or an *incorrect* one, where eventually all choices go against the fashion's true value. The model uses a deterministic model of choice, which means that the agents choose the action (to adopt or reject the fashion) with the greatest evidence for its correctness, based on observations of other agents and their own private information, or make a 50/50 random choice if the evidence for "adopt" and "reject" is equal.

Bikhchandani et al., presented a high level analysis of their model, which lacks mathematical details. Our aim is to provide a detailed Bayesian model that accounts for the uncertainty about the private information of other agents. We also wish to investigate the impact of agents making choices non-deterministically, via random weighted choice as this probabilistic choice model is claimed to be psychologically more realistic [18,21].

In the model of Bikhchandani et al., the first agent in the chain of observed agents is assumed to be the first to make a decision to adopt or reject the fashion. This makes its choice highly influential, as its action is known to correspond directly to its private signal. Moreover, this is unrealistic in many settings. An agent may know that the fashion has been around for a while, so it could estimate a number of prior agents whose actions were unobserved. Our model therefore uses a prior probability distribution over the count of positive perceptions of the fashion by these unobserved agents. Even if this is a completely uninformative prior distribution, it weakens the dominance of the first agent.

2   Prior Work

Besides Bikhchandani et al., many other researchers have highlighted the importance of information cascades. Benerji et al., [2] introduced a model to investigate herd behaviour to understand how people adopt others' actions while ignoring their own information. They showed that people observe others' actions and tend to act in the same way because they believe the previous people have better information than them. Easley et al., [9] presented a theoretical and experimental study of herding behaviour. They presented a Bayesian model for sequential decision-making where people consider the counts of the previous actions and choose the most common one.

Vany et al., [7] developed an agent-based model to compare the theoretical aspects of Bikichandani's concept. Specially, they analysed how people are attracted to watch a specific movie, as they have multiple choices. The key aspect of this model is how an agent will be highly influenced by the nearest neighbour's action as well as the popularity of different movies. In the same fashion, Lee et al., [11] examined how online reviews of a movie are socially influenced [20] by two different groups such as a general crowd and friends. They concluded that the reviews of the popular movies show a cascading behaviour. However, people tend to follow friend ratings regardless of popularity, since these have more impact than the general crowd rating. Similarly Liu et al., [13,14] analysed how information cascades occur in e-book marketing. Particularly, for both paid and free e-books they experimented to find the effect of information cascades, and found that an information cascade has a strong impact when selecting paid e-books in comparison with free books.

Anderson et al., [1] designed a laboratory experiment to show how an information cascade occurs. It became apparent that people at some stage discard their own knowledge and continue to follow others. Huber et al., [10] used functional magnetic resonance imaging of experimental participants' brains to research how a cascade can be stimulated by individual preference. They concluded from their findings that overweighting personal information can trigger and stop the information cascade.

Watts [23,24] developed a model to show how agents' actions interact with neighbours' actions by setting a simple threshold rule. Cheng et al., [6] addressed the prediction of a cascade when sharing a picture post in Facebook. They found that the size of an information cascade can be predicted by its temporal (observed time) and structural (caption, language and content) features. Lu et al., [17] proposed a system to analyse the collective behaviour of information cascades by analysing a huge social media data set.

3   The Information Cascade Model of Bikhchandani et al.

Bikhchandani et al., [3] considered a sequence of individuals who will choose between accepting (A) or rejecting (R) a fashion or fad. The model assumes that there is some true value $V \in \{0, 1\}$ representing the benefit of following the fashion/fad. Every individual perceives a private signal $X_i \in \{H, L\}$, representing a "high" or "low" perception of V. As shown in Table 1 a "high" perception of V has probability p for $V = 1$ and $1-p$ for $V = 0$, and vice versa for "low" perceptions.

In the "basic model" considered by Bikhchandani et al., each agent considers the actions of earlier agents in the sequence, and takes those actions of adopt or reject as a proxy for what each of those agents perceived their X_i which is unknown by observing agents. The agent can count all of the previous accepts or rejects, adds a count 0 or 1 (respectively) given his own information (L or H), and then chooses his action based on the action with the greatest count. Here we notice that the actions of agents earlier in the chain are repeatedly used as evidence by later agents, and their impact may therefore be exaggerated.

The "general model" of Bikhchandani et al., states that an agent will make its decision based on the expected value of V given the agent's private signal and observations of other agents' actions. Bikhchandani et al., gave the following definition of agent $n+1$'s expectation of V given his/her private signal x and observation history A_n: $V_{n+1}(x; A_n) \equiv E[V|X_{n+1} = x, X_i \in J_i(A_{i-1}, a_i)$, for all $i \leq n]$. Here, A_{i-1} is the sequence of prior actions that agent i has observed and $J_i(A_{i-1}, a_i)$ is a set of possible signals that would have led individual i to choose action a_i given A_{i-1}. Individual $n + 1$ adopts if $V_{n+1}(x; A_n) \geq C$, where C is the cost of adoption[1]. However, no computational account is given of how this expected value is determined by the agent. Their general model also considers that the X_i values may be drawn from finite ordered set rather than the two options H and L. But we do not consider this case.

Bikhchandani et al., found that "An informational cascade occurs if an individual's action does not depend on his private signal". Hence, he ignores his private signal and will adopt based on the prior agents' actions alone. This is true for all subsequent agents too, so they follow their predecessors and create a cascade. If $V = 1$, a cascade can be either a correct cascade, where all adopt, or an incorrect cascade, where all reject, and vice versa for $V = 0$.

---

[1] This cost is not used in our model.

Bikhchandani et al., showed that once the cascade starts it will last forever even if it is incorrect. They also discussed the fragility of cascades. For instance, cascades can be broken if public information is revealed.

Our aim is to create a Bayesian model of an information cascade that captures the uncertainty about prior agents' private information. We avoid the strong influence of the first agent's action on later agent's action through the ability to model a probability distribution over the information of unobserved prior agents. The model of Bikhchandani et al., uses a deterministic model of choice in which an agent ranks options and chooses the highest ranked one. This deterministic technique[2] is commonly used in economic models [5]. Inspired by the work of Luce, [18,21] we consider the effects on cascades if agents use weighted non-deterministic choice when choosing to adopt or reject. This means that choice is probabilistic and an agent may choose randomly from a set of weighted choices, in proportion to their weights. This has been claimed to be more psychologically plausible than deterministic choice [21].

Table 1. Signal probabilities [3]

Gain of adopting	$P(X_i = H \mid V)$	$P(X_i = L \mid V)$
$V = 1$	p	$1 - p$
$V = 0$	$1 - p$	p

4   Our Model and Approach

In this section we present our Bayesian model of information cascades. We define the following variables:

- $V \in \{0,1\}$, is the true value of the fad/fashion.
- $X_i \in \{H, L\}$, is the private signal of the agent: high or low. This represents agent i's possibly incorrect perception of V.
- $A_i \in \{A, R\}$, is the action of the agent: adopt or reject.
- C_i is a count of how many times H appears in the observations of prior agents: $C_i = C_0 + |X_i : X_i = H, 1 \leq i \leq n|$. This will be probabilistically inferred by each agent since it cannot be directly perceived.
- k is an estimated number of prior agents who made choices that were not observed by any of the agents. C_0 is the count of H signals observed by these prior agents. As this is unknown, our model uses an estimated probability distribution for C_0.
- p is the signal accuracy, which is assumed to be the same for all agents.

---

[2] Luce refers to this as *algebraic choice* due to the common use of algebraic rather than probabilistic models in economics [18].

The dependencies between these variables are shown using a probabilistic graphical model [4] in Fig. 1, which is expressed from the viewpoint of agent 4. k and p are constants, but the other nodes are random variables. Shaded nodes represent observed variables, and X_i is known by agent i. A_4 is shown as a rectangle, as this is a decision node. Agent 4 will choose A if $P(V = 1 \mid X_4, A_1, A_2, A_3) > 0.5$, R if this probability is less than 0.5, and otherwise will make a 50/50 choice between A and R. An equivalent choice procedure involving C_i is given at the end of this section.

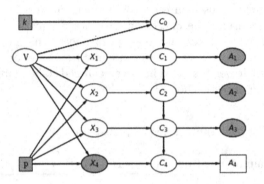

Fig. 1. Probabilistic graphical model of information cascade from agent 4's viewpoint

The information cascade model is used as follows. V and C_i are conditionally independent given C_{i-1} and X_i, therefore:

$$P(V, C_i \mid C_{i-1}, X_i) = p(V \mid C_{i-1}, X_i)\, p(C_i \mid C_{i-1}, X_i) \qquad (1)$$

Each agent i maintains a joint probability distribution over V and C that is conditional on the actions observed so far. This is $p(V, C_0) = p(V)\, p(C_0 \mid V)$ for the first agent. We use a uniform prior over V and a binomial distribution for C_0 given V:

$$P(C_0 = c \mid V = 0) = (1 - p)^c p^{k-c} \quad \text{and} \quad P(C_0 = c \mid V = 1) = p^c (1 - p)^{k-c} \qquad (2)$$

For $i > 1$, agent i will observe the actions of all prior agents $j < i$ and compute the joint conditional distribution $p(V, C_j \mid C_0, A_1, \cdots, A_j)$. Agents act and are observed sequentially, so it will already have computed $p(V, C_{j-1} \mid C_0, A_1, \cdots, A_{j-1})$.[3] Once it observes A_j, it first uses Bayes' Theorem to compute $P(X_j \mid A_1, \cdots, A_j)$:

$$P(X_j \mid A_1, \cdots, A_j) \propto P(X_j \mid A_1, \cdots, A_{j-1})\, P(A_j \mid X_j, A_1, \cdots, A_{j-1}) \qquad (3)$$

---

[3] C_0 appears as a condition whenever a sequence of action variables does. Henceforth, we omit it for brevity.

where:

$$P(X_j \mid A_1, \cdots, A_{j-1})$$
$$= \sum_{v \in \{0,1\}} P(X_j \mid V = v, A_1, \cdots, A_{j-1}) P(V = v \mid A_1, \cdots, A_{j-1}) \tag{4}$$
$$= \sum_{v \in \{0,1\}} P(X_j \mid V = v) P(V = v \mid A_1, \cdots, A_{j-1})$$

$$P(A_j \mid X_j, A_1, \cdots, A_{j-1}) = P(A_j \mid X_j, C_{j-1}) \tag{5}$$

The last line of Eq. 4 holds because X_j depends only on V. Equation 5 holds because, $P(C_{j-1})$ contains all the knowledge inferred from observing $A_1, \cdots, A_{j-1}$.

$P(A_j \mid X_j, C_{j-1})$ is calculated as shown in Tables 2 and 3 for the deterministic and non-deterministic models of choice, respectively. In the tables, C_{j-1}^{+1} denotes a new random variable formed by shifting C_{j-1} right by one count value. i.e. $C_{j-1}^{+1} = c \iff C_{j-1} = c - 1$. This represents the addition of the count 1 for $X_j = H$ to C_{j-1}.

Table 2. $P(A_j \mid X_j, C_{j-1})$ for deterministic choice

X_j	Condition on C_{j-1}	$P(A_j = A)$	$P(A_j = R)$
H	$P(C_{j-1}^{+1} > \frac{k+j}{2}) > P(C_{j-1}^{+1} < \frac{k+j}{2})$	1	0
	$P(C_{j-1}^{+1} > \frac{k+j}{2}) < P(C_{j-1}^{+1} < \frac{k+j}{2})$	0	1
	$P(C_{j-1}^{+1} > \frac{k+j}{2}) = P(C_{j-1}^{+1} < \frac{k+j}{2})$	0.5	0.5
L	$P(C_{j-1} > \frac{k+j}{2}) > P(C_{j-1} < \frac{k+j}{2})$	1	0
	$P(C_{j-1} > \frac{k+j}{2}) < P(C_{j-1} < \frac{k+j}{2})$	0	1
	$P(C_{j-1} > \frac{k+j}{2}) = P(C_{j-1} < \frac{k+j}{2})$	0.5	0.5

Table 3. $P(A_j \mid X_j, C_{j-1})$ for non-deterministic choice

X_j	$P(A_j = A)$	$P(A_j = R)$
H	$P(C_{j-1}^{+1} > \frac{k+j}{2}) + \frac{1}{2}P(C_{j-1}^{+1} = \frac{k+j}{2})$	$P(C_{j-1}^{+1} < \frac{k+j}{2}) + \frac{1}{2}P(C_{j-1}^{+1} = \frac{k+j}{2})$
L	$P(C_{j-1} > \frac{k+j}{2}) + \frac{1}{2}P(C_{j-1} = \frac{k+j}{2})$	$P(C_{j-1} < \frac{k+j}{2}) + \frac{1}{2}P(C_{j-1} = \frac{k+j}{2})$

Agent i can then compute $p(V, C_j \mid A_1, \cdots, A_j)$ as follows:

$$P(V = v, C_j = c \mid A_1, \cdots, A_j) =$$
$$P(V = v, C_{j-1} = c \mid A_1, \cdots, A_{j-1}) P(X_j = L \mid A_1, \cdots, A_j) + \tag{6}$$
$$P(V = v, C_{j-1} = c - 1 \mid A_1, \cdots, A_{j-1}) P(X_j = H \mid A_1, \cdots, A_j)$$

When it is agent i's turn to act, it will know $P(V = v, C_{i-1} = c \mid A_1, \cdots, A_{i-1})$ and will have its own signal X_i to calculate $P(C_i \mid C_{i-1}, X_i)$ as follows. Since V and C_i are conditionally independent given C_{i-1} and X_i, we have:

$$P(C_i = c \mid C_{i-1}, X_i = x) = \begin{cases} P(C_i = c-1) & \text{if } x = H \\ P(C_i = c) & \text{if } x = L \end{cases} \tag{7}$$

Finally, as agent i now has a probability distribution over C_i, it can choose between the options A and R by comparing $p_1 = P(C_i > \frac{k+i}{2} \mid \cdots)$, $p_2 = P(C_i < \frac{k+i}{2} \mid \cdots)$ and $p_3 = P(C_i = \frac{k+i}{2} \mid \cdots)$. For deterministic choice, if $p_1 > p_2$ it chooses A, and if $p_2 > p_1$ it chooses R. Otherwise it tosses an evenly weighted coin to choose between the two options. For non-deterministic choice, a random weighted choice is made with weights $p_1 + \frac{p_3}{2}$ for A and $p_2 + \frac{p_3}{2}$ for R.

5 Experiment and Results

5.1 Deterministic Model

As a first step we implemented[4] a deterministic choice model [3] using our Bayesian approach. Our model uses the probability distribution $P(C_i \mid C_{i-1}, X_i)$ to choose actions.

We ran cascade simulations 1000 times for 100 agents for different values of $v \in \{0, 1\}$, $p \in \{0.5, 0.6, 0.7, 0.8, 0.9\}$ and $k \in \{1, 20, 40\}$. In a single graph we plot two lines, red and green, for each run. The green line indicates the cumulative frequency of acceptances (A) and the red line indicates the same for rejections (R). Figures 2a and 2b illustrate this type of plot for a single run for a chain of 10 agents where the choices are A, A, A, R, R, A, A, A, A, A, (cascade, majority of agents are accepting) and A, A, R, A, A, R, R, A, R, A (no cascade, mixture of As and Rs) respectively. A cascade is shown when one line extends upwards and covers the entire range while the other line stays at the bottom. Cascades do not occur if lines stay in the middle of the image. For our experiment with 100 agents Figs. 3, 4 and 5 show the outcome of simulation which start with 1, 20 and 40 prior agents, respectively, for $V = 1$. We have separate graphs for each value of $p \in \{0.5, 0.6, 0.7, 0.8, 0.9\}$. It is evident from the graphs that there is always a high chance of cascades where everyone adopts when $V = 1$ and everyone rejects when $V = 0$. The results for $V = 0$ are similar to those for $V = 1$, except that the colours are swapped as R is dominant when $V = 0$. These graphs are similar to the results obtained from Bikhchandani's original model [3].

---

[4] The implementation of our model in Python can be found at https://github.com/ashalya86/Information-cascade-models.

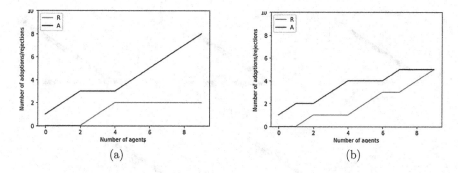

(a)   (b)

Fig. 2. Graph for a single simulation of cascading and non cascading patterns

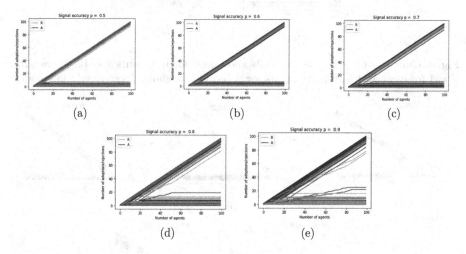

(a)   (b)   (c)

(d)   (e)

Fig. 3. Cumulative frequencies of adopts and rejects for 100 agents over 1000 runs with $V = 1$ for each p with 1 prior agent for deterministic choice (best viewed in colour)

5.2   Non-deterministic Model

We wish to investigate how the deterministic model of choice in the model of Bikhchandani et al., impacts their results, given that non-deterministic choice has been described as more psychologically plausible [21]. We modified our implementation to pick an action using random weighted choice (Table 3). As a result, even if the most likely optimal choice is to adopt, the agent could still choose the less likely one and reject.

As for the deterministic choice model, in a single graph we plot cumulative frequency of acceptances (A) and rejections (R) for 1000 runs of 100 agents for each p. The plots of cascades which begin with 1, 20 and 40 prior agents for $V = 1$, are seen in Figs. 6, 7, 8. The results for $V = 0$ are similar to $V = 1$, except that the colours are swapped as R is dominant when $V = 0$.

Simulation results suggest that for high accuracy perception of the true value of a choice ($p \in \{0.8, 0.9\}$, Figs. 6d, 6e, 7d and 7e), cascades still occur, but for

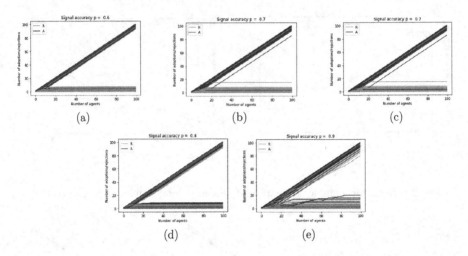

Fig. 4. Cumulative frequencies of adopts and rejects for 100 agents over 1000 runs with $V = 1$ for each p with 20 prior agents for deterministic choice (best viewed in colour)

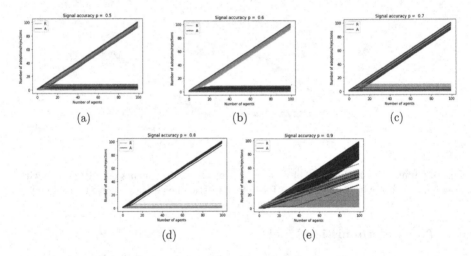

Fig. 5. Cumulative frequencies of adopts and rejects for 100 agents over 1000 runs with $V = 1$ for each p with 40 prior agents for deterministic choice (best viewed in colour)

lower accuracy perception, cascades are replaced by a bias towards one choice that is greater than would be expected if only the odds of correct vs. incorrect perception were considered (Figs. 6a, 6b, 7a and 7b). Although the ratio of choosing As over Rs starts with 0.6 and 0.4 for $p = 0.6$, one choice becomes increasingly dominant and it still shows the possibility of no cascade occurring (Figs. 6b and 7b).

According to Bikhchandani's model, the first agent's private information can be uniquely determined from its action, which makes its choice highly influen-

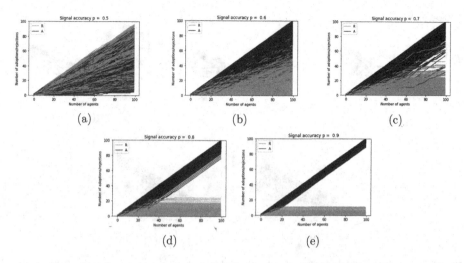

Fig. 6. Cumulative frequencies of adopts and rejects for 100 agents over 1000 runs with $V = 1$ for each p with 1 prior agent for non deterministic choice (best viewed in colour)

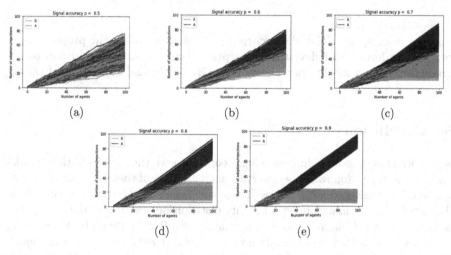

Fig. 7. Cumulative frequencies of adopts and rejects for 100 agents over 1000 runs with $V = 1$ for each p with 20 prior agents for non deterministic choice (best viewed in colour)

tial. Therefore, our model starts by assuming there are some unobserved agents present and uses a prior distribution over C and V.

For instance, suppose there are assumed to be 20 unobserved prior agents. Then the model creates a uniform prior for V and a binomial distribution over the count of prior H signals given V, in terms of p, for 20 prior agents. We then do the Bayesian inference. We obtained a significant change in cascades while plotting the cascade with different numbers of prior agents. We notice

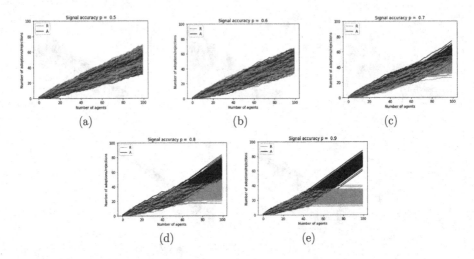

Fig. 8. Cumulative frequencies of adopts and rejects for 100 agents over 1000 runs with $V = 1$ for each p with 40 prior agents for non deterministic choice (best viewed in colour)

that the prior agents delay the occurrence of cascades. While the proportions of two choices have wider deviation for 1 prior agent (Figs. 6b, 6c, 6d and 6e), it gradually reduces for 20 prior agents (Figs. 7b, 7c, 7d and 7e) and 30 (Figs. 8b, 8c, 8d and 8e)

6   Conclusion

An information cascade happens when people observe the actions of their predecessors and try to follow these observations regardless of their own private information. We presented a full Bayesian account based on the model of Bikhchandani et al., [3]. We maintain a probability distribution over V and the (unknown) counts of high (H) signals received by the agents. Rather than always choosing the most likely option, agents make a weighted choice between Adopt and Reject. We do not assume that the first agent that was observed was the first to consider the fad. Instead, we incorporate prior knowledge of unobserved agents. This means that first (observed) agent's choice is less dominant than in the earlier model. Our findings show that prior agents delay the occurrence of cascades. Furthermore, in contrast to the predictions of Bikhchandani et al., our results show that cascades will not necessarily occur. The graphs obtained show that, for lower accuracy perception, cascades occur with much less probability. However, as p gets high, there is a high chance of cascades.

While people may not be good at Bayesian reasoning, as used in our model, we believe that appropriate software using our model could support users to assess the evidence from others' choices, including the possible presence of unobserved agents. This could help to reduce the likelihood of cascades. Using a plugin or extension in social media or market place could help people make their choices by analysing the observations including probability distributions over the counts of the private signals of prior actors using our Bayesian approach. Not only would this help individuals to make appropriate choices, but also businesses might find it beneficial to analyze the diffusion of information in the launch of products [19]. Investors might find it useful when understanding stock markets and prediction markets. Government and political parties could obtain better predictions of get the actual information of people's opinions during election campaigns.

Acknowledgements. This work was supported by the Marsden Fund Council from New Zealand Government funding, managed by Royal Society Te Apārangi.

References

1. Anderson, L.R., Holt, C.A.: Information cascades in the laboratory. Am. Econ. Rev. **87**, 847–862 (1996)
2. Banerjee, A.V.: A simple model of herd behavior. Q. J. Econ. **107**(3), 797–817 (1992). https://doi.org/10.2307/2118364
3. Bikhchandani, S., Hirshleifer, D., Welch, I.: A theory of fads, fashion, custom, and cultural change as informational cascades. J. Polit. Econ. **100**(5), 992–1026 (1992)
4. Bishop, C.M.: Pattern Recognition and Machine Learning, 1st edn. Springer-Verlag, New York (2006). https://link.springer.com/book/9780387310732
5. Blavatskyy, P.R.: Dual choice axiom and probabilistic choice. J. Risk Uncertain. **61**(1), 25–41 (2020). https://doi.org/10.1007/s11166-020-09332-7
6. Cheng, J., Adamic, L., Dow, P.A., Kleinberg, J.M., Leskovec, J.: Can cascades be predicted? In: Proceedings of the 23rd International Conference on the World Wide Web - WWW 2014, pp. 925–936. ACM Press (2014). https://doi.org/10.1145/2566486.2567997
7. De Vany, A., Lee, C.: Information cascades in multi-agent models. Technical report, University of California, Irvine, Department of Economics (1999). http://pages.stern.nyu.edu/~wgreene/entertainmentandmedia/Cascades.pdf
8. Duan, G.: Whinston: informational cascades and software adoption on the Internet: an empirical investigation. MIS Q. **33**(1), 23 (2009). https://doi.org/10.2307/20650277
9. Easley, D., Kleinberg, J.: Networks, Crowds, and Markets: Reasoning About A Highly Connected World. Cambridge University Press, UK (2010)
10. Huber, R.E., Klucharev, V., Rieskamp, J.: Neural correlates of informational cascades: brain mechanisms of social influence on belief updating. Soc. Cogn. Affect. Neurosci. **10**(4), 589–597 (2015). https://doi.org/10.1093/scan/nsu090
11. Lee, Y.J., Hosanagar, K., Tan, Y.: Do I follow my friends or the crowd? Information cascades in online movie ratings. Manage. Sci. **61**(9), 2241–2258 (2015). https://doi.org/10.1287/mnsc.2014.2082
12. Liu, C., Wang, W., Jiao, P., Chen, X., Sun, Y.: Cascade modeling with multihead self-attention. In: 2020 International Joint Conference on Neural Networks (IJCNN), pp. 1–8. IEEE (2020). https://doi.org/10.1109/IJCNN48605.2020.9207418
13. Liu, Q., Zhang, L.: Information cascades in online reading: an empirical investigation of panel data. Libr. Hi Tech **32**(4), 687–705 (2014). https://doi.org/10.1108/LHT-06-2014-0052

14. Liu, Q., Zhang, X., Li, Y.: The influence of information cascades on online reading behaviors of free and paid e-books. Libr. Inf. Sci. Res. **42**(1), 101001 (2020). https://doi.org/10.1016/j.lisr.2019.101001

15. Liu, Q., Zhang, X., Zhang, L., Zhao, Y.: The interaction effects of information cascades, word of mouth and recommendation systems on online reading behavior: an empirical investigation. Electron. Commer. Res. **19**(3), 521–547 (2018). https://doi.org/10.1007/s10660-018-9312-0

16. Lohmann, S.: Collective action cascades: an informational rationale for the power in numbers. J. Econ. Surv. **14**(5), 654–684 (2002)

17. Lu, Y., et al.: Exploring the collective human behavior in cascading systems: a comprehensive framework. Knowl. Inf. Syst. **62**(12), 4599–4623 (2020). https://doi.org/10.1007/s10115-020-01506-8

18. Luce, R.D., Suppes, P.: Preference, utility, and subjective probability. In: Luce, Duncan, R., Bush, R.R., Galanter, E. (eds.) Handbook of Mathematical Psychology, vol. 3, p. 162. John Wiley & Sons (1965)

19. Mangold, W.G., Faulds, D.J.: Social media: the new hybrid element of the promotion mix. Bus. Horiz. **52**(4), 357–365 (2009)

20. Peng, S., Yang, A., Cao, L., Yu, S., Xie, D.: Social influence modeling using information theory in mobile social networks. Inf. Sci. **379**, 146–159 (2017). https://doi.org/10.1016/j.ins.2016.08.023

21. Pleskac, T.J.: Decision and choice: Luce's choice axiom. In: International Encyclopedia of the Social & Behavioral Sciences, pp. 895–900. Elsevier (2015). https://doi.org/10.1016/B978-0-08-097086-8.43031-X

22. Wang, T., Wang, D.: Why Amazon's ratings might mislead you: the story of herding effects. Big Data **2**(4), 196–204 (2014). https://doi.org/10.1089/big.2014.0063

23. Watts, D.J.: A simple model of global cascades on random networks. In: Proceedings of the National Academy of Science, pp. 4766–5771 (2022)

24. Watts, D.J., Dodds, P.S.: Influentials, networks, and public opinion formation. J. Consum. Res. **34**(4), 441–458 (2007). https://doi.org/10.1086/518527

Interactions Between Social Norms and Incentive Mechanisms in Organizations

Ravshanbek Khodzhimatov[1]([✉])(iD), Stephan Leitner[2](iD), and Friederike Wall[2](iD)

[1] Digital Age Research Center, University of Klagenfurt, 9020 Klagenfurt, Austria
`ravshanbek.khodzhimatov@aau.at`
[2] Department of Management Control and Strategic Management, University of
Klagenfurt, 9020 Klagenfurt, Austria
`{stephan.leitner,friederike.wall}@aau.at`

Abstract. We focus on how individual behavior that complies with
social norms interferes with performance-based incentive mechanisms
in organizations with multiple distributed decision-making agents. We
model social norms to emerge from interactions between agents: agents
observe other the agents' actions and, from these observations, induce
what kind of behavior is socially acceptable. By complying with the
induced socially accepted behavior, agents experience utility. Also, agents
get utility from a pay-for-performance incentive mechanism. Thus, agents
pursue two objectives. We place the interaction between social norms and
performance-based incentive mechanisms in the complex environment of
an organization with distributed decision-makers, in which a set of inter-
dependent tasks is allocated to multiple agents. The results suggest that,
unless the sets of assigned tasks are highly correlated, complying with
emergent socially accepted behavior is detrimental to the organization's
performance. However, we find that incentive schemes can help offset the
performance loss by applying individual-based incentives in environments
with lower task-complexity and team-based incentives in environments
with higher task-complexity.

Keywords: Agent-based modeling and simulation · NK-framework ·
Emergence · Socially accepted behavior

1 Introduction

Norms are defined as behavior that is common within a society or as rules that
are aimed at maintaining specific patterns of behavior which are acceptable to
(the majority) of a society [33]. In line with this definition, Sen and Airiau [35]
stress that norms facilitate coordination – they refer to Lewis [28] who argues:
*"Everyone conforms, everyone expects others to conform, and everyone has good
reason to conform because conforming is in each person's best interest when
everyone else plans to conform"*, and conclude that norms can be interpreted as
external correlating signals that promote behavioral coordination.

© Springer Nature Switzerland AG 2022
A. Theodorou et al. (Eds.): COINE 2021, LNAI 13239, pp. 111–126, 2022.
https://doi.org/10.1007/978-3-031-16617-4_8

Despite being a focus of research in many scientific disciplines, a consensus about the ontology of norms has not yet been reached [31]. In this paper, we follow the classification introduced by Tuomela et al. [37], who distinguish between four types of norms, namely (i) rule norms, (ii) proper social norms, (iii) moral norms, and (iv) prudential norms (see also [33]). They argue that the (i) *rule norms* can be either formal or informal. The former are articulated and written with formal sanctions and brought into existence by an authority, the latter are articulated but usually not written down, associated with informal sanctions and brought into existence by group members' mutual implicit or explicit agreement. Morris-Martin et al. [33] add that rule norms are often also referred to as laws. With respect to (ii) *social norms*, Tuomela et al. [37] distinguish between *conventions*, which apply to an entire community, society or social class, and *group-specific norms*, which are specific to one or more groups, but not to the entire society. This understanding of social norms is in line with the definition introduced in Cialdini et al. [9], who add that social norms are usually not accompanied by enforcing laws. Mahmoud et al. [30] stress that social norms can be interpreted as informal rules and standards which entail what others expect, e.g., in terms of behavior, and have a non-obligatory character. The latter implies that social norms are self-enforcing and that there are often social processes underlying norms that ensure that non-conforming results in a social punishment [4,35]. Thus, obeying social norms is often regarded to be rational due to the threat of social sanctions [14]. Finally, Morris-Martin et al. [33] and Tuomela et al. [37] line out that (iii) *moral norms* are intended to appeal an individual's conscience and (iv) *prudential norms* usually follow the principles of rationality.

In this paper, we adopt the notion of (ii) *social norms* introduced above. Their presence has been widely recognized in the academic literature. The field of multi-agent systems is, for example, concerned with the emergence of social norms and their enforcement in agent societies. Recent reviews of research on norms in multi-agent systems are provided by Morris-Martin et al. [33] and Alechina et al. [2]. Cranefield et al. [11] line out that the way norms are included in decision making algorithms needs to be explicitly formulated by the designer, while for human agents, norms (and values) are highly entrenched in the decision making process. This is in line with Kohlberg [24], who argues that individuals have an endogenous preference to conform to the behavior of their peers, which is why social norms play a central role in a multiplicity of contexts in which humans interact and make decisions, such as decisions between different courses of action in organizations or in politics [35].

We apply social norms to the context of organizations which consist of collaborative and distributed decision makers and focus on the interaction between emergent social norms (at the level of individuals) and performance-based incentives, the behavioral implications of this interaction, and its consequences for the performance of the overall system.[1] By doing so, we focus on social norms which emerge from past decisions of fellow agents within an organization [8].

The remainder of this paper is organized as follows: Sect. 2 reviews the research on social norms, Sect. 3 describes the structure and methodology we use to model the simulation of organizational environment with emergent social norms and varying performance-based incentives, Sect. 4 elaborates on results and findings, and Sect. 5 concludes this paper.

2   Related Work

Considering social norms as key-factors which drive individual behavior is not a new issue in research. Early work on this topic goes back to social approval of individual behavior [18,36]. A recent survey of interactions between social norms and incentives is provided by Festre [15], who argues that social norms are supplementary motives to self-interest, which is commonly assumed for economic agents. He presents the following two empirical findings to support this assertion: (i) a large proportion of Americans do not apply for welfare programs, even when they are eligible [32], and (ii) in donations to charity, whether the list of contributors is published or not, has an effect on the total amount donated [3,17]. Festre [15] claims that the reason for this behaviour can be traced back to social norms.[2]

Festre [15] reviews current studies on social norms in economic theory and concludes that there might be two explanations for social norms as a driver of individual behavior: (i) the individual desire for conformity and (ii) positive externalities. For (i) the individual desire for conformity, she argues that individuals care about their social status (e.g., in terms of popularity or respect) and therefore want to conform to social norms. This explanation is in line with previous studies [6,38]. With respect to (ii) positive externalities, Festre [15] refers to Coleman [10], who lines out that situations, in which the same outcome satisfies the interests of others, enforce social norms. Consequently, since everyone has incentives to reward others for working towards this outcome, all individuals have two sources of utility: the reward for the effort one made towards the outcome (i.e., the incentives), and the rewards provided by others for helping to achieve that outcome (in terms of social approval). This argumentation is also in line with Janssen et al. [21] and Huck et al. [19], who argue that individual behavior is driven by multiple forces and that interactions may exist among these

---

[1] Note that along with social norms at the individual level, previous research also addresses social norms at the level of organizations: Dowling et al. [12], for example, conceptualize organizational legitimacy as congruence between the social values associated with an organization's action and the norms of acceptable behavior in the social system of the organization. This paper, however, focuses on social norms *within* an organization.

[2] For extensive discussions on the role of social norms in behavioral control, the reader is also referred to [25,39], and most recently [29] and the literature cited in these studies.

forces (e.g., in terms of reinforcement or weakening). Festre [15] adds that previous research has shortcomings in the way it deals with behavioral responses to norms or changes in norms, and that the interaction between *endogenous* social norms and incentives should be further addressed. The latter is also in line with Kübler [25], who argues that social norms have been considered as being exogenous (and, thus, not emergent) for (too) long. Some work in the field of psychology addresses social norms, but puts the focus on the emergence in the sense of learning which type of behavior is socially approved: Paluck et al. [34], for example, are concerned with evolving norms in the context of social networks in schools and Ehrhart et al. [13] address citizenship behavior in organizational units. Previous research in the field of economics has, amongst others, addressed how performance-based incentives can change the meaning of following a social norm [19,25], and how incentive framing and social norms interact with respect to behavioral implications [29]. Moreover, previous research has found that, under specific circumstances, monetary incentives can crowd out incentives provided by intrinsic factors, such as social norms [5,21].

We implement emergent social norms in the sense of Cialdini et al. [8], who state that social norms emerge from the shared knowledge about the past behavior of peers and are determined by the strength of social interactions and the similarity of decisions, regardless of the impact of the norms on the outcomes. Thus, we focus on the behavior that is *normal* in the population, rather than what is declared (morally or otherwise) to be a desired behavior [1,8]. This allows us to model the social norms solely as an emergent phenomenon without imposing the desirability qualities to particular actions.

Fischer and Huddart [16] similarly acknowledge that social norms can emerge endogenously: they argue that there is a complex relationship between individual behavior and social norms within an organization, as they are mutually dependent. If an agent's peers are members of the same organization, individual behavior determines the organization's social norms, which, in turn, influence individual behavior. They acknowledge, however, that individual behavior of the members of an organization is affected not only by social norms but also by other means of behavioral control, such as incentive systems. They conclude that social norms (i) emerge endogenously within organizations from the individual behavior of the organization's members and their interaction, and (ii) might be endogenously affected by choices related to organizational design elements. They explicitly point out that further investigation of the interaction between social norms and incentives is required. This is where we place our research: we study how social norms affect the performance in organizations with collaborative and distributed decision makers and how they interact with performance-based incentive mechanisms.

3   Model

This section introduces the model of a stylized organization which is implemented as a collective of P agents facing a complex task. The task environment is based on the NK-framework [23,26,41]. Agents face the dilemma of pursuing two objectives simultaneously, namely, to conform to emergent social norms and to maximize their individual (performance-based) utility. We model agents to employ the approach of goal programming to dissolve this dilemma and observe how interactions between social norms and (performance-based) incentives affect the organization's performance for $t = \{1, 2, \ldots, T\}$ periods. The task environment, in which the organization operates, is introduced in Sec. 3.1, while Sects. 3.2 and 3.3 characterize the agents and describe how social norms emerge, respectively. Section 3.4 describes the agents' search for better performing solutions to the decision problem and the approach of goal programming is introduced in Sec. 3.5. Finally, Sect. 3.6 provides an overview of the sequence of events during simulation runs.

3.1   Task Environment

We model an organization that faces a complex decision problem that is expressed as the set of M binary choices. The decision problem is segmented into sub-problems which are allocated to P agents, so that each agent faces an N-dimensional sub-problem. We denote the organization's decision problem by an M-dimensional bitstring $\mathbf{x} = (x_1, x_2, \ldots, x_M)$, where $M = N \cdot P$, bits x_i represent single tasks, and $x_i \in \{0, 1\}$ for $i \in \{1, 2, \ldots, M\}$. Without loss of generality, we model tasks to be assigned to agents sequentially, such that agent 1 is responsible for tasks 1–4, agent 2 – for tasks 5–8, and so forth. Formally, agent $p \in \{1, 2, \ldots, P\}$ is responsible for the following vector of tasks:

$$\mathbf{x}^p = (x_1^p, \ldots, x_N^p) = \left(x_{N \cdot (p-1)+1}, \ldots, x_{N \cdot p} \right) \tag{1}$$

Every task x_i for $i \in \{1, 2, \ldots, M\}$ is associated with a uniformly distributed performance contribution $\phi(x_i) \sim U(0, 1)$. The decision problem is *complex* in that the performance contribution $\phi(x_i)$, might be affected not only by the decision x_i, but also by decisions x_j, where $j \neq i$. We differentiate between two types of such inter-dependencies: (a) *internal* inter-dependencies within $\mathbf{x}^p$, in which interdependence exists between the tasks assigned to agent p, and (b) *external* inter-dependencies between $\mathbf{x}^p$ and $\mathbf{x}^q$, in which interdependence exists between the tasks assigned to agents p and q, where $p \neq q$. We control inter-dependencies by parameters K, C, S, so that every task interacts with exactly K other tasks internally and C tasks assigned to S other agents externally [22]. Figure 1 illustrates four stylized interaction structures considered in this paper. The figure features $M = 16$ tasks equally assigned to $P = 4$ employees for different levels of complexity.

Based on the structure outlined above, we can formally describe the performance contribution of decision x_i as follows:

$$\phi(x_i) = \phi(x_i, \underbrace{x_{i_1}, \ldots, x_{i_K}}_{\substack{K \text{ internal} \\ \text{interdependencies}}}, \underbrace{x_{i_{K+1}}, \ldots, x_{i_{K+C \cdot S}}}_{\substack{C \cdot S \text{ external} \\ \text{interdependencies}}}), \tag{2}$$

where $\{i_1, \ldots, i_{K+C \cdot S}\} \subset \{1, \ldots, M\} \backslash i$, and the parameters satisfy $0 \leq K < N$, $0 \leq C \leq N$, and $0 \leq S < P$. Using Eq. 2, we compute performance landscapes for all agents. We indicate time steps by $t \in \{1, 2, \ldots, T\}$. Let $\mathbf{x}_t^p$ and $\mathbf{x}_t$ be a vector of decisions of agent p and a vector of decisions of all agents at time t, respectively. Then the performance achieved by agent p at time step t is:

$$\phi_{own}(\mathbf{x}_t^p) = \frac{1}{N} \sum_{x_i \in \mathbf{x}_t^p} \phi(x_i), \tag{3}$$

and the organization's performance at time step t is:

$$\phi_{org}(\mathbf{x}_t) = \frac{1}{P} \sum_{p=1}^{P} \phi(\mathbf{x}_t^p) . \tag{4}$$

In order to capture diversity (or similarity) in the sub-problems allocated to agents, we consider the correlations between the performance landscapes using the methodology described in Verel et al. [40]. The performance contributions of every set of N tasks assigned to agent p are correlated to the performance contributions of the sets of N tasks assigned to $P-1$ other agents with a constant correlation coefficient $\rho \in [0, 1]$. When $\rho = 0$ and $\rho = 1$, agents operate on perfectly distinct and perfectly identical performance landscapes, respectively.

3.2 Agents' Performance-Based Incentives

The agents' compensation is composed of a fixed and a variable component: without loss of generality, we normalize the former to 0. The latter is based on agent p's own performance ϕ_{own} (see Eq. 3), and the residual performance ϕ_{res} resulting from decisions of all other agents. Let $\mathbf{x}_t^{-p}$ be a vector of decisions of all agents other than p:

$$\mathbf{x}_t^{-p} = \{\mathbf{x}_t^q : q \in \{1, \ldots, P\} \backslash p\} \tag{5}$$

Then, the residual performance is defined as the mean of own performances of every agent other than p:

$$\phi_{res}(\mathbf{x}_t^{-p}) = \frac{1}{P-1} \cdot \sum_{\mathbf{x} \in \mathbf{x}_t^{-p}} \phi_{own}(\mathbf{x}), \tag{6}$$

and agent p's variable compensation component follows the linear incentive scheme[3]:

$$\phi_{inc}(\mathbf{x}_t^p, \mathbf{x}_t^{-p}) = \alpha \cdot \phi_{own}(\mathbf{x}_t^p) + \beta \cdot \phi_{res}(\mathbf{x}_t^{-p}), \tag{7}$$

where $\alpha + \beta = 1$.

---

[3] In our context linear incentives are as efficient as other contracts inducing non-boundary actions. See [16, p. 1461].

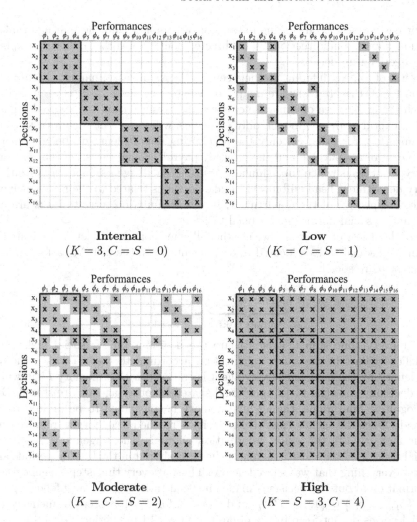

Fig. 1. Stylized interdependence structures with $M = 16$ tasks equally assigned to $P = 4$ agents for different levels of complexity. The crossed cells indicate inter-dependencies as follows: let (i, j) be coordinates of a crossed cell in row-column order, then performance contribution $\phi(x_i)$ depends on decision x_j.

3.3 Social Norms

We implement the emergent social norms using a version of the Social Cognitive Optimization algorithm [42]. The algorithm features *social sharing libraries*, where agents share and observe the information (i.e., the previous decisions) which they consider in their decision-making later. In our implementation, every

agent has an individual sharing library (as a memory), and the sharing of information happens unidirectionally in directed social networks. Below we explain
this algorithm in detail.

First of all, we differentiate between two types of tasks, namely *private* and
social tasks. Private tasks are unique to agents, i.e., these tasks cover activities
which are in the area of expertise of a specific agent; within the stylized organization captured by our model, only one agent will carry out such a task. In an
organization, for example, only the accounting department will be responsible
for the accounts payable and the monthly payroll. Social tasks, on the contrary,
are types of tasks which (in a similar way) concern all agents. In an organization,
every department head will have to make decisions related to their management
style, irrespective of the department. In our formulation, private tasks are not
relevant to social norms, while social tasks are.

Without loss of generality we use the following convention: let N_s indicate the
number of social tasks allocated to each agent. Then the last N_s tasks assigned
to agent p are social:

$$\mathbf{x}^p = (\underbrace{x_1^p, \ldots, x_{N-N_s}^p}_{\text{private tasks}}, \underbrace{x_{N-N_s+1}^p, \ldots, x_N^p}_{\text{social tasks}}) \tag{8}$$

At every time step t, agents share the decisions on N_s social tasks with
D fellow agents in the same organization according to the network structure
predefined by the modeler.[4] Every agent is endowed with a memory L^p in which
the decisions on social tasks, made and shared by other agents, are stored. Due
to cognitive limitations, the agent's memory is considered to be limited to T_L
periods. Once the agents' cognitive capacity is reached, they forget (remove from
their memory L^p) the oldest information on their fellow agents' decisions on
social tasks, i.e., they just remember what was shared in the last T_L periods and
forget everything that was shared before. Thus, at every time step t, agent p gets
information about the decisions made on social tasks $\mathbf{x}_{soc}^q$ from D fellow agents
$q \in \{p_1, \ldots, p_D\} \subseteq \{1, \ldots, P\} \backslash p$, and stores it for T_L time steps in memory L^p.
Social norms do not form in the organization until time period T_L.

The extent to which agent p's decision at time t, $\mathbf{x}_t^p$, complies with the emergent social norm is computed as a match rate of the social bits in the memory:

$$\phi_{soc}^p(\mathbf{x}_t^p) = \begin{cases} \dfrac{1}{N_s \cdot |L_t^p|} \displaystyle\sum_{\mathbf{x} \in L_t^p} h(\mathbf{x}_{soc}^p, \mathbf{x}), & t > T_L \\ 0, & t \leq T_L \end{cases} \tag{9}$$

where $|L_t^p|$ is the number of entries in agent p's memory at time t and $h(\mathbf{x}, \mathbf{y})$
for two equal-length bitstrings $\mathbf{x}$ and $\mathbf{y}$ of size J is the number of positions at
which the corresponding bits are equal:

---

[4] We use the bidirectional *ring network* topology, in which each node is connected to
exactly two other nodes with reciprocal unidirectional links, where nodes represent
agents and the links represent sharing of information.

$$h(\mathbf{x}, \mathbf{y}) = \sum_{i=1}^{J} [x_i == y_i] . \tag{10}$$

If the statement inside the bracket is true, it equals 1, and 0 otherwise [20].

3.4   Discovering New Solutions to the Decision Problem

At time t, agent p can observe its own performance in the last period, $\phi_{own}(\mathbf{x}_{t-1}^p)$, and the decisions of all agents in the organization in the last period *after* they are implemented, $\mathbf{x}_{t-1}$.

In order to come up with new solutions to their decision problems, agents perform a search in the neighbourhood of $\mathbf{x}_{t-1}$ as follows: agent p randomly switches one decision $x_i \in \mathbf{x}^p$ (from 0 to 1, or vice versa), and assumes that other agents will not switch their decisions[5]. We denote this vector with one switched element by $\hat{\mathbf{x}}_t^p$.

Next, the agent has to make a decision whether to stick with the status quo, $\mathbf{x}_t^p$, or to switch to the newly discovered $\hat{\mathbf{x}}_t^p$. The rule for this decision is described in the next subsection.

3.5   Balancing Performance-Based Incentives and Social Norms and Making a Decision

Agents pursue two objectives simultaneously: they aim at maximizing their performance-based incentives formalized in Eq. 7 and, at the same time, want to comply with the social norms as formalized in Eq. 9. In order to balance these two objectives, agents follow the approach of *goal programming* [7] as described below.

Let g_{soc} and g_{inc} be the goals that agents have for $\phi_{soc}(\mathbf{x}_t^p)$ and $\phi_{inc}(\mathbf{x}_t^p, \mathbf{x}_t^{-p})$, respectively[6]. Agent p wants to achieve both goals, so that:

$$\phi_{soc}(\mathbf{x}_t^p) \geq g_{soc}, \text{ and} \tag{11a}$$

$$\phi_{inc}(\mathbf{x}_t^p, \mathbf{x}_t^{-p}) \geq g_{inc} \tag{11b}$$

Let $d_{soc}(\mathbf{x}_t^p)$ and $d_{inc}(\mathbf{x}_t^p, \mathbf{x}_t^{-p})$ be the under-achievements of the set of decisions $(\mathbf{x}_t^p, \mathbf{x}_t^{-p})$ on the goals regarding social norms and performance-based incentives respectively (see Eqs. 7 and 9):

$$d_{soc}(\mathbf{x}_t^p) = \max\{g_{soc} - \phi_{soc}(\mathbf{x}_t^p), 0\}, \tag{12}$$

$$d_{inc}(\mathbf{x}_t^p, \mathbf{x}_t^{-p}) = \max\{g_{inc} - \phi_{inc}(\mathbf{x}_t^p, \mathbf{x}_t^{-p}), 0\} \tag{13}$$

---

[5] Levinthal [27] describes situations in which agents switch more than one decision at a time as *long jumps* and states that such scenarios are less likely to occur, as it is hard or risky to change multiple processes simultaneously.

[6] Note that agents are homogeneous with respect to goals and that goals are constant over time.

As mentioned before, agent p discovers $\hat{\mathbf{x}}_t^p$ – an alternative configuration to the decision at t, but can only observe what other agents implemented at the previous time period, $\mathbf{x}_{t-1}^{-p}$. Given p's information, this agent makes the decision to either implement $\hat{\mathbf{x}}_t^p$ or to stick with $\mathbf{x}_{t-1}^p$ at t and chooses $\mathbf{x}_t^p$ according to the following rule:

$$\mathbf{x}_t^p = \argmin_{\mathbf{x} \in \{\mathbf{x}_{t-1}^p, \hat{\mathbf{x}}_t^p\}} w_{soc} \cdot d_{soc}(\mathbf{x}) + w_{inc} \cdot d_{inc}(\mathbf{x}, \mathbf{x}_{t-1}^{-p}), \qquad (14)$$

where w_{soc} and w_{inc} represent the weights for the goal for compliance with the social norms (g_{soc}) and goal for performance-based incentives (g_{inc}) respectively.

3.6   Process Overview, Scheduling and Main Parameters

The simulation model has been implemented in Python 3.7.4. Every simulation round starts with the initialization of the agents' performance landscapes, the allocation of tasks to $P = 4$ agents[7], and the generation of an N-dimensional bitstring as a starting point of the simulation run (see Sect. 3.1). After initialization, agents perform the *hill climbing* search procedure outlined above (see Sects. 3.4 and 3.5) and share information regarding their social decisions in their social networks (see Sect. 3.3). The observation period T, the memory span of the employees T_L, and the number of repetitions in a simulation, R, are exogenous parameters, whereby the latter is fixed on the basis of the coefficient of variation. Figure 2 provides an overview of this process and Table 1 summarizes the main parameters used in this paper.

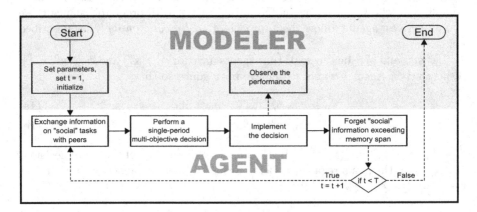

Fig. 2. Process overview. Upper actions are performed by the modeler and lower actions are performed by agents

---

[7] For reliable results, we generate the entire landscapes before the simulation, which is computationally feasible for $P = 4$ given modern RAM sizes. Our sensitivity analyses with simpler models without entire landscapes, suggest that the results also hold for larger population sizes.

Table 1. Main parameters

Parameter	Description	Value
M	Total number of tasks	16
P	Number of agents	4
N	Number of tasks assigned to a single agent	4
$[K, C, S]$	Internal and external couplings	$[3, 0, 0]$, $[1, 1, 1]$, $[2, 2, 2]$, $[3, 4, 3]$
ρ	Pairwise correlation coefficient between tasks assigned to different agents	0.3
T_L	Memory span of agents	20
N_S	Number of social tasks	2
D	Level of social connection (network degree)	2
T	Observation period	500
R	Number of simulation runs per scenario	300
$[g_{inc}, g_{soc}]$	Goals for performance-based incentives $(\phi_{inc}(\mathbf{x}_t^p, \mathbf{x}_t^{-p}))$ and compliance with the social norms $(\phi_{soc}(\mathbf{x}_t^p))$	$[1.0, 1.0]$
$[w_{inc}, w_{soc}]$	Weights for performance-based incentives $\phi_{inc}(\mathbf{x}_t^p, \mathbf{x}_t^{-p})$ and compliance with the social norms $\phi_{soc}(\mathbf{x}_t^p)$	$[1, 0]$, $[0.7, 0.3]$, $[0.5, 0.5]$
$[\alpha, \beta]$	Shares of own and residual performances included in the performance-based incentive scheme	$[1, 0]$, $[0.75, 0.25]$, $[0.5, 0.5]$, $[0.25, 0.75]$

4 Results

4.1 Performance Measure

We indicate the solution (at the system's level) implemented at time step t and simulation run $r \in \{1, \dots, R\}$ by $\mathbf{x}_t^r$, and the associated performance by $\phi_{org}^r(\mathbf{x}_t^r)$ (see Eq. 4). As the performance landscapes on which agents operate are randomly generated, for every simulation run, we normalize the performances by the maximum performances per landscape to ensure comparability. We indicate then normalized performance achieved by the organization at time step t in simulation run r by

$$\Phi[r, t] = \frac{\phi_{org}^r(\mathbf{x}_t^r)}{\max\limits_{\mathbf{x} \in [0,1]^M} \{\phi_{org}^r(\mathbf{x})\}} \qquad (15)$$

We denote the average performance at t by:

$$\overline{\Phi}[t] = \frac{1}{R} \sum_{r=1}^{R} \Phi[r, t], \qquad (16)$$

In Sect. 4.2, we report the *distance to maximum performance* as a performance measure. Note that this measure captures the cumulative distance

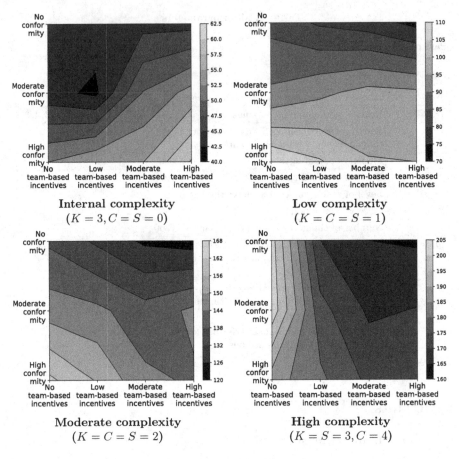

Fig. 3. Contour plots for cumulative distances $d(\overline{\Phi})$ to the maximum attainable performance for different scenarios. The lower (higher) values mean better (worse) performance for organization and are indicated by lighter (darker) tones

between the average performances achieved throughout the observation period and the maximum performance attainable (which equals 1 by construction), and lower (higher) values of the distance indicate higher (lower) performance:

$$d(\overline{\Phi}) = \sum_{t=1}^{T} \left(1 - \overline{\Phi}[t]\right) \tag{17}$$

4.2 Results of the Simulation Study

The parameters summarized in Table 1 result in $4 \cdot 3 \cdot 4 = 48$ different scenarios for 4 levels of complexity (internal, low, moderate, and high), 3 pairs of weights for performance-based incentive and compliance with social norms (high, moderate, and zero weight on social norms), and 4 different settings for the performance-based incentive schemes (zero, low, moderate, and high team-based incentives).

The results are presented in Fig. 3. The contours indicate ranges of similar distance values, where darker (lighter) colors indicate larger (smaller) values for the distance to maximum. In other words, the lighter contours represent higher organizational performance and are more desirable, while the darker contours represent lower organizational performance and are less desirable. In each plot, the performance-based incentive scheme (α and β) and the pairs of weights for incentives and social norms (w_{inc} and w_{soc}) are presented as the horizontal and the vertical axes, respectively. Please note that performance-based incentive schemes that put full weight on the performance achieved by the agents individually are included on the left hand side on horizontal axes (i.e., $\alpha = 1$ and $\beta = 0$), while moving to the right decreases the weight of individual performance and increases the weight of residual performance (until $\alpha = 0.25$ and $\beta = 0.75$). On the vertical axes, scenarios in which agents put strong emphasis on complying with social norms, are included at the bottom (i.e., $w_{inc} = 0.5$ and $w_{soc} = 0.5$), while moving upwards decreases the extent to which agents care about social norms (until $w_{inc} = 1$ and $w_{soc} = 0$). The 4 contour plots correspond to 4 different levels of complexity presented in Fig. 1.

Looking at the ranges of the plots (the minimal and maximal values), we observe that as the complexity increases, the average performance drops for all social norm weights and incentive schemes. This finding is in line with previous research [22,27].

For scenarios in which agents put full emphasis on performance-based incentives and do not care about complying with social norms (i.e., upper parts of subplots, where $w_{inc} = 1$ and $w_{soc} = 0$), we can observe that the choice of the incentive scheme does not have an effect on performance in the absence of external interdependencies (see Fig. 3(a)). However as soon as there are external interdependencies, even if the task's complexity is relatively low (see Fig. 3(b)), the team-based incentive schemes result in a better performance.[8] This positive effect of team-based incentive mechanisms increases with the external complexity of the task environment (see Fig. 3 (b,c,d)). This finding emphasizes the importance of differentiating between internal and external interdependencies among tasks when designing incentive mechanisms. A stronger focus of incentives on the residual performance (higher values of β) appears to offset some of the negative effects associated with task complexity only in cases in which the complexity is not internal (i.e., when $C, S > 0$). This finding, therefore, extends the literature that states that residual performance is suitable in presence of externalities [16], by specifying the nature of these externalities. We also find that the pattern described above is robust in presence of social norms (i.e., on lower parts of subplots, the similar effect is observed).

We also observe that as the agents start putting higher weights on the social norms (i.e. moving down the vertical axis), the contours get darker, meaning that the performance drops. This represents that complying to social norms can come

---

[8] Please note that task complexity in Fig. 3(b) is relatively low, since every task is coupled with $K + C \cdot S = 2$ other tasks. In Fig. 3(a), on the contrary, each task is coupled with $K + C \cdot S = 3$ other tasks.

at a cost for performance, as agents have to consider multiple objectives. However, as the (external) complexity increases (Fig. 3 (b, c, d)), the extent of this effect declines, and in situations with high (external) complexity (see Fig. 3 (d)) we observe that the contours are almost vertical, meaning that social norms do not cause a significant decline in the performance. This can be explained by the coordinating function of social norms, which can be observed when the task environment is too complex to solve individually without any coordination. Apart from that, our sensitivity analyses show that the decline in performance related to social norms, disappears for cases with higher correlation among agents' performance landscapes even for environments with lower complexity.

5   Conclusion

In this paper, we proposed a model of an organization which is composed of autonomous and collaborative decision making agents facing a complex task. Agents pursue two objectives simultaneously, i.e., they aim at maximizing their performance-based incentives and, at the same time, want to comply to the social norms emerging in their social networks. In our analysis, we focus on the interplay between performance-based incentives and social norms. Our main results are the following: First, if agents focus on performance-based incentives only, the choice of the type of incentive scheme has marginal effects in task environments with low level of complexity. As complexity increases, team-based incentives become more beneficial. However, in environments where inter-dependencies (no matter how high) exist only within tasks allocated to the same agent, the incentive schemes have zero effect on the performance. Second, if agents focus on complying to social norms, this comes at the cost of performance at the level of the system (except for scenarios when agents' task environments are highly correlated). Third, whether team-based performance can offset negative effects on performance, caused by agents that aim at complying to social norms, is substantially affected by the level of task complexity. For highly complex tasks, team-based incentives appear to be beneficial, while the opposite is true for task environments with a low level of complexity.

Our work is, of course, not without its limitations. First, we treat compliance and non-compliance to social norms equally. In reality, however, non-compliance to social norms might lead to more fatal consequences than "over-compliance" [15]. Future work might want to investigate this issue. Second, we limit the number of agents to 4 and consider ring networks only. It might be a promising avenue for future research to increase the number of agents and test the effect of other network topologies on the dynamics emerging from social norms. Finally, it might be an interesting extension to model the transformation of social norms into values by adjusting the task environment dynamically.

References

1. Ajzen, I.: The theory of planned behavior. Organ. Behav. Human Decis. Process. **50**(2), 179–211 (1991)
2. Alechina, N., Dastani, M., Logan, B.: Norm specification and verification in multi-agent systems. J. Appl. Logics-IFCoLog J. Logics Appl. **5**(2), 457–490 (2018)
3. Andreoni, J., Petri, R.: Social Motives to Giving: Can These Explain Fund Raising Institutions? University of Wisconsin, Technical report (2000)
4. Axelrod, R.: The Complexity of Cooperation: Agent-Based Models of Competition and Collaboration. Princeton University Press, Princeton (1997)
5. Benabou, R., Tirole, J.: Intrinsic and extrinsic motivation. Rev. Econ. Stud. **70**(3), 489–520 (2003)
6. Bernheim, B.D.: A theory of conformity. J. Polit. Econ. **102**(5), 841–877 (1994)
7. Charnes, A., Cooper, W.W.: Management models and industrial applications of linear programming. Manag. Sci. **4**(1), 38–91 (1957)
8. Cialdini, R., Reno, R., Kallgren, C.: A focus theory of normative conduct: recycling the concept of norms to reduce littering in public places. J. Pers. Social Psychol. **58**, 1015–1026 (1990)
9. Cialdini, R.B., Trost, M.R.: Social Influence: Social Norms, Conformity and Compliance. McGraw-Hill, New York (1998)
10. Coleman, J.S.: Free riders and zealots: the role of social networks. Sociol. Theory **6**(1), 52–57 (1988)
11. Cranefield, S., Winikoff, M., Dignum, V., Dignum, F.: No pizza for you: value-based plan selection in BDI agents. In: IJCAI, pp. 178–184 (2017)
12. Dowling, J., Pfeffer, J.: Organizational legitimacy: social values and organizational behavior. Pac. Sociol. Rev. **18**(1), 122–136 (1975)
13. Ehrhart, M.G., Naumann, S.E.: Organizational citizenship behavior in work groups: a group norms approach. J. Appl. Psychol. **89**(6), 960 (2004)
14. Elster, J.: Social norms and economic theory. J. Econ. Perspect. **3**(4), 99–117 (1989)
15. Festre, A.: Incentives and social norms: a motivation-based economic analysis of social norms. J. Econ. Surv. **24**(3), 511–538 (2010)
16. Fischer, P., Huddart, S.: Optimal contracting with endogenous social norms. Am. Econ. Rev. **98**(4), 1459–1475 (2008)
17. Glazer, A., Konrad, K.A.: A signaling explanation for charity. Am. Econ. Rev. **86**(4), 1019–1028 (1996)
18. Hayek, F.A.: Studies in Philosophy, Politics and Economics. University of Chicago Press, Chicago (1967)
19. Huck, S., Kübler, D., Weibull, J.: Social norms and economic incentives in firms. J. Econ. Behav. Organ. **83**(2), 173–185 (2012)
20. Iversion, K.E.: A Programming Language. Wiley, Hoboken (1962)
21. Janssen, M.C.W., Mendys-Kamphorst, E.: The price of a price: on the crowding out and in of social norms. J. Econ. Behav. Organ. **55**(3), 377–395 (2004)
22. Kauffman, S.A., Johnsen, S.: Coevolution to the edge of chaos: coupled fitness landscapes, poised states, and coevolutionary avalanches. J. Theor. Biol. **149**(4), 467–505 (1991). https://doi.org/10.1016/S0022-5193(05)80094-3
23. Kauffman, S.A., Weinberger, E.D.: The NK model of rugged fitness landscapes and its application to maturation of the immune response. J. Theor. Biol. **141**, 211–245 (1989)
24. Kohlberg, L.: The psychology of moral development: essays on moral development, vol. 2 (1984)

25. Kübler, D.: On the regulation of social norms. J. Law Econ. Organ. **17**(2), 449–476 (2001)
26. Leitner, S., Wall, F.: Multiobjective decision making policies and coordination mechanisms in hierarchical organizations: results of an agent-based simulation. Sci. World J. (2014). https://doi.org/10.1155/2014/875146
27. Levinthal, D.A.: Adaptation on rugged landscapes. Manag. Sci. **43**(7), 934–950 (1997)
28. Lewis, D.: Convention: A Philosophical Study. John Wiley & Sons, Hoboken (1969)
29. Lieberman, A., Duke, K.E., Amir, O.: How incentive framing can harness the power of social norms. Organ. Behav. Human Decis. Processes **151**, 118–131 (2019)
30. Mahmoud, M.A., Ahmad, M.S., Mostafa, S.A.: Norm-based behavior regulating technique for multi-agent in complex adaptive systems. IEEE Access **7**, 126662–126678 (2019)
31. Mellema, R., Jensen, M., Dignum, F.: Social rules for agent systems (2020)
32. Moffitt, R.: An economic model of welfare stigma. Am. Econ. Rev. **73**(5), 1023–1035 (1983)
33. Morris-Martin, A., De Vos, M., Padget, J.: Norm emergence in multiagent systems: a viewpoint paper. Auton. Agents Multi-Agent Syst. **33**(6), 706–749 (2019). https://doi.org/10.1007/s10458-019-09422-0
34. Paluck, E.L., Shepherd, H.: The salience of social referents: a field experiment on collective norms and harassment behavior in a school social network. J. Pers. Social Psychol. **103**(6), 899 (2012)
35. Sen, S., Airiau, S.: Emergence of norms through social learning. In: IJCAI, vol. 1507, p. 1512 (2007)
36. Smith, A.: The theory of moral sentiments, vol. 1. J. Richardson (1822)
37. Tuomela, R., Bonnevier-Tuomela, M.: Norms and agreement. Eur. J. Law Phil. Comput. Sci. **5**, 41–46 (1995)
38. Veblen, T.: The Theory of the Leisure Class. Houghton Mifflin, Boston (1973)
39. Vendrik, M.C.M.: Dynamics of a household norm in female labour supply. J. Econ. Dyn. Control **27**(5), 823–841 (2003)
40. Verel, S., Liefooghe, A., Jourdan, L., Dhaenens, C.: On the structure of multiobjective combinatorial search space: Mnk-landscapes with correlated objectives. Eur. J. Oper. Res. **227**(2), 331–342 (2013)
41. Wall, F., Leitner, S.: Agent-based computational economics in management accounting research: opportunities and difficulties. J. Manag. Account. Res. (2020). https://doi.org/10.2308/JMAR-19-073
42. Xie, X.F., Zhang, W.J., Yang, Z.L.: Social cognitive optimization for nonlinear programming problems. In: Proceedings. International Conference on Machine Learning and Cybernetics, vol. 2, pp. 779–783. IEEE (2002)

Learning for Detecting Norm Violation
in Online Communities

Thiago Freitas dos Santos[✉], Nardine Osman, and Marco Schorlemmer

Artificial Intelligence Research Institute, IIIA-CSIC Barcelona, Catalonia, Spain
thiago@iiia.csic.es

Abstract. In this paper, we focus on normative systems for online communities. The paper addresses the issue that arises when different community members interpret these norms in different ways, possibly leading to unexpected behavior in interactions, usually with norm violations that affect the individual and community experiences. To address this issue, we propose a framework capable of detecting norm violations and providing the violator with information about the features of their action that makes this action violate a norm. We build our framework using Machine Learning, with Logistic Model Trees as the classification algorithm. Since norm violations can be highly contextual, we train our model using data from the Wikipedia online community, namely data on Wikipedia edits. Our work is then evaluated with the Wikipedia use case where we focus on the norm that prohibits vandalism in Wikipedia edits.

Keywords: Norms · Norm violation detection · Machine learning · Wikipedia norms

1 Introduction

The aligned understanding of a norm is an essential process for the interaction between different agents (human or artificial) in normative systems. Mainly because these systems take into consideration norms as the basis to specify and regulate the relevant behavior of the interacting agents [9]. This is especially important when we consider online communities in which different people with diverse profiles are easily connected with each other. In these cases, misunderstandings about the community norms may lead to interactions being unsuccessful. Thus, the goals of this research are: 1) to investigate the challenges associated with detecting when a norm is being violated by a certain member, usually due to a misunderstanding of the norm; and 2) to inform this member about the features of their action that triggered the violation, allowing the member to change their action to be in accordance with the understanding of the community, thus helping the interactions to keep running smoothly. To tackle these goals, our main contribution is to provide a framework capable of detecting norm violation and informing the violator of why their action triggered a violation detection.

The proposed framework is using data, that belongs to a specific community, to train a Machine Learning (ML) model that can detect norm violation. We

© Springer Nature Switzerland AG 2022
A. Theodorou et al. (Eds.): COINE 2021, LNAI 13239, pp. 127–142, 2022.
https://doi.org/10.1007/978-3-031-16617-4_9

chose this approach based on studies showing that the definition of what is norm violation can be highly contextual, thus it is necessary to consider what a certain community defines as norm violation or expected behavior [2,4,16].

To investigate norm violations, this work is specifically interested in norms that govern online interactions, and we use the Wikipedia community as a testbed, focusing on the article editing actions. This area of research is not only important due to the high volume of interactions that happen on Wikipedia, but also for the proper inclusion and treatment of diverse people in these online interactions. For instance, studies show that, when a system fails to detect norm violations (e.g., hate speech or gender, sexual and racial discrimination), the interactions are damaged, thus impacting the way people interact in the community [8,11].

Previous works have dealt with norms and normative systems, proposing mechanisms for norm conflict detection [1], norm synthesis [12], norm violation on Wikipedia [3,17] and other online communities, such as Stack Overflow [5] and Reddit [4]. However, our approach differs mainly in three points: 1) implementing an ML model that allows for the interpretation of the reasons leading to detecting norm violation; 2) incorporating a taxonomy to better explain to the violator which features of their actions triggered the norm violation, based on the results provided by our ML model; and 3) codifying actions in order to represent them through a set of features acquired from previous knowledge about the domain, which is necessary for the above two points. Concerning the last point, we note that our framework does not consider the action as is, but a representation of that action in terms of features and the relation of those features to norm violation (as learned by the applied ML model). For the Wikipedia case, we represent the action of editing articles based on the categorization introduced in [17], with features such as: the measure of profane words, the measure of pronouns, and the measure of Wiki syntax/markup (the details of these are later presented in Sect. 4.2).

To build our proposed framework, this work investigates the combination of two main algorithms: 1) the Logistic Model Tree, the algorithm responsible for classifying an article edit as a violation or not; and 2) the K-Means, the clustering algorithm responsible for grouping the features that are most relevant for detecting a violation. The information about the relevant features is then used to navigate the taxonomy and get a simplified taxonomy of these relevant features.

Our experiments describe how the ML model was built based on the training data provided by Wikipedia, and the results of applying this model to the task of vandalism detection in Wikipedia's article edits illustrate how our approach can reach a precision of 78,1% and a recall of 63,8%. Besides, the results also show that our framework can provide information about the specific group of features that affect the probability of an action being considered a violation, and we make use of this information to provide feedback to the user on their actions.

The remainder of this paper is divided as follows. Section 2 presents the basic mechanisms used by our proposed framework. Section 3 describes our framework, while Sect. 4 presents its application to the Wikipedia edits use case, and Sect. 5 presents our experiment and its results. The related literature is presented in Sect. 6. We then describe our conclusions and future work in Sect. 7.

2   Background

This section aims to present the base concepts upon which this work is built. We first start with the description of the taxonomy, which we intend to use to formalize a community's knowledge about the features of the actions. Next, we describe the ML algorithms applied to build our framework. First, the Logistic Model Tree (LMT) algorithm, which is used to build the model responsible for detecting possible vandalism; and second, the K-Means algorithm, responsible for grouping the features of the action that are most relevant for detecting violation.

2.1   Taxonomy for Action Representation

In the context of our work, an action (executed by a user in an online community) is represented by a set of features. Each of these features describes one aspect of the action being executed, i.e., the composing parts of the action. The goal of adopting this approach is to equip our system with an adaptive aspect, since by modelling an action as a set of features allows the system to deal with different kinds of actions (in different domains). For example, we could map the action of participating in an online meeting by features, such as: amount of time present in the meeting; volume of message exchange; and rate of interaction with other participants. Besides, in the context of norm violation, the proposed approach can use these features to explain which aspects of an action were problematic.

Defining an action through its features gives information about different aspects of the action that might have triggered a violation. However, it is still necessary to find a way to present this information to the violators. The idea is that this information must be provided in a human-readable way, allowing the users to understand what that feature means and how different features are related to each other. With these requirements in mind, we propose the use of a taxonomy to present this data. This classification scheme provides relevant information about concepts of a complex domain in a structured way [7], thus handling the requirements of our solution.

We note that, in this work, the focus is not on *building* a taxonomy of features. Instead, we assume that the taxonomy is provided with their associated norms. Our system uses this taxonomy, navigating it to select the relevant features. The violator is then informed about the features (presented as a subsection of the larger taxonomy) that triggered the violation detected by our model.

2.2   Logistic Model Tree

With respect to the domain of detecting norm violations in online communities, interpreting the ML model is an important aspect to consider. Thus, if a community is interested in providing the violator with information about the features of their action that are indicative of violation, then the proposed solution needs to work with a model that can correctly identify these problematic features.

In this work, we are interested in supervised learning, which is the ML task of finding a map between the input and the output. Several algorithms exist that implement the concepts of supervised learning, e.g., artificial neural networks and tree induction. We are most concerned with the ability of these algorithms to generate interpretable outputs, i.e., how the model explains the reasons for taking a certain decision. As such, the algorithm we chose that contains this characteristic is the tree induction algorithm.

The ability to interpret the tree induction model is provided by the way a path is defined in this technique (basically a set of *if-then* statements), which allows our model to find patterns in the data, present the path followed by the model and consequently provide the reasons that lead to that conclusion.

Although induction trees have been a popular approach to solve classification problems, this algorithm also presents some disadvantages. This has prompted Landwehr et al. [10] to propose the Logistic Model Tree (LMT) algorithm, which adds logistic regression functions at the leaves of the tree.

In logistic regression, there are two types of variables: the independent and the dependent variables. The goal is to find a model able to describe the effects of the independent variables on the dependent ones. In our context, the output of the model is responsible for predicting the probability of an action being classified as norm violation.

Dealing with odds is an interesting aspect present in logistic regression, since the increase in a certain variable indicates how the odds changes for the classification output, in this case the odds indicate the effect of the independent variables on the dependent ones. Besides, another important aspect is the equivalence of the natural log of the odds ratio and the linear function of the independent variables, represented by Eq. 1:

$$ln(\frac{p}{1-p}) \leftarrow \beta_0 + \beta_1 x_1 \tag{1}$$

where ln is the logarithm of the odds ratio, p [0,1] is the probability of an event occurring. β represents the parameters of the model, in our case the weights for features of the action. After calculating the natural logarithm, we can then use the inverse of the function to get our estimated regression equation:

$$\hat{p} \leftarrow \frac{\epsilon^{\beta_0 + \beta_1 x_1}}{1 + \epsilon^{\beta_0 + \beta_1 x_1}} \tag{2}$$

where $\hat{p}$ is the probability estimated by the regression model.

With these characteristics of logistic regression, we can see how this technique can be used to highlight attributes (independent variables) that have relevant influence over the output of the classifier probability.

Landwehr et al. [10] demonstrate how neither of the two algorithms described above (Tree Induction and Logistic Regression) is better than the other. Thus, to tackle the issues present in these two algorithms, LMT adds to the leaves of the tree a logistic regression function.

Figure 1 presents the description of a tree generated by the LMT algorithm. With a similar process as the standard decision tree, the LMT algorithm obtains a probability estimation as follow: first, the feature is compared to the value associated with that node. This step is repeated until the algorithm has reached a leaf node, when the exploration is completed. Then the logistic regression function determines the probabilities for the class, as described by Eq. 2.

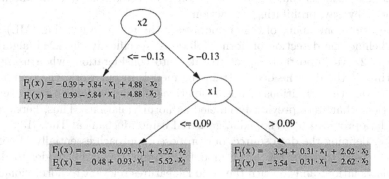

Fig. 1. An example of a tree built by the LMT algorithm [10]. X_1 and X_2 are features present in the dataset. F_1 and F_2 are the equations found by the logistic regression model, describing the weights for each feature present in the training dataset.

2.3 K-Means Clustering Method

K-Means is a clustering algorithm with the goal of finding a number K of clusters in the observed data, attempting to group the most 'similar' data points together. This algorithm has been used successfully in different applications, such as feature learning [15] and computer vision [20]. To achieve this goal, K-Means clusters the data using the nearest mean to the cluster center (calculating the squared Euclidean distance), thus reducing the variance within the group [14].

In this work, the K-Means algorithm can be used to group the features that may indicate an action as violation (we use the features' weights multiplied by their input values as indication of relevance for the classification probability). First, after detecting a possible violation, the ML model provides the K-Means algorithm with the set of features present in the logistic regression and their associated values (the input multiplied by the weight). Then, based on the values of these features, the algorithm is responsible for separating the features in two groups: 1) those that our model found with highest values, i.g., the most relevant for the vandalism classification; and 2) those with the lowest values, e.g., less relevant for the vandalism classification. Lastly, the output of K-Means informs the framework which are the most relevant features for detecting violations (i.e. the first group), which the framework can then use to navigate the taxonomy and present a selected simplified taxonomy of relevant features to the violator.

3   Framework for Norm Violation Detection (FNVD)

This section presents the main contribution of our work, the framework for norm violation detection (FNVD). The goal of this framework is to be deployed in a normative system so that when a violation is detected, the system can enforce the norms by, say, prohibiting the action.

The main component of our framework is the machine learning (ML) algorithm behind the detection of norm violations, specifically the LMT algorithm of Sect. 2.2. An important aspect to take into consideration, when using this algorithm, is the data needed to train the model. In our work, the community must provide the definitions of norm violations through a dataset that exemplifies actions that were previously labeled as norm violations. Thus, here we are using data provided by Wikipedia, gathered using Mechanical Turk [13].

After defining the data source, our proposed approach essentially 1) collects the data used to train the LMT model; 2) trains the LMT model to detect possible violations and to learn the action's features relevant to norm violations; and 3) when violations are detected, according to the LMT model's results, then the action responsible for the violation is rejected and the violator is informed about the features of their action that triggered the model output. Furthermore, in both cases (when actions are labelled as violating norms or not), we suggest that the framework collects feedback from the members of the community, which can then be used as new data to retrain the ML model. This is important as we strongly believe that communities and their members evolve, and what may be considered a norm violation today might not be in the future. For example, imagine a norm that states that hate speech is not allowed. Agreeing on the features of hate speech may change from one group of people to another and may also change over time. Consider the evaluation of the N-word, which is usually seen as a serious racial offense and can automatically be considered a text that violates the "no hate speech" norm. However, imagine a community of African Americans frequently saluting each other with the phrase "Wussup nigga" and the ML model classifying their text as hate speech. Clearly, human communities do not always have one clear definition of concepts like hate speech, violation, freedom of speech, etc. The framework, as such, must have a mechanism to adapt to the views of the members of its community, as well as adapt to the views that may change over time. While we leave the adaptation part for future work, we highlight its need in this section, and prepare the framework to deal with such adaptions, as we illustrate in Fig. 2.

To further clarify how our framework would act to detect a norm violation when deployed in a community, it is essential to explore the diagram in Fig. 2. Step 0 represents the training process of the LMT model, which is a fundamental part of our approach because it is in this moment that the rules for norm violation

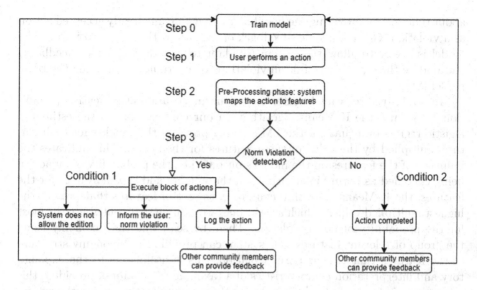

Fig. 2. How the framework works when deployed in an online community.

are specified. Basically, after training the model, our framework would have identified a set of rules that describe norm violation. We can portray these rules as a conjunction of two elements: 1) the tree that is built by the LMT algorithm on top of the collected data; and 2) the weights presented in the leaves of the tree. These weights are the parameters of the estimated regression equation that defines the probability of norm violation (depicted in Eq. 2). With the trained LMT model, the system starts monitoring every new action performed in the community (Step 1). In Step 2, the system maps the action to features that the community defined as descriptive of that action, which triggers the LMT model to start working to detect if that action is violating (or not) any of the norms. Step 3 presents the two different paths that can be executed by our system. If the action is detected as violating a norm (Condition 1), then we argue that the system must execute a sequence of steps to guarantee that the community norms are not violated: 1) the system does not allow the action to persist (i.e., action is not executed); 2) the system presents to the user information about which action features were the most relevant for our model to detect the norm violation, and the taxonomy of the relevant features is presented; 3) the action is logged by the system, allowing other community members to give feedback about the edit attempt, thus providing the possibility of these members flagging the action as a non-violation. The feedback collected from the users can later be used to continuously train (Step 0) our LMT model (future work). However, if the executed action is not detected as violating a norm (Condition 2), then the system can proceed as follows. The action persists in the system (i.e., action is executed), and since any model may incorrectly classify some norm violation as non-violation, the system allows the members of the community to give feedback about that action, providing the possibility of flagging an already accepted action as a violation. Getting people's feedback on violations that go unnoticed by the model is a way to allow the system to adapt to new data (people's feedback) and update the definitions of norm violations by continuously training the LMT model (Step 0).

To obtain the relevant features for the norm violation classification (Condition 1), we use the K-Means algorithm. In our context, due to the estimated logistic regression equation, the LMT model provides the weights for each feature multiplied by the value of these features for the action. This indicates the influence of the features on the model's output (i.e., the probability of an action being classified as norm violation). With the weights and specific values for the features, the K-Means algorithm can group the set of features that present the highest multiplied values, which are the ones we assume that contribute the most for the probability of norm violation. Then, by searching the taxonomy using the group of relevant features, our system can provide the taxonomy structure of the features that trigger norm violation, this is useful due to the explanatory and interpretation characteristics of a taxonomy. The aim of providing this information is to clarify to the member of the community performing the action, what are the problematic aspects of their action as learned by our model.

4   The Wikipedia Vandalism Detection Use Case

We focus on the problem of detecting vandalism in Wikipedia article edits. This use case is interesting because Wikipedia is an online community where norms such as 'no vandalism' may have different interpretations by different people. In what follows, we first present the use case's domain, followed by the taxonomy used by our system, and finally, an illustration of how our proposed framework may be applied to this use case.

4.1   Domain

Wikipedia [18] is an online encyclopedia, containing articles about different subjects in any area of knowledge. It is free to read and edit, thus any person with a device connected to the internet can access it and edit its articles. Due to the openness and collaborative structure of Wikipedia, the system is subject to different interpretations of what is the community's expectation concerning how content should be edited. To help address this issue, Wikipedia has compiled a set of rules, the Wikipedia norms [13], to maintain and organize its content.

Since we are looking for an automated solution for detecting norm violations by applying machine learning mechanisms, the availability of data becomes crucial. Wikipedia provides data on what edits are marked as vandalism, where vandalism annotations were provided by Amazon's Mechanical Turk. Basically, every article edit was evaluated by at least three people (Mechanical Turks) that decided whether the edit violates the 'no vandalism' norm or not. In the context of our work, the actions performed by the members of the community are the

Wikipedia users' attempts to edit articles, and the norm is *"Do not engage in vandalism behavior"* (which we refer to as the 'no vandalism' norm). It is this precise dataset that we have used to train the model that detects norm violations. We present an example of what is considered a vandalism in a Wikipedia article edit, where a user edited an article by adding the following text: *"Bugger all in the subject of health ect."*

4.2   Taxonomy Associated with Wikipedia's 'No Vandalism' Norm

An important step in our work is to map actions to features and then specify how they are linked to each other. We manually created a taxonomy to describe these features by separating them in categories that describe their relation with the action.[1] In this work, we consider the 58 features described in [17] and 3 more that were available in the provided dataset: LANG_MARKUP_IMPACT, the measure of the addition/removal of Wiki syntax/markup; LANG_EN_PROFANE_BIG and LANG_EN_PROFANE_BIG_IMPACT, the measure of addition/removal of English profane words. In the dataset, features ending with _IMPACT are normalized by the difference of the article size after edition. The main objective of this taxonomy is to help our system present to the violator an easy-to-read explanation of the reasons why their article edit was marked as violating a norm by our model, specifying the features with highest influence to trigger this violation.

To further explain our taxonomy approach, we present in Fig. 3 the constructed taxonomy for Wikipedia's 'no vandalism' norm. We observe that features can be divided in four main groups. The first is user's direct actions, which represent aspects of the user's article editing action, e.g., adding a text. This group is further divided in four sub-groups: a) written edition, which contains features about the text itself that is being edited by the user; b) comment on the edition, which contains features about the comments that users have left on that edition; c) article after edition, which contains features about how the edited article changed after the edition was completed; and d) time of edition, which contains features about the time when the user made their edition. The second group is the user's profile, general information about the user. The third is the page's history, how the article changed with past editions. The last group is reversions, which is essentially information on past reversions.[2] In total, these groups have 61 features, but due to simplification purpose, Table 1 only presents a subset of those features.

4.3   FNVD Applied to Wikipedia Vandalism Detection

It this section, we first describe an example of how our framework can be configured to be deployed in the Wikipedia community. First, the community provides the features and the taxonomy describing that feature space (see Fig. 3). Then,

---

[1] For the complete taxonomy, the reader can refer to https://bit.ly/3sQFhQz.

[2] A reversion is when an article is reverted back to a version before the vandalism occurred.

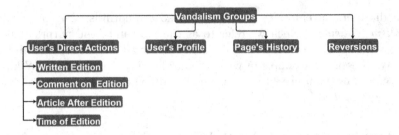

Fig. 3. Taxonomy associated with Wikipedia's 'no vandalism' norm.

Table 1. Example of Features present in the taxonomy groups.

Group	Features
Written edition	LANG_ALL_ALPHA; LANG_EN_PRONOUN
Comment on edition	COMM_LEN; COMM_LEN_NO_SECT
Article after edition	SIZE_CHANGE_RESULT; SIZE_CHANGE_CHARS
Time of edition	TIME_TOD; TIME_DOW
User's profile	HIST_REP_COUNTRY; USER_EDITS_DENSITY
Page's history	PAGE_AGE; WT_NO_DELAY
Reversions	HASH_REVERTED; HASH_IP_REVERT

our framework trains the LMT model to classify norm violations based on the data provided (Step 0 of Fig. 2), which must contain examples of what that community understands as norm violation and regular behavior.

In the context of vandalism detection on Wikipedia, the relevant actions performed by the members of the community are the attempts to edit Wikipedia articles. Following the diagram in Fig. 2, when a user attempts to edit an article (Step 1), our system will analyze this edit. We note here that our proposed LMT model does not work with the action itself, but the features that describe it. As such, it is necessary to first find the features that represent the performed action. Thus, in Step 2, there is a pre-processing phase responsible for mapping actions to the features associated to the norm in question. For example, an article about Asteroid was edited with the addition of the text *"i like man!!"*. After getting this edition text, the system can compute the values (as described in [17]) for the 61 features, which are used to calculate the vandalism probability. For brevity reasons, we only show the values for some of these features:

1. LANG_ALL_ALPHA, the percentage of text which is alphabetic: 0,615385;
2. WT_NO_DELAY, the calculated WikiTrust score: 0,731452;
3. HIST_REP_COUNTRY, measure of how users from the same country as the editor behaved: 0,155146.

After calculating the values for all features, the LMT model can evaluate if this article edit is considered 'vandalism' or not. In the case of detecting vandalism (Condition 1 of Fig. 2), the system does not allow the edition to be recorded on the Wikipedia article, and it presents to the violator two inputs. The first is the set of features of their edit that have the highest influence on the model's decision to detect the vandalism. To get this set, after calculating the probability of vandalism (as depicted in Eq. 2), the LMT model provides the features that present a positive relationship with the output. These 'positive features' are then used by K-Means to create the group with the most relevant ones (Table 2 presents an example of this process). The second input is the selected part of the taxonomy related to chosen set of features, providing further explanation of those features that triggered the norm violation. Additionally, the system will log the attempt to edit the article, which eventually may trigger feedback collection that can at a later stage be used to retrain our model.

Table 2. List of features that positively affects the probability of vandalism detection. Total Value is the multiplication between the feature's values and the features' weights. The most relevant features, as found by K-Means, are marked with an (*).

Features	Total value
WT_NO_DELAY*	1.08254896
HIST_REP_COUNTRY*	0.899847
LANG_ALL_ALPHA*	0.7261543
HASH_REC_DIVERSITY	0.15714292
WT_DELAYED	0.12748878
LANG_ALL_CHAR_REP	0.12
HIST_REP_ARTICLE	0.093548

The features WT_NO_DELAY, $HIST\_REP\_COUNTRY$ and $LANG\_ALL$ $\_ALPHA$ were indicated by K-Means as the most relevant for the classification of vandalism. With this information, our framework can search the taxonomy for the relevant features and then automatically retrieve the simplified taxonomy structure for these three specific features, as shown in Fig. 4.

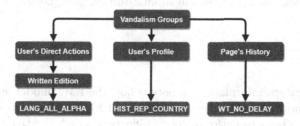

Fig. 4. Taxonomy for part of the features that were most relevant for the vandalism classification. These features are then presented to the user with a descriptive text.

However, in case the system classifies the article edit as 'non-vandalism' (Condition 2 of Fig. 2), the Wikipedia article is updated according to the user's article edit and community members may provide feedback on this new article edit, which may later be used to retrain our model (as explained in Sect. 3).

5   Experiments and Results

The goal of this section is to describe how the proposed approach was applied for detecting norm violation in the domain of Wikipedia article edits, with an initial attempt to improve the interactions in online communities. Then, we demonstrate and discuss the results achieved.

5.1   Experiments

Data on vandalism detection in Wikipedia articles [17] were used for the experiments. This dataset has 61 features and 32,439 instances for training (with 2,394 examples of vandalism editions and 30,045 examples of regular editions). The model was trained with WEKA [19] and evaluated using 10 folds cross-validation.

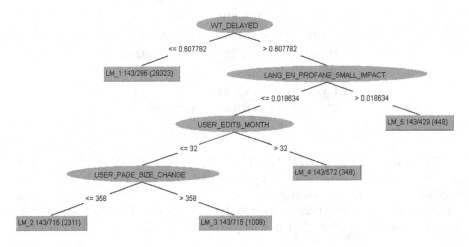

Fig. 5. The built model for the vandalism detection, using Logistic Model Tree.

5.2   Results

The first important information to note is how the LMT model performs when classifying vandalism in Wikipedia editions. In Fig. 5, it is possible to see the model that was built to perform the classification task.[3] The tree has four decision nodes and five leaves in total. Since the LMT model uses logistic regression

---

[3] Trained model available at: https://bit.ly/3gBBkwP.

at the leaves, the model has five different estimated logistic regression equations, each of these equations outputs' the probability of an edition being a vandalism.

The LMT model correctly classifies 96% of instances in general. However, when we separate the results in two groups, vandalism editions and regular editions, it is possible to observe a difference in the model's performance. For the regular editions, the LMT model achieves a precision of 97,2%, and a recall of 98,6%. While for vandalism editions, the performance of the model drops, with a precision of 78,1% and a recall of 63,8%. This decrease can be explained by how the dataset was separated and the number of vandalism instances, which consequently leads to an unbalanced dataset. In the dataset, the total number of vandalism instances is 2,394 and the other 30,045 instances are of regular editions. A better balance between the number of vandalism editions and regular edition should improve our classifier, thus in the future we are exploring other model configurations (e.g., ensemble models) to handle data imbalance.

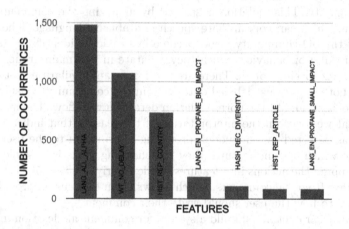

Fig. 6. Number of occurrences of relevant features in vandalism detection.

The influence of each feature on determining the probability of a norm violation is provided by the LMT model (as assumed in this work, feature influence is model specific, meaning that a different model can find a different set of relevant features). The graph in Fig. 6 shows the number of times a feature is classified as relevant by the built model. Some features appear in most of the observations, indicating how important they are to detect vandalism. Future work shall investigate if this same behavior (some features present in the actions have more influence than other features to define the norm violation probability) can be detected in other domains.

"LANG_ALL_ALPHA" recurrently appears as relevant when vandalism is detected. This happens because this feature presents, as estimated by the LMT model, a positive relationship with the norm violation, meaning that when a vandalism edition is detected, this feature is usually relevant for the classification.

6   Related Work

In this section, we present the most relevant works related to that reported in this paper. Specifically, we reference the relevant literature that uses ML solutions to learn the meaning of a violation, then use that to detect violations in online communities. In addition to the specific works presented below, it is also worth to mention a survey that studies a variety of research in the area, focusing on norm violation detection in the domains of hate speech and cyberbullying [2].

Also investigating norm violation in Wikipedia but using the dataset from the comments on talk page edits, Anand and Eswari [3] present a Deep Learning (DL) approach to classify a comment as abusive or not. Although the use of DL is an interesting approach to norm violation detection, we focus on offering interpretability, i.e., providing features our model found as relevant for the detection of norm violation. While the DL model in [3] does not provide such information.

The work by Cherian et al. [5] explores norm violation on the Stack Overflow (SO) community. This violation is studied by analyzing the comments posted on the site, which can contain hate speech and abusive language. The authors state that the SO community could become less toxic by identifying and minimizing this kind of behavior, which they separate in two main groups: generic norms and SO specific norms. There are two important similarities between our works: 1) both studies use labeled dataset from the community, considering the relevant context; and 2) the norm violation detection workflow. The main difference is that we focus on the interpretation of the reasons that indicate a norm violation as detected by our model, providing information to the user so they can decide which specific features they are changing. This is possible because we are mapping the actions into features, while Cheriyan at al. [5] work directly with the text from the comments, which allows them to focus on providing text alternatives to how the user should write their comment.

Chandrasekaran et al. [4] build a system for comment moderation in Reddit, named Crossmod. Crossmod is described as a sociotechnical moderation system designed using participatory methods (interview with Reddit moderators). To detect norm violation, Crossmod uses a ML back-end, formed by an ensemble of classifiers. Since there is an ensemble of classifiers, the ML back-end was trained using the concept of cross-community learning, which uses data from different communities to detect violation in a specific target community. Like our work, Crossmod uses labeled data from the community to train the classifiers and the norm violation detection workflow follows the same pattern. However, different from our approach, Chandrasekaran et al. [4] use textual data directly, not mapping to features. Besides, Crossmod do not provide to the user information on the parts of the action that triggered the violation classifier.

Considering another type of ML algorithm, Di Capua et al. [6] build a solution based on Natural Language Processing (NLP) and Self-Oganizing Map (SOM) to automatically detect bullying behavior on social networks. The authors decided to use an unsupervised learning algorithm because they wanted to avoid the manual work of labeling the data, the assumption is that the dataset is huge and by avoiding manual labelling, they would also avoid imposing a priori bias about the possible classes. This differs from our assumptions since we regard the data/feedback from the community as the basis to deal with norm violation.

One interesting aspect about these studies is that they are either in the realm of hate speech or cyberbullying, which can be understood as a sub-group of norm violation by formalizing hate speech and cyberbullying in terms of norms that a community should adhere to. Researchers are interested in these fields mainly due to the damage that violating these norms can cause in the members of an online community, and due to the available data to study these communities.

7   Conclusion and Future Work

The proposed framework, combining machine learning (Logistic Model Trees and K-Means) and taxonomy exploration, is an initial approach on how to detect norm violations. In this paper, we focused on the issue of norm violation assuming violations may occur due to misunderstandings of norms originated by the diverse ways people interpret norms in an online community. To study norm violation, our work used a dataset from Wikipedia's vandalism edition, which contains data about Wikipedia article edits that were considered vandalism.

The framework described in this work is a first step towards detecting vandalism, and it provides relevant information about the problems (features) of the action that led to vandalism. Further investigation is still needed to get a measure of how our system would improve the interactions in an online community. The experiments conducted in our work show that our ML model has a precision of 78,1% and a recall of 63,8% when classifying data describing vandalism.

Future work is going to focus on the use of feedback from the community members to continuously train our ML model, as explained in Sect. 3. The idea is to apply an online training approach to our framework, so when a community behavior changes, that would be taken to indicate a new view on the rules defining the norm, and our ML model should adapt to this new view.

Throughout this investigation, we have noticed that the literature mostly deals with norm violation that focus either on hate speech or cyberbullying. We aim that our approach can be applied to other domains (not only textual), thus we are planning to explore domains with different actions to analyze how our framework deals with a different context (since these domains would have a different set of actions to be executed in an online community).

Acknowledgements. This research has received funding from the European Union's Horizon 2020 FET Proactive project "WeNet - The Internet of us", grant agreement No 823783, as well as the RecerCaixa 2017 funded "AppPhil" project.

References

1. Aires, J.P., Monteiro, J., Granada, R., Meneguzzi, F.: Norm conflict identification using vector space offsets. In: IJCNN, pp. 1–8 (2018)

142   T. Freitas dos Santos et al.

2. Al-Hassan, A., Al-Dossari, H.: Detection of hate speech in social networks: a survey on multilingual corpus. In: 6th International Conference on Computer Science and Information Technology, pp. 83–100 (2019)
3. Anand, M., Eswari, R.: Classification of abusive comments in social media using deep learning. In: 2019 3rd International Conference on Computing Methodologies and Communication (ICCMC), pp. 974–977 (2019)
4. Chandrasekharan, E., Gandhi, C., Mustelier, M.W., Gilbert, E.: Crossmod: a cross-community learning-based system to assist reddit moderators. In: Proceedings of ACM Human-Computer Interaction, vol. 3(CSCW) (2019)
5. Cheriyan, J., Savarimuthu, B.T.R., Cranefield, S.: Norm violation in online communities-a study of stack overflow comments. arXiv preprint arXiv:2004.05589 (2020)
6. Di Capua, M., Di Nardo, E., Petrosino, A.: Unsupervised cyber bullying detection in social networks. In: ICPR, pp. 432–437 (2016)
7. Fiedler, K.D., Grover, V., Teng, J.T.: An empirically derived taxonomy of information technology structure and its relationship to organizational structure. J. Manag. Inf. Syst. 13(1), 9–34 (1996)
8. Gray, K.L.: Gaming out online: black lesbian identity development and community building in xbox live. J. Lesbian Stud. 22(3), 282–296 (2018)
9. Jones, A.J., Sergot, M., et al.: On the characterisation of law and computer systems: the normative systems perspective. In: Deontic Logic in Computer Science: Normative System Specification, pp. 275–307 (1993)
10. Landwehr, N., Hall, M., Frank, E.: Logistic model trees. Mach. Learn. 59(1–2), 161–205 (2005)
11. McLean, L., Griffiths, M.D.: Female gamers' experience of online harassment and social support in online gaming: a qualitative study. Int. J. Mental Health Addict. 17(4), 970–994 (2019)
12. Morales, J., Wooldridge, M., Rodríguez-Aguilar, J.A., López-Sánchez, M.: Off-line synthesis of evolutionarily stable normative systems. Auton. Agents Multi-agent Syst. 32(5), 635–671 (2018)
13. Potthast, M., Holfeld, T.: Overview of the 1st international competition on wikipedia vandalism detection. In: CLEF (2010)
14. Rai, P., Singh, S.: A survey of clustering techniques. Int. J. Comput. Appl. 7(12), 1–5 (2010)
15. Rubaiat, S.Y., Rahman, M.M., Hasan, M.K.: Important feature selection accuracy comparisons of different machine learning models for early diabetes detection. In: International Conference on Innovation in Engineering and Technology, pp. 1–6 (2018)
16. van der Torre, L.: Contextual deontic logic: normative agents, violations and independence. Ann. Math. Artif. Intell 37(1–2), 33–63 (2003)
17. West, A.G., Lee, I.: Multilingual vandalism detection using language-independent & ex post facto evidence. In: CLEF Notebooks (2011)
18. Wikipedia contributors: Wikipedia — Wikipedia, the free encyclopedia (2021). https://en.wikipedia.org/wiki/Wikipedia. Accessed 22 Feb 2021
19. Witten, I.H., Frank, E., Hall, M.A.: The WEKA workbench. In: Data Mining: Practical Machine Learning Tools and Techniques, pp. 403–406. Morgan Kaufmann (2011)
20. Zheng, X., Lei, Q., Yao, R., Gong, Y., Yin, Q.: Image segmentation based on adaptive k-means algorithm. EURASIP J. Image Video Process. 2018(1), 1–10 (2018)

Solving Social Dilemmas by Reasoning About Expectations

Abira Sengupta[1](✉), Stephen Cranefield[1](✉), and Jeremy Pitt[2]

[1] University of Otago, Dunedin, New Zealand
abira.sengupta@postgrad.otago.ac.nz, stephen.cranefield@otago.ac.nz
[2] Imperial College London, London, UK
j.pitt@imperial.ac.uk

Abstract. It has been argued that one role of social constructs, such as institutions, trust and norms, is to coordinate the expectations of autonomous entities in order to resolve collective action situations (such as collective risk dilemmas) through the coordination of behaviour. While much work has addressed the formal representation of these social constructs, in this paper we focus specifically on the formal representation of, and associated reasoning with, the expectations themselves. In particular, we investigate how explicit reasoning about expectations can be used to encode both traditional game theory solution concepts and social mechanisms for the social dilemma situation. We use the Collective Action Simulation Platform (CASP) to model a collective risk dilemma based on a flood plain scenario and show how using expectations in the reasoning mechanisms of the agents making decisions supports the choice of cooperative behaviour.

Keywords: Collective action · Social dilemmas · Event calculus · Expectations

1 Introduction

Collective action takes place when a group of people come together to act in certain ways that will benefit the group as a whole [17]. People have different characteristics—some are more willing to achieve collective benefits rather than their own. In addition, social norms [21], reputation, trust and reciprocity motivate individuals to cooperate [22]. Collective action often fails when individuals are not interested in cooperating or coordinating with each other because there is a conflict between self-interest and collective interest. Thus, individuals pursue their own interests rather than long-term cooperation [20] and ultimately no benefit of collective action occurs [8]. For example, the free-rider problem is a type of social dilemma. A free-rider is someone, who can access a collective benefit without contributing or incurring any cost [3,11].

Collective action or social dilemmas are well-known problems, which have been analysed in many studies using the method of game theory. Simple game

© Springer Nature Switzerland AG 2022
A. Theodorou et al. (Eds.): COINE 2021, LNAI 13239, pp. 143–159, 2022.
https://doi.org/10.1007/978-3-031-16617-4_10

theory models of social dilemmas predict that cooperation is not rational. However, human society suggests that cooperation can occur due to psychological and social motivations such as benevolence and social norms [2], internal motivations (e.g. altruism, fairness norms), rational expectations (e.g. focal points), and social choice mechanisms (e.g. voting and bargaining) [13].

Game theory is predicated on solution concepts such as the Nash Equilibrium. This becomes complex to reason about for a large number of agents and does not seem realistic as a method of human reasoning. In particular, there is a lack of consideration of the (bounded) reasoning processes that can lead community members to participate in collective action [27].

Unlike game theory, which assumes that the problem has already been encoded into a concise representation based on payoffs, we aim to develop a *generic* computational mechanism that can be customised to individual problems by using explicit representations of social knowledge. We posit that this knowledge can often be encoded in the form of expectations, and thus wish to investigate the role of social expectations in agent-reasoning mechanisms when faced with collective action problems. Here we investigate how agents might explicitly reason about social knowledge to generate cooperative behaviour in social dilemma situations.

Game theoretic approaches require the agent to understand the strategic structure of the 'game' in the form of matrix (for a normal form game) or tree (for extended form of game) [24]. For simple standard forms of games (e.g., the Prisoner's Dilemma) it is reasonable to assume that an agent can infer the game structure and payoffs. However, while various forms of expectation have been modelled using game theory, for example, the Confidence game [10], where payoffs depend on agents' beliefs that represent expectations, the plain-plateau scenario [14], where a credible commitments creates an expectation, and the Bravery game [10], where bold and timid decision-making creates expectations, we think these are less amenable to a utility-based encoding inferred by an agent (rather than a programmer).

As an alternative, or additional, form of reasoning, we believe that maintaining explicit representations of expectations, and their fulfilment and violation, will allow *generic* (scenario-specific) reasoning mechanisms to be developed, such as those discussed here: the selection between alternative game structures based on credible commitments (Sect. 2) and moving away from utilities in favour of agent strategies that choose between expectation-violating and non-expectation-violating actions (Sect. 5).

Social expectations can play an important role in allowing cooperation to occur [6]. In this area, Pitt et al. have developed a computational model for self-governance of common-pool resources based on Ostrom's principles [25]. Ostrom and Ahn [23] also investigated three forms of social mechanisms that seem to foster cooperation in collective action problems: those forms are trustworthiness, social network connections and the observed conformance.

To investigate the use of reasoning about expectations to resolve a social dilemma, we model the plain-plateau scenario using the Collective Action

Simulation Platform (CASP) [6] and demonstrate how its support for expectation-based reasoning allows cooperation to take place in this scenario.

The structure of this paper is as follows. In Sect. 2 we describe the plain-plateau scenario. Section 3 highlights the related concepts and platform. Section 4 describes the modelling of the plain-plateau scenario using CASP. Section 5 describes the norm-based solution to the plain-plateau scenario. The outline of a potential team reasoning approach to the plain-plateau scenario is discussed in Sect. 6. Section 7 discusses future work and concludes the paper.

2   The Plain-Plateau Scenario

Klein [14] introduced a scenario that we refer to as the plain-plateau scenario. In this scenario, the objective of the author was to show how it can be rational for a government to restrict its future choices. The scenario models a society where people can choose to live in a river plain where they can access water easily; otherwise, they can live on a plateau. When living in the river plain, there is a risk of flooding. The government's objective is to maximize the collective utility of the citizens. Klein models each citizen's utility as a concave (logarithmic) function of their wealth and house value. Therefore in this scenario when the government has full discretionary power (the "discretionary regime"), there is common knowledge that it is in the government's best interest to compensate citizens whose houses have flood damage by taxing citizens living on the plateau. Thus, citizens who live in the flood plain and suffer due to flood damage can expect to be bailed out by the government. Klein shows that this leads to a prisoner's dilemma game between the citizens, where choosing the plateau is cooperation and choosing the plain is defection.

To avoid the prisoner's dilemma situation, the government can adopt the "rule-based regime" where it removes its own discretionary ability to provide compensation. This can be seen as a binding announcement that the government will not bail out any citizens who have flood damage. In this case, the government will have no reason to tax citizens who are living on the plateau. Therefore, this announcement avoids the prisoner's dilemma.

Sequence of Events. Figure 1 shows the occurrence of the events in the plain-plateau scenario. There are multiple rounds in which citizens choose where to live. Within each round, the events are as follows: 'receive income' is the first step, in which citizens receive wealth. The next step 'choose location' is when agents choose a location to live in (the scenario assumes that their houses can be easily moved). Next there is a possible flood occurrence with probability p. After a flood occurs, if the government has discretionary power then it will tax and compensate for flood damage; however, if the government is following the rule-based regime then there is no compensation. In the next step citizens can repair their houses if they have flood damage. Finally, citizens can consume the remaining money at the 'consume' step.

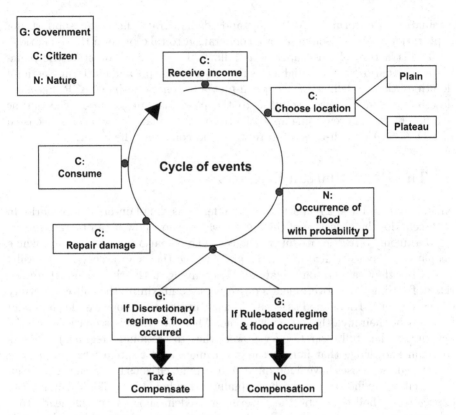

Fig. 1. Sequence of events in the plain-plateau scenario

Although the plain-plateau scenario is, in general, an n-person game, Klein models this as an extensive form game with two players [14] as illustrated in Fig. 2. This scenario involves the government and two citizens, citizen_1 and citizen_2, and two action choices, plain and plateau. In this figure, single arrows define the strategies under the rule-based regime and double arrows show strategies under the discretionary regime. At state 2, the decision nodes for citizen_2 form a single information state, i. e. citizen_2 is not aware of what choice was made by citizen_1. When under the full discretionary power of the government, citizens are better off to live on the plain as the government's rational choice is to redistribute income to compensate for damage. Given Klein's specific values for periodic income, house values on the plain and plateau, the probability of a flood, and the amount of flood damage, the government's payoff (social utility) is then 0.666. On the other hand when the government follows the rule-based regime, citizens are better to move to the plateau position and the government's payoff is 0.730.

A Nash equilibrium is "a set of strategies, one for each of the n players of a game, that has the property that each player's choice is his best response to the choices of the $n-1$ other players" [12]. It is interpreted as a potential stable point resulting from agents adjusting their behaviour to search for strategy

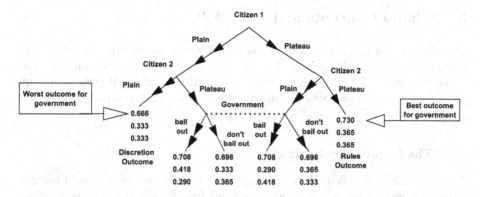

Fig. 2. Extensive form of plain-plateau game Payoffs are listed in the order: ruler, citizen_1, citizen_2. Single arrows show strategies under the rule-based regime. Double arrows show strategies under the discretionary-based regime, redraw from [14].

choices that will give them better results. In particular, a Nash equilibrium is a self-enforcing agreement, which does not need any external power, because due to self-interest, players will follow the agreement if others do.

The prisoner's dilemma game is a paradox in decision analysis, which shows why two completely rational individuals will not cooperate, even though they would be better off to do so if both of them made that choice [7]. In this game, the highest reward for each party occurs when both players choose to cooperate. However purely rational individuals in the prisoner's dilemma game will defect on each other [7]. Figure 3(a) shows that the discretionary power of the government leads to a prisoner's dilemma situation with the Nash equilibrium (plain, plain) and payoffs (0.333, 0.333) even though there will be no plateau-dweller for the government to tax. On the other hand, Fig. 3(b) shows that the expectation of citizens under the rule-based regime of the government changes the game to one with a different Nash value, (plateau, plateau) and the payoffs (0.365, 0.365).

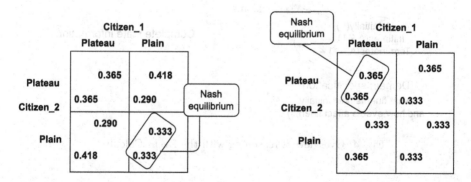

Fig. 3. (a) The prisoner's dilemma game under the discretionary regime and Nash equilibrium (plain, plain) and payoff (0.333, 0.333) [14]. (b) The game under the rule-based regime with Nash equilibrium (plateau, plateau) and payoff (0.365, 0.365)

3   Related Concepts and the CASP Platform

The objective of this study is to model and solve the social dilemmas based on the expectations of the agents. This section introduces relevant concepts and tools. We use the CASP platform which is an extension of the Repast Simphony agent-based simulation tool that incorporates an event calculus engine to reason about the physical and social effects of actions.

3.1   The Event Calculus (EC)

We use the Event Calculus to model the effects of events in the plain-plateau scenario—both physical (e.g. damage resulting from flooding) and social (e.g. the conditional expectation resulting from a government's credible commitment that in the case of flooding no bail-outs will occur). The Event Calculus (EC) is a logical language and deductive mechanism to model the effects of actions on information about the state of the world [6,15]. Figure 4 illustrates how the Event Calculus enables a form of reasoning known as temporal projection. This logical language refers to "what's true when given what happens when and what actions do" [28]. In the figure, the "what happened when" is a narrative of events (e.g. HappensAt(A,T)) and "what fluents hold initially" and "how events affect fluents" are represented by the vocabulary of the Event Calculus (e.g. Initially(F), Initiates(A,F,T) and Terminates(A,F,T)).

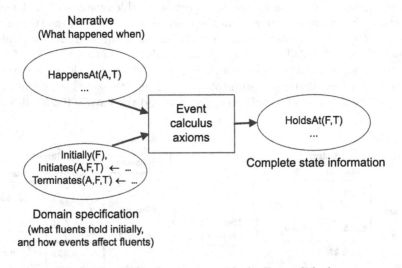

Fig. 4. Overview of reasoning with the Event Calculus

The Event Calculus models fluents and events. A fluent is a "quantity such as 'the temperature in the room' whose numerical value is subject to variation" [28]. In our work, fluents are Boolean, e.g. damage(Agent, Amount). The EC contains an inertia principle, which specifies that the value of a fluent remains the same until an event occurs that changes the value.

In this work, we have represented both physical state and social knowledge using a form of the Event Calculus that has discrete time steps [18]. Within the discrete time points we are able to assign labels to states. Moreover, the EC is extended with the notion of expectations, and their fulfilment and violation [5].

3.2   Expectations

An expectation is a future-directed belief that an agent has an active interest in monitoring [4]. Expectations may be inferred from obligations, commitments, credible announcements, experience, etc. For example, in a circus, a ringmaster may expect his acrobats to form a tower-shaped structure. He needs to know whether his expectation is true or not in future, because he has the liability to entertain the audience. In this scenario his belief about his acrobats creates his expectation.

We model expectations based on the logic of Cranefield [5]. We define a fluent $exp\_rule(Cond, Exp)$ to state the existence of a conditional rule of expectation: $Cond$ represents a condition on the past and present, and constraint Exp is an expectation regarding the future. If $Cond$ holds then the formula Exp is expected. $Cond$ and Exp are formed from fluents, event occurrences denoted $happ(Events)$, Boolean operators, and (for Exp only) Linear Temporal Logic operators e. g. $\bigcirc$ (next), $\Diamond$ (eventually) and $\Box$ (always). A fluent of the form @L can also be used to test if the current state is associated with the label L. We use labels to model the steps within each cycle in the plain-plateau scenario (e.g. 'receive income' and 'change location').

When the condition of an exp_rule fluent is true, the expectation Exp becomes active, denoted by a fluent $exp(Exp)$. An expectation records a state of affairs that is expected to occur, but may not. This will be considered fulfilled or violated if the expectation evaluates to true or (respectively) false in the current or a future state [26]. When this occurs, the Event Calculus engine asserts a *fulf* or *viol* event to the narrative. Exp may contain temporal operators, so its truth may not be known in the current state. However, it may be able to be partially evaluated. Suppose $exp(p \wedge \bigcirc q)$ holds in the current state (time t), i. e. $p \wedge \bigcirc q$ is expected where p and q are fluents. If p holds at t then at the next time point $t + 1$, the formula $exp(q)$ holds. In other words, q is expected to hold at $t + 1$.

Our Event Calculus implementation provides a *what-if* predicate that takes two alternative event lists (E1 and E2) as arguments and considers, in turn, what fluents and violation and fulfilment events would occur if each list of events were to occur at the current timepoint. It instantiates two output arguments: the consequences that will result from the occurrence of E1 but not E2, and those that will result from E2 but not E1. This can be used as a simple form of look-ahead to help an agent choose between two actions.

3.3   The Collective Action Simulation Platform (CASP)

To simulate agent decision-making with knowledge-based expectations, we use the Collective Action Simulation Platform (CASP), which is an extension of the Java-based Repast Simphony simulation platform [19]. This allows us to model the effects of actions using a version of the Discrete Event Calculus [18] implemented in Prolog. It is enhanced by the logic of expectations described above.

Agents can take on roles in an institution by asserting to Prolog that certain institution-related events have occurred: joining an institution, adding a role, changing roles and dropping a role. CASP detects these new events in the Event Calculus narrative, and loads a set of rules associated with each current role into a rule engine[1] associated with each agent. When the rule engine is run at the start of a simulation step, these rules recommend the actions that are relevant to the agent's current role, given the current state (as determined by the rules' conditions, which may query both the Event Calculus state and the agent's instance variables in Java). Then the agent can run scenario-specific code to select one of the actions to perform [6]. Both decisions may involve querying the current state recorded in the Event Calculus engine. In this work, we have modelled the plain-plateau scenario using CASP.[2]

4   Modelling the Plain-Plateau Scenario Using CASP

In this section of the paper, we investigate how expectation-based reasoning supports various stages of decision-making in the plain-plateau scenario.

Within the scenario we have two types of agents, Government and Citizen, and there are two institutions, Government and Citizens. The Citizens institution has roles Plain-dweller and Plateau-dweller, which determine the actions available to the agents in these two locations, plain and plateau. The Government institution has the roles Discretionary regime and Rule-based regime.

Information about the agents, their institutions, roles and their possible actions in the simulation is presented in Table 1. If the government has the rule-based regime role, then it will perform no action (and specifically no taxation and compensation). If the government has the discretionary regime role then its possible actions are to compensate citizens whose houses have been damaged due to flooding by taxing citizens who are living on the plateau. If a citizen has the role plateau-dweller, then the citizen can stay in that role or change to the plain-dweller role to stay in the plain. If a citizen changes role from plateau-dweller to plain-dweller and due to flooding gets damage, then he/she will repair their damage. On the other hand, when the citizen has the role plain-dweller after joining the institution, the citizen either can stay in that role or change to the plateau-dweller role to stay on the plateau. The physical effect of changing a

---

[1] https://github.com/maxant/rules.

[2] Source code can be found at https://github.com/abira-sengupta/casp-Plain_Plateau_2021.

Table 1. Roles and actions in the plain-plateau Scenario

Agent	Institution	Role	Possible actions
Government	Government	Rule-based regime	None
Government	Government	Discretionary regime	Tax and compensate
Citizen	Citizens	Plateau-dweller	Receive income, change role, consume, stay plain
Citizen	Citizens	Plain-dweller	Receive income, change role, repair, consume, stay plateau

villager's role is modelled by an Event Calculus rule that changes a "location" fluent. At the beginning of each cycle, a citizen receives income. The citizen can repair his/her damaged house, and in the end, the citizen can consume the remaining money.

Here are examples of the EC clauses used in the simulation:

```
initiates(join(government_agent, government, rulesbasedregimerole),
       exp_rule(damage(A,_), not(happ(compensate(A,_)))), _).
```

This EC clause states that if the government joins the institution government with the rule-based regime role then this creates an expectation rule, which says that if a citizen gets damage then there will be no compensation for that citizen.

```
initiates(receive_income(A,RMoney), wealth(A,NMoney), T) :-
    holdsAt(wealth(A,OMoney), T),
    NMoney is OMoney + RMoney.
```

This EC clause updates the wealth fluent for an agent when a receive_income event occurs. The income is added to the existing wealth.

```
initiates(change_role(A,citizens, _, citizens_plaindwellerrole),
        location(A,plain), T) :-
    holdsAt(member(A,citizens), T).

initiates(change_role(A, citizens, _, citizens_plateaudwellerrole),
        location(A,plateau), T) :-
    holdsAt(member(A,citizens), T).
```

These EC clauses define the scenario-specific effects of the change_role event for each citizen. Changing to the citizens_plaindwellerrole causes a citizen's location to change to the plain, and changing to citizens_plateaudwellerrole causes the location to change to the plateau.

```
initiates(flood, damage(A,D), T) :-
    holdsAt(location(A,plain), T),
    \+ holdsAt(damage(A,_), T),
```

```
flood_causes_damage(D).

initiates(flood, damage(A,D), T) :-
    holdsAt(damage(A,CD), T),
    initial_house_on_plain_value(V),
    flood_causes_damage(FD),
    D is min(FD + CD, V).

terminates(flood, damage(_,_), _).
```

These EC clauses, the flood event initiates damage for each citizen in the plain. If no damage already exists, a new damage fluent is created. If there is an existing damage fluent, the new fluent records the increased damage, up to the value of the house. Any existing damage fluent is terminated as it is now replaced with an updated one.

```
initiates(taxed(A,Tax), wealth(A,New), T) :-
    holdsAt(wealth(A,Old), T),
    New is Old - Tax.
```

This EC clause updates the wealth fluent for an agent when a taxed event occurs. The tax is deducted from the existing wealth.

```
initiates(compensate(A,Money), wealth(A,New), T) :-
    holdsAt(wealth(A,Old), T),
    New is Old + Money.
```

This EC clause defines the compensate event with two arguments, a citizen agent (A) and money. It initiates a wealth fluent that updates a citizen's wealth with the amount of compensation.

```
initiates(consumed(A), wealth(A,0), _).
```

This EC clause states that a citizen consumes all the remaining money when the consumed event occurs. The three clauses above have accompanying terminates clauses to remove existing fluents recording damage (for the flood event) and wealth (for taxed and compensate events).

Figure 5 shows how expectations are used in the simulation. At the beginning of the simulation, the government can join the institution either with the rule-based regime role or the discretionary regime role. If the government joins the institution with the rule-based regime role, then an Event Calculus rule initiates an expectation rule for all citizens as shown above, labelled 'exp-rule 1' in the figure. This expectation rule states that if any citizen gets damage (damage(A,_)) then it is expected that no compensation will be made for that citizen (not(happ(compensate(A,_)))). On the other hand if the government has full discretionary power then there is no expectation rule generated. When citizens are initiated in the simulation, they check for the existence of this expectation rule. A citizen knows it could be playing one of two possible games. Under

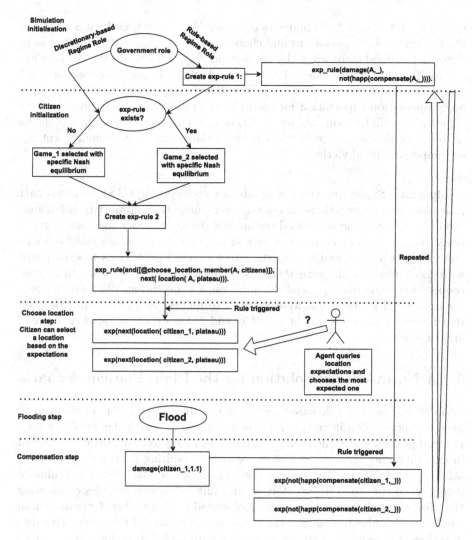

Fig. 5. Role of expectations in the plain-plateau scenario

the existence of this expectation rule, Game_2 (Fig. 3(b)) will be selected with
the Nash equilibrium (plateau, plateau). Otherwise, Game_1 (Fig. 3(a)) will be
selected with the Nash equilibrium (plain, plain). The Nash equilibrium[3] is represented as a second exp_rule fluent, labelled 'exp-rule 2'. In the diagram we
assume the location is the plateau. After this expectation rule is triggered in the
choosing location step, corresponding expectations will be generated for every
citizen. Here the exp fluents are created with the expected location of plateau for

---

[3] While we currently use the Nash equilibrium of these games to create these expectations, in principle they could be learned from experience.

citizen_1, and citizen_2. To make its own location decision, each citizen queries the EC engine for expectations and chooses the most commonly expected location. At the flood step, when the flood event occurs it creates the damage fluent for the citizens who moved to the flood plain. In our scenario, citizen_1 gets damage after the flooding step. This fluent triggers exp-rule 1, creating a no compensation expectation for each affected citizen. Any violations of these expectations will be computed by our EC engine and could by used by the agents in this reasoning, e.g. to revise their belief in the government's commitment not to compensate flood victims.

Evaluation. Simulating the plain-plateau scenario using CASP confirms that reasoning with expectations successfully generated the appropriate behaviour: cooperation under the rule-based regime and defection under the discretionary-based regime. This illustrates how reasoning about expectations using the Discrete Event Calculus and a simulation tool (CASP) allowed us to experiment with mechanisms from game theory and behavioural game theory to explain cooperation resolution of social dilemma using expectations. The explicit representations of expectations were used: 1) to model the government's decision that no compensation would be possible, and 2) the expected location choice of other agents.

5   A Norms-Based Solution for the Plain-Plateau Scenario

Klein notes that the rule-based regime is not the only possible mechanism to promote cooperation in the plain-plateau scenario. In particular, he discusses a range of possible social mechanisms. From Klein's suggestions, we are interested in experimenting with the use of expectations resulting from *social norms* to achieve coordination. We propose that an agent uses the Event Calculus to detect when expectations are violated and fulfilled, which includes considering the effects of their own actions. This look-ahead uses our *what-if* mechanism in the Event Calculus to compare the normative outcomes of two alternative lists of actions. Currently, our citizen agents are hard-coded to prefer sets of actions that will cause no violations over those that will. More generally, this decision could be based on an agent-specific strategy using psychological properties such as *boldness* and *vengefulness* (governing the probability of norm-violation and punishment), as in Axelrod's work on the evolution of cooperation [1]. This would provide a *generic* approach to collective action through properties that are transferable across scenarios, leveraging a *generic* ability to detect potential *norm* violations through the Event Calculus enhanced with expectation-based reasoning without requiring any changes to the code.

In application to the plain-plateau scenario, suppose that the citizens notice the cost in overall lost utility if anyone chooses to live in the plain[4], suffers flood

---

[4] In this paper, we do not consider possible mechanisms for such a *norm* to emerge, but instead assume it holds initially.

damage, and triggers taxation and compensation. A *norm* may then emerge stating that no one should live in the plain. This norm can be expressed by the following expectation rule, stating that no citizen should move to the plain.

```
exp_rule(member(A,citizen), never(location(A,plain))).
```

This expectation rule, however, may not be sufficient to encourage citizens to cooperate. In this situation, we may require a *metanorm*, stating that if the *norm* is violated, any citizen of the institution who moves to the plain can be expected to be punished by those citizens who remain on the plateau:

```
exp_rule(and([happ(viol(never(location(A, plain)))),
        location(B,plateau)]),
      happ(punish(B,A))).
```

Figure 6 depicts our use of expectations in a simulation of the plain-plateau scenario in which agents are aware of *norm* (and *metanorm*) violations.

Event Calculus *initially* clauses create the *exp_rule* fluents for the *norm* and *metanorm* above. At each step of the plain-plateau cycle, agents choose between a pair of actions recommended by one of the roles they hold. The rules of the plain-dweller and plateau-dweller roles are triggered in the choose location step of the plain-plateau cycle, and recommend the options of moving or staying. We add a new role possible-viol-punisher for agents that will consider punishing violations of the *norm*. This contains rules to propose punishing all agents in the plain (if there are any and this agent is on the plateau), or not to punish them, and these are applicable in a new step of the plain-plateau cycle: consider_punishment.

These rules recommend symbolic abstract actions that we can translate to an institutional action, such as change role. Counts-as relations (stored in the Prolog database) are used to make these mappings.

Previously, we had two citizen roles: plain-dweller and plateau-dweller. Each of these roles has rules proposing the action options of staying or moving. We now have a new role called possible-viol-punisher, which represents agents who are aware of the *metanorm* and may choose to punish; it includes rules to propose punishing or not punishing.

Our event calculus *what-if* predicate is now used to consider two options: move or stay, or punish or do not punish (depending on the current step in the simulation cycle), and determines whether one rule produces a violation while the other does not, then chooses the non-violating option (or a random choice if there is no potential violation). If both choices will lead to violation, the cost of each violation is assessed (using domain-specific knowledge) and the less costly option is chosen. If the costs are equal, a random choice is made.

Consider, an agent *a* living on the plateau, and two agents *b* and *c* who have moved to the plain (we assume they are not aware of the *norm* or do not use our violation-avoiding action choice mechanism). If *a* does not have the possible-viol-punisher role, then no punishment will occur. If *a* has that role, but the metanorm does not exist, then neither the punish nor do not punish options will

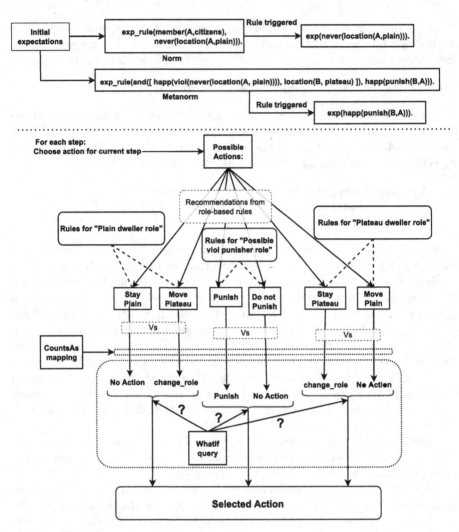

Fig. 6. *Norm* and *metanorm* of the plain-plateau scenario

result in a violation, so a chooses between them randomly. If we now add the metanorm, then a will always punish, as the do not punish choice will violate the metanorm.

6   Toward a Team Reasoning Approach

We are also interested in reasoning with the expectations underlying team reasoning [16,29]. We intend to use CASP and the EC to show how agents can make action decisions based on the common expectation not to achieve their own individual pay off but instead to achieve the team payoff. Lecouteux [16] outlined the following "team reasoning schema" (given here for a two-agent team in a social dilemma):

- A certain pair of agents are the members of the team.
- Each member identifies with the team.
- Team members must choose between the joint strategies (C,C), (C,D), (D,C) and (D,D). where C stands for cooperation and D for defection.
- The team prefers a strategy that maximises the collection team payoff: (C,C)
- Each member wants to choose what the team prefers, so each of us should choose C.

del Corral de Felipe [9] states some properties of group agency that can be modelled as expectations. For example, membership of a "collective agent", e.g. a team, implies commitment to a certain *ethos* as a reason for thinking and acting as a team member. In the context of a game theory style interaction defined by a pay-off matrix, that ethos (as expressed in the team reasoning schema above) might be for each member to make decisions that optimise the collective team payoff rather than the individual payoff. This could be expressed by the following expectation rule:

```
exp_rule(and([member(Ag, Team, Role), game(Team,G),
            team_optimal(Role,G,Act), @action_time]),
        happ(Ag,Act))
```

This states that, for an agent in a team with a specified role, if the team is playing a given game, and it is optimal for the team for an agent in that role to perform action Act, then once it is time to act, the agent is expected to perform Act.[5]

7 Conclusion and Future Work

In this paper, we have presented an approach to agent-based simulation to show how cooperation towards collective action can be achieved based on reasoning about expectations. To present this investigation we have used the CASP simulation framework, which allows agents to query Event Calculus fluents representing social knowledge during their reasoning.

Currently, in our initial simulation of the plain-plateau scenario (without norms) the expectation rule expressing the expected locations of citizens was created at the start of the simulation. This was based on the presence or absence of the government announcement, leading to knowledge of the game being played (Fig. 3(a) or (b)), and then the computation of its Nash Equilibrium. In general, we do not plan to rely on the use of Nash Equilibrium. Expectation rules such as this can come from other sources, such as advice from other agents, or learning from observation.

---

[5] This requires a slight extension of our expectation language to allow an actor to be named in a happ term.

A feature of our Event Calculus dialect that has not been used in the plain-plateau simulation so far is the detection of expectation violations and ful-filments. Consider the no-compensation expectations shown at the bottom of Fig. 6. If it turns out that compensation is made to any citizen with flood dam-age, despite these expectations existing, the Event Calculus engine will create a violation event corresponding to each of these expectations. The agents could choose to monitor for such violations, which may cause them to revise their opinion of the game being played between agents. They could then alter the expectation rule about the location of agents after the next choose_location step (the plain will now be the rational choice). This will in turn cause them to choose the plain.

There are several directions for future work. We can find out various solution concepts to solve the collective action problems in a uniform way. This paper discussed expectation-based reasoning in the context of a specific scenario. How-ever, we seek to explore the use of expectation-based reasoning as a general mechanism that can also model other solutions to social dilemmas, e.g. choices influenced by social norms, social capital, team reasoning [16] etc. In future work, we will investigate the role that expectations play in these social mechanisms to facilitate cooperation in the plain-plateau scenario and in other scenarios.

Acknowledgement. This work was supported by the Marsden Fund Council from New Zealand Government funding, managed by Royal Society Te Apārangi.

References

1. Axelrod, R.: An evolutionary approach to norms. Am. Polit. Sci. Rev. **80**(4), 1095–1111 (1986)
2. Bicchieri, C., Muldoon, R., Sontuoso, A.: Social norms. In: Zalta, E.N. (ed.) The Stanford Encyclopedia of Philosophy. Metaphysics Research Lab, Stanford University, winter 2018 edn. (2018)
3. Booth, A.L.: The free rider problem and a social custom model of trade union membership. Q. J. Econ. **100**(1), 253–261 (1985)
4. Castelfranchi, C.: Mind as an anticipatory device: for a theory of expectations. In: De Gregorio, M., Di Maio, V., Frucci, M., Musio, C. (eds.) BVAI 2005. LNCS, vol. 3704, pp. 258–276. Springer, Heidelberg (2005). https://doi.org/10.1007/11565123_26
5. Cranefield, S.: Agents and expectations. In: Balke, T., Dignum, F., van Riemsdijk, M.B., Chopra, A.K. (eds.) COIN 2013. LNCS (LNAI), vol. 8386, pp. 234–255. Springer, Cham (2014). https://doi.org/10.1007/978-3-319-07314-9_13
6. Cranefield, S., Clark-Younger, H., Hay, G.: A collective action simulation platform. In: Paolucci, M., Sichman, J.S., Verhagen, H. (eds.) MABS 2019. LNCS (LNAI), vol. 12025, pp. 69–80. Springer, Cham (2020). https://doi.org/10.1007/978-3-030-60843-9_6
7. Dal Bó, P., Fréchette, G.R.: Strategy choice in the infinitely repeated prisoner's dilemma. Am. Econ. Rev. **109**(11), 3929–52 (2019)
8. Dawes, R.M.: Social dilemmas. Ann. Rev. Psychol. **31**(1), 169–193 (1980)

9. del Corral de Felipe, M.: The role of commitment in the explanation of agency: From practical reasoning to collective action. Ph.D. thesis, National University of Distance Education (UNED), Spain (2012)
10. Geanakoplos, J., Pearce, D., Stacchetti, E.: Psychological games and sequential rationality. Games Econ. Behav. 1(1), 60–79 (1989)
11. Hardin, R., Cullity, G.: The free rider problem. In: Zalta, E.N. (ed.) The Stanford Encyclopedia of Philosophy (2013)
12. Holt, C.A., Roth, A.E.: The Nash equilibrium: a perspective. Proc. Natl. Acad. Sci. 101(12), 3999–4002 (2004)
13. Holzinger, K.: The problems of collective action: a new approach. MPI Collective Goods Preprint No. 2003/2, SSRN (2003). https://doi.org/10.2139/ssrn.399140
14. Klein, D.B.: The microfoundations of rules vs. discretion. Const. Polit. Econ. 1(3), 1–19 (1990)
15. Kowalski, R., Sergot, M.: A logic-based calculus of events. In: Foundations of Knowledge Base Management, pp. 23–55. Springer, Heidelberg (1989). https://doi.org/10.1007/978-3-642-83397-7_2
16. Lecouteux, G.: What does "we" want? Team reasoning, game theory, and unselfish behaviours. Revue d'Économie Politique 128(3), 311–332 (2018)
17. Lee, B.H., Struben, J., Bingham, C.B.: Collective action and market formation: an integrative framework. Strat. Manag. J. 39(1), 242–266 (2018)
18. Mueller, E.T.: Commonsense Reasoning. Morgan Kaufmann, Boston (2006)
19. North, M.J., et al.: Complex adaptive systems modeling with Repast Simphony. Complex Adapt. Syst. Model. 1(1), 3 (2013)
20. Olson, M.: The Theory of Collective Action: Public Goods and the Theory of Groups. Harvard University Press, Cambridge (1965)
21. Ostrom, E.: Collective action and the evolution of social norms. J. Econ. Perspect. 14(3), 137–158 (2000)
22. Ostrom, E.: Analyzing collective action. Agric. Econ. 41, 155–166 (2010)
23. Ostrom, E., Ahn, T.K.: Foundations of social capital (2003)
24. Peters, H.: Game Theory: A Multi-leveled Approach. Springer, Heidelberg (2015). https://doi.org/10.1007/978-3-540-69291-1
25. Petruzzi, P.E., Busquets, D., Pitt, J.: Social capital as a complexity reduction mechanism for decision making in large scale open systems. In: 2014 IEEE Eighth International Conference on Self-Adaptive and Self-Organizing Systems, pp. 145–150. IEEE (2014)
26. Ranathunga, S., Purvis, M., Cranefield, S.: Integrating expectation handling into Jason (2011)
27. Reuben, E.: The Evolution of Theories of Collective Action. MPhil thesis, Tinbergen Institute (2003)
28. Shanahan, M.: The event calculus explained. In: Wooldridge, M.J., Veloso, M. (eds.) Artificial Intelligence Today. LNCS (LNAI), vol. 1600, pp. 409–430. Springer, Heidelberg (1999). https://doi.org/10.1007/3-540-48317-9_17
29. Sugden, R.: The logic of team reasoning. Phil. Explor. 6(3), 165–181 (2003)

Author Index

Printed in the United States
by Baker & Taylor Publisher Services

Printed in the United States
by Baker & Taylor Publisher Services